Financing Politics

Money, Elections and Political Reform

POLITICS AND PUBLIC POLICY SERIES

Advisory Editor

Robert L. Peabody

Johns Hopkins University

Financing Politics

Money, Elections and Political Reform

HERBERT E. ALEXANDER

Congressional Quarterly Press

A DIVISION OF CONGRESSIONAL QUARTERLY INC.

1414 22nd Street, N.W., Washington, D.C. 20037

Photo Credits: p. 23, Smithsonian Institution;
p. 67, Library of Congress.

Library of Congress Cataloging in Publication Data

Alexander, Herbert E
    Financing politics.

    Bibliography: p. 283
    Includes index.
    1. Elections—United States—Campaign funds.
I. Title.
JK1991.A6797   329'.025'0973   76-22558
ISBN 0-87187-098-3

*To Nancy, Michael,
Andrew and Kenneth*

Table of Contents

Foreword

A prominent West Coast legislator once referred to money as "the mother's milk of politics." In *Financing Politics: Money, Elections and Political Reform,* Herbert E. Alexander suggests why money and politics are so intimately related. As the director of the Citizens' Research Foundation, the principal private organization collecting campaign finance statistics for more than a decade, Dr. Alexander has long been recognized as the nation's leading authority on the issue of electoral reform. In 1962-63 he served as executive director of President Kennedy's Commission on Campaign Costs. It was this group's recommendations which have formed the basis for many of the landmark reforms in campaign finance carried out in the early 1970s.

Financing Politics is the first book in Congressional Quarterly Press' new Politics and Public Policy Series. These supplementary textbooks in political science, each to be written by a leading authority, are designed for use in courses in American government, political parties, interest groups and public policy formation.

Dr. Alexander's book is a thorough study, well-grounded in history. It focuses upon an issue that reflects the basic structure and processes of our democratic system—the financing of electoral politics. He treats how money is raised, where it comes from, how it is spent and the myriad attempts to regulate its use in national and state elections.

Moreover, his book is the only up-to-date treatment of the problem. It covers the principal legislation passed in 1971 and 1974—the Federal Election Campaign Act (FECA) of 1971, the Revenue Act of 1971 (containing the presidential election checkoff provisions) and the 1974 Amendments to FECA. *Financing Politics* also examines *Buckley v. Valeo*, the crucial Supreme Court decision Jan. 30, 1976, that overturned portions of these earlier acts, and the subsequent response of the 94th Congress to the court's decision. The likely impact of 1976 legislation revamping the Federal Election Commission and changing the rules of electoral politics is assessed.

Never before, in such a relatively brief time frame (1971-1976), have so many fundamental changes in electoral reform taken place. In the process, the rules of the game were rather drastically altered. And, of course, the impact of this new legislation is still unfolding.

Through this book we are able to take a close look at these major electoral reforms. They are evaluated in the context of steadily expanding campaign costs; an enhanced role for media politics, especially television; and the special import of Watergate and its aftermath. The pattern of big contributors seeking favors, ambassadors on the auction block, corporations funneling illegal millions into campaigns—all contributed to the zeal with which a majority of the House and Senate reacted in the 1970s.

Financing Politics begins with a discussion of the election reformer in the 1970s: in an age of media politics, where money talks, how can democratic principles be maintained? How can the individual citizen have an impact on the choice of candidates and the outcomes of elections? Chapter 2 is devoted to a detailed examination of the increasing costs of political campaigns, especially for the presidency.

Although money is generally a basic condition for success at the polls, the high spender does not always win. Chapter 3 details why this is the case, with examples from recent elections.

Who puts up the money? Chapter 4 traces the impact of large contributions from the days of the "spoils system," through the contributions of the Rockefellers and the Mellons, down to such contemporary "big money" donors as W. Clement Stone and Stewart Mott. The development of direct mail solicitation as an alternative is also explored.

Wherever important political decisions are being made, the special interests cannot be far away. Marxists as well as pluralists can agree about that. Chapter 5 outlines the extent to which corporations, labor unions and other interests, legally or illegally, have had an impact on elections.

Chapter 6 examines the drives for electoral reform in both the pre- and post-Watergate eras. The focus is upon the 1971, 1974 and 1976 Federal Election Campaign Acts, their legislative history, major provisions and the problems that have been encountered in implementation. Reform efforts from earlier years are given ample treatment.

During the same period that federal laws governing campaign financing were undergoing such change, many states also experimented with reform. These experiences are described and analyzed at length in Chapter 7.

Chapters 8, 9, and 10 provide case studies on the campaign finance practices in the federal elections of 1972, 1974 and 1976. The latter chapter reviews the experience of governmental funding for the presidential primaries, nominating conventions and the general election of 1976.

In his closing chapter, Professor Alexander becomes future oriented. What is the probable impact of a continued escalation of the price of running for political office? Is public financing a genuine solution or mainly just a means of returning incumbents to office and perpetuating the two-party system? How can present laws be modified so as to ensure broader and more intensive participation by the citizenry?

Financing Politics cannot supply easy answers to these or broader questions of democratic governance. But this factual, comprehensive and tightly reasoned study would seem to be must reading for all those who are interested in the relationship of money to politics.

Robert L. Peabody

Preface

I have tried to convey to the reader a sense of the unprecedented changes that have occurred in recent years relating to the ways elections are conducted and financed in the United States. More data are available now than ever before because of the public disclosure provisions of federal reform legislation enacted in 1971, 1974 and 1976 and many state reform laws passed since 1972. The history of that legislation and its impact on the electoral system is discussed in detail. In addition, an attempt is made to bring together insights from numerous studies of campaign finance in order to put reform and its ramifications in perspective.

Special thanks are due to Mike McCarroll, vice president and general manager of Lexington Books, D.C. Heath and Company, for permission to use materials, including tables and appendices, from my book, *Financing the 1972 Election,* published by D.C. Heath and Company.

Acknowledgment is made to Charles Smith, editor-in-chief of The Free Press, for permission to capsulize in Chapter 9 several case studies from a book I edited, *Campaign Money: Reform and Reality in the States,* published by The Free Press in 1976. I also thank the authors of the chapters covered: William Endicott, William Mansfield, Robert Healy, Sam Roberts, Brian T. Usher, and Al Polczinski.

Some historical data are derived from an article, "Financing Presidential Campaigns," which the author published in *History of American Presidential Elections, 1789-1968,* Arthur M. Schlesinger Jr., (editor), Volume IV, New York, Chelsea House Publishers with McGraw-Hill, 1971. I appreciate the permission given by Chelsea House for use of materials from that article.

The thinking about reform and its implications is taken in part from an article the author wrote, entitled "Rethinking Election Reform," in *The Annals, Political Finance: Reform and Reality,* May 1976. Permission has been granted by the *Annals.*

Special thanks go to Fred Wertheimer, Common Cause vice president for operations, for permission to use 1974 data collected by Common Cause and described in its publication, "The Political Money Tree," *In Common: The Common Cause Report from Washington,* Volume 7, Number 2, Spring 1976. This material is used in Chapter 9.

I am happy to thank members of the staff of Citizens' Research Foundation for their devotion and help: John M. Fenton, for editorial assistance; Linda Y. Sheldon, for editorial and typing assistance and preparing the bibliography; Gloria Cornette for important contributions during the book's preparation; and Jean Soete for all her help.

Robert E. Cuthriell, research director of Congressional Quarterly, was especially helpful in his editorial suggestions and added immeasurably to the final product. I also want to thank Professor Robert L. Peabody, advisory editor of this series for the Congressional Quarterly Press.

I always appreciate the cooperation and encouragement received from officers and members of the Board of Trustees of the Citizens' Research Foundation, but the presentation is mine and does not reflect their views.

Herbert E. Alexander
Princeton, New Jersey

Financing Politics

**Money, Elections
and Political Reform**

1

Introduction:
New Age of Reform

From time to time public issues surface which pose fundamental challenges to our democratic system. Such were the issues, for example, of black and women's suffrage, of the civil and voting rights movements.

In the late 1960s and first half of the 1970s, another such issue surfaced—election reform, with particular focus on those laws regulating the ways in which money is raised, handled and spent in American political campaigns. Already well underway, particularly in the states, before the name Watergate became a synonym for political corruption and unfair practices, the election reform movement was given new impetus by that series of events. Indeed, of the many issues thrust into the public consciousness by the Watergate affair, none were more profound than those relating to the electoral process. What is at stake in the issue of election reform is the determination of who will write and implement the laws by which we are governed.

Although given distinct dimensions by the "climate of Watergate," a new reform movement in the 1970s contained nonetheless many of the classic elements associated with political reform generally, and as such provides a notable case study of how and why such movements wax and wane, with attendant clashes of interest groups, and how, often, they produce consequences unanticipated by either their supporters or opponents.

Many of the reforms that were enacted from 1971 through 1976 tended to restrict and limit forms of electoral participation rather than to enlarge them. Designed to curb the influence of wealth and special interests in politics, some of the reforms were so exclusionary that the Supreme Court partially struck them down Jan. 30, 1976, in the case of *Buckley v. Valeo.*[1]

Rules Change Again in 1976

When President Gerald Ford signed legislation reconstituting the Federal Election Commission (FEC) on May 11, 1976, the rules governing the conduct of elections in the United States changed for the fourth time in six years. In its January decision the Supreme Court had struck down several major provisions of the 1974 Amendments[2] to the Federal Election Campaign Act of 1971 (FECA).[3] In order for the commission to continue carrying on its executive and enforcement functions—including the certification of matching public funds to presidential candidates during the 1976 primary campaigns—the court said that all six members of the election commission would have to be appointed by the President. In addition, the court rejected expenditure limits for candidates who do not receive public funds and for individuals and organizations so long as their activities are not coordinated with candidate committees.

Congress wrestled with the legislation, which would be known as the 1976 Amendments[4] to FECA, for three months and during the latter part of that period no matching public funds were available to presidential primary contenders, most of whom by then were in desperate need of the funds to meet budgeted expenditures. Much of the delay was due to contention over provisions dealing with restrictions on the fund-raising ability of corporate and union political action committees. Another controversial provision, allowing either house of Congress to veto commission regulations, was objected to by some members of Congress and President Ford. And while maneuvering on the bill within Congress and between Congress and the President continued through the spring, candidates for elective office in 1976 were forced to campaign without knowledge of what the final election rules would be.

Disputes, lapses and uncertainties are nothing new in the history of recent election law reform. The fact that election law has been treated so cavalierly by the federal government, and by some state governments as well, may be partly responsible for the low levels of public confidence in our electoral system. At the federal level, the sequence of recent election law changes has been:

- The comprehensive Federal Election Campaign Act of 1971 became effective on April 7, 1972, in mid-campaign, causing many problems in educating participants and obtaining compliance;
- The 1974 Amendments only partly became effective Jan. 1, 1975, because the FEC had not been appointed on time and did not become a functioning agency until the following April 14;
- The *Buckley v. Valeo* decision occurred in mid-campaign in 1976, causing further disruptions;
- The delay in reconstituting the Federal Election Commission, finally accomplished by the 1976 Amendments, resulted in the temporary suspension of matching funds and lack of enforcement capability by the FEC.

It is possible that Congress will modify federal election laws again before the 1978 elections. If so, each of four successive federal elections will have been conducted under different laws. These events illustrate the rough and uncertain road to modern reform of election law.

Shape of Reform in the 1970s

During the first half of the 1970s, federal laws regulating election campaigns were changed fundamentally—in the Federal Election Campaign Act of 1971, the Revenue Act of 1971, and in the FECA Amendments of 1974, which significantly altered both the 1971 enactments. From 1972 to 1976, 49 states also revised their laws regulating political money. The states undertook much experimentation, living up to their description by Justice Louis D. Brandeis as "laboratories of reform."

Although there has been little uniformity in the laws governing political finance which have been enacted in this

3

new age of reform, certain patterns can be discerned. The regulations have taken three basic forms, each of which will be discussed at greater length later. Stated briefly, they are:

1. *Public Disclosure.* To provide the public, both during and after campaigns, with knowledge of monetary influences upon its elected officials and to help curb excesses and abuses by increasing the political risk for those who would undertake such practices, laws were enacted requiring extensive and detailed public reporting of campaign fund data.

2. *Expenditure Limits.* To meet the problems created by some candidates having more funds than others and by rising costs, limitations on campaign expenditures were imposed.

3. *Contribution Restrictions.* To meet the problems of candidates obligating themselves to certain interests, prohibitions were enacted against contributions from certain sources and ceilings placed on individual and group contributions. Both at the federal level and in some states, partial government funding now is provided for, making available alternative sources of funds to replace sources that have been prohibited or limited.

This recent wave of reform, a tide unmatched since the Populists and Muckrakers triggered reform at the turn of the century, has been primarily an effort to improve a system perceived by many as fraught with favoritism and corruption. It has been widely felt in recent years that the American system of financing elections through sometimes secret, often unlimited private donations has given undue influence in politics and government to wealthy or well-organized donors at the expense of the unorganized public.

THE CONSEQUENCES OF REFORM

Reform is not neutral. When the rules of the game are changed, advantages shift and institutions change—sometimes in unforeseen ways. As Douglas Rae has pointed out,[5] election laws can be used—in fact are being used— as instruments to achieve certain political goals. Laws that regulate relationships between candidates and political parties, and between citizens and politicians, and that affect the relative power of interest groups and political parties, are bound to influence the entire political process and change the ways in which citizens, candidates, parties and other groups participate and interact.

The ways we regulate political finance affect numerous concerns central to the vitality of our democracy; to the integrity of the election process; to levels of public confidence in the election process; to the robustness of our public dialogue; to the freedom to criticize and to challenge effectively those in control of government; to the survival of political parties and the durability of the two-party system; to the participation by citizens in the political process; and to the effectiveness of groups in our pluralistic society.

The problem of the election reformer in the final third of the 20th century is how to apply democratic principles to elections in an age of media politics, seemingly dominated by an atmosphere of dollar politics. The costs reported for Richard Nixon's successful campaign to retain the presidency in 1972—some $61-million—were six times those reported for John Kennedy's attaining that office in 1960. Kennedy's costs, in turn, were one hundred times those to elect Abraham Lincoln a century earlier. The electoral process today has come to be a classic case of conflict between the democratic goal of full public dialogue in free elections and the conditions of an economic marketplace.

In retrospect, some of the celebrated political reforms of the last half century have caused serious, unintended problems. For example, in the interest of taking the selection of candidates out of the hands of a few party bosses, the primary system was inaugurated. But the characteristics of that widely accepted system—primary costs are high, candidates are numerous, voter turnout is low, and political parties are weaker because their nomination function has been removed—make primaries far from the kind of referenda reformers in the early 20th century envisioned.

So too in today's reform movement, no doubt changes are being generated that will have unexpected impact on the political system. Many of the new laws are already being challenged in the courts, and we shall probably experience a decade of litigation in the "government-in-the-sunshine"[6] and political finance areas. Just as the past decade was marked by a series of conflicting court decisions in respect to obscenity and pornography, the years ahead probably will see the same kind of inconsistent and contradictory rulings in election law.

Although the impact of the Supreme Court's decision has not been fully measured in terms of how workable and equitable a system of regulation will be left intact, no doubt a watershed period in the history of regulation has begun. While the reformers' thrust had been in the direction of restricting large contributions and special interests, the court's ruling was in the direction of re-opening channels for big money to enter politics. While the reformers' thrust had been in the direction of limiting campaign expenditures, the court's ruling was in the direction of permitting unlimited individual expenditures by a candidate for his own campaign, and by individuals and groups so long as their activity is independent of coordination with the candidate's campaign.

Before *Buckley v. Valeo,* the reform movement had achieved comprehensive and stringent regulation both at the federal level and in many of the states. This was no "fake reform" but a far-reaching one that was changing the system radically. Reformers often fear the dangers of incomplete reform but were on the way to achieving a real one when the Supreme Court slowed its momentum.

In the wake of the Supreme Court decision, the reform problem remains: how to improve political dialogue, attract a more attentive and well-informed electorate, encourage citizens to participate in the political process as workers, contributors and voters, and yet diminish financial inequalities among candidates and political parties, reduce the dominance of big money, while opening opportunities for well-qualified persons to become candidates? The questions to be asked are whether the expenditure limits mean there will be more or less communication between candidates and voters and whether the contribution limits and the expenditure limits encourage more competition, favor incumbents, or discriminate among candidates in differing jurisdictions and circumstances? The questions to be asked about government funding of political campaigns are how it will alter the political process, whether government intrusion will be an opening wedge for control over various political activities and whether floors (or minimal levels of financial support) are or are not better than ceilings or limits on spending?

The consensus of opinion among reformers and their supporters (apparently, at least since Watergate, a majority of citizens) seems to be that democratic principles cannot be upheld in the atmosphere of unfettered and often unpublicized campaign fund raising and spending that traditionally prevailed in America. The secrecy or incomplete disclosure surrounding political giving permitted widespread abuses that at times constituted a fundamental corruption of the election process. Revelations that milk producers sought to keep price supports high by their large campaign contributions and allegations that Vice President Spiro Agnew had been the recipient of kickbacks from Maryland state contractors who were also campaign contributors provide dramatic evidence of the corruption of political money that can occur at both the federal and state levels.

NEW AGE OF REFORM

Until Watergate and other recent scandals brought intense scrutiny to the role that money plays in U.S. elections, reform of the political finance system since about the turn of the century invariably yielded piecemeal legislation which, ironically, may have helped further the very corruption that was the original target. The controls imposed by the legislation were mostly negative, restricting spending even as needs and costs were rising.

To prevent candidates from becoming obligated to special interests, limits were set on the amount of contributions. Funds from suspect sources or heavily regulated industries were prohibited. To dilute the "spoils system," career civil servants were protected from political demands for cash. If there was danger that partisans would dominate the airwaves, all sides were guaranteed equal opportunity for free time—although opportunities to buy time were equal only for those who could pay for it. One after another, traditional sources of political funds were cut off without provision for new sources of supply.

The impact of new technology—television, jets, polling—has been felt increasingly in politics, causing costs to mount and outpace contributions. The givers, often large contributors and special interests, were squeezed to give more. New contributors and new sources emerged as improved solicitation and collection systems developed with computerized mail drives and sophisticated fund-raising organizations. Labor and business pioneered in forming political action committees to raise funds and support candidates. Other organizations, especially trade associations, then peace groups, environmentalists and other issue-oriented groups, emulated them. Millionaire candidates raised the ante for other candidates, escalating costs but also focusing attention on wealth as a fact in electoral candidacy.

Negative Character of Laws

Through the years, there were few compensatory positive features to the generally negative character of laws regarding political finance. Historically, when the assessment of government employees was prohibited, no alternative means were provided to ease fund-raising problems or to reduce political costs; the gap or income loss was filled by corporate contributions. When corporate giving was prohibited, again no statutory alternatives were enacted; the gap was filled by contributions of wealthy individuals. When the wealthy were restricted in their giving (although there were many loopholes in these restrictions), again no legislation was enacted to help make available new sources of funds; the gap this time was filled by a miscellany of means, such as fund-raising dinners and other devices still in use.

It was not until 1974 that the historical pattern was reversed at the federal level; when strict limitations on contributions were imposed, reducing sources of money, the gap in lost revenue was filled by money from a new source, the government, at least for presidential elections. In *Buckley v. Valeo,* the Supreme Court upheld both of these provisions—contribution limits and government funding—of the 1974 election law.

Efforts are under way in Congress to extend government funding to congressional campaigns. And a number of states have begun programs of increased government assistance, through direct or indirect means, to candidates and in some cases to political parties.

DIMENSIONS OF THE PROBLEM

The American system of government is rooted in the egalitarian assumption of "one man, one vote," but, like all democracies, it is confronted with an unequal distribution of economic resources. The attempt to reconcile the inequalities lies at the base of the problem of money in politics.

The problems of financing political campaigns are widespread; few candidates or political committees have found satisfactory ways of meeting the necessary expenses in competing in a system of free elections.

The implications of the ways in which we finance our politics are many. Affected are: candidates at all levels, from the White House to the courthouse, in both the nominating and electing phases of the electoral process; the two-party system and the structure of each party; and the decision-making process and public policy at all levels.

Scores of millions of dollars are needed—and spent—to elect our public officials at all levels of government. Consider the following:

- In 1952, about $140-million was spent on elective and party politics at all levels of government. By 1972, the costs rose to $425-million, more than three times as much.
- More than 500,000 public offices, from President to the proverbial dogcatcher, are filled by election in the United States, yet federal and state constitutions contain few provisions for the necessary—and costly—campaigns.

- In some states a campaign for the U.S. Senate may cost more than ten times the salary paid to the winner during his term of office.
- The annual budgets of the major national party committees, such as the Republican National Committee and the Democratic National Committee, run several million dollars even in nonelection years—the size of the budget of a small corporation.
- The electorate is expanding and well dispersed in urban, suburban and rural areas. The development of communications media makes it easier—but also more costly—to carry on political campaigns.

These items add up to an important fact: Money—lots of it—is essential to the smooth conduct of our system of free elections. If one considers how much is spent in this country each year on chewing gum or cosmetics, the $425-million does not seem overwhelming. It can be considered the cost of tuition for educating the American people on the issues confronting them. True, political campaigns are not always edifying, but they nevertheless contribute significantly to the public dialogue in a democracy.

Our discussion so far suggests several crucial questions for citizens in a democracy:

What effect has money on the ideal of equality of opportunity to serve in public office?

Is the man of little or no wealth disadvantaged in entering public life?

Can the poorly financed candidate win nomination or election?

Is the voice of the political contributor—particularly the big contributor—more influential than the voice of the average citizen?

Can political costs be reduced without damage to our democratic system?

We shall deal with these questions in detail in later chapters.

Focusing primarily on the financing of presidential elections—about which most is known—will permit us to point up the problems and prospects of political finance. But it should be remembered these problems are as urgently felt by candidates for public office at other levels as well, though on a smaller scale.

The next several chapters begin our consideration of political finance by exploring how much campaigns cost, where the money comes from and how it is spent.

NOTES

1. 424 U.S. 1 (1976).
2. P.L. 93-443.
3. P.L. 92-225.
4. P.L. 94-283.
5. Douglas W. Rae, *The Political Consequences of Electoral Laws* (New Haven: Yale University Press, 1967).
6. "Sunshine" laws are those designed to make public and illuminate information about influences on the governmental decision-making process. As used here, the term applies to disclosure required by law of political contributions and expenditures, lobbying registration and disclosure, laws regulating conflict of interest, and personal disclosure by public officials (and in some cases, candidates) of their individual or family assets, liabilities and interests, or of their income tax returns.

2

Dollar Politics:
Increasing Costs of Campaigns

Seeking, acquiring, maintaining and extending political power require both human energies and material resources. Material resources are increasingly important in an age in which the stump speech has given way to campaigning by jet plane, to political polls and to the media blitz.

— In virtually all societies, money is a significant medium by which command over both energies and resources can be achieved.[1] The great distinguishing characteristics of money are that it is transferable and convertible without necessarily revealing its original source. These are obvious advantages in politics.

Money is convertible into other resources. It will buy goods, and it will also buy human energy, skills and services. The obverse also obtains. Other resources, in turn, can be converted into political money through the incumbent's advantages of public office, for example, in awarding contracts and jobs, in controlling the flow of information and in making decisions. Skillful use of ideology, issues and the perquisites or promises of office attract financial support to political actors—in legitimate forms as contributions or dues, or in such unethical or illegitimate forms as those involved in recent years in the cases of Senator Thomas Dodd, Bobby Baker, Spiro Agnew, and, of course, Watergate.

— The convertibility of money, then, makes the financing of politics a significant component of the governing processes of all but the most primitive societies. But money is symbolic. The deeper competition is for power or prestige or for other values. In this sense, money is instrumental, and its importance is in the ways in which it is used by people to try to gain influence, or is converted into other resources, or used in combination with other resources, to achieve political power. Because of its universality, money is a tracer element in the study of political power. Light thrown upon transactions involving money illuminates political processes and behavior and improves our understanding of the flows of influence and power.

Political Power

But power is distributed unequally in society; it does not vary directly with wealth, status, skill, or any other single characteristic. Rather, degree of power is determined by many such factors, no one of which stands alone and no one of which has meaning unless related to the purposes of the individual and the environment in which he or she acts. So money is but one element in the equation of political power. But it is the common denominator in the shaping of many of the factors comprising political power, because it buys what is not or cannot be volunteered. Giving money permits numbers of citizens to share in the energy that must go into politics. In relatively affluent America, many individuals find it easier to show their support for a candidate or their loyalty to a party by writing a check than by devoting time to campaign or political work. Of course, most citizens have no special talent for politics, or they will not give their time, so money is a happy substitute and at the same time a means of participation in a democracy. If money is considered as a substitute for service, however, it does not require as firm a commitment; for example, one might give money to both parties, but one is less likely to give time to both. Money has an advantage over service, however, in that it is not loaded down with the personality or idiosyncrasies of the giver.

In every society in which free elections have been held, the problem of who pays the political bills—and why—has arisen. The problem is how to reconcile a theory of democratic government with a set of economic conditions—for example, how to hold to the equalitarian assumption of "one man, one vote" in the face of the fact that in a democracy there is an unequal distribution of economic resources.

The problem is compounded if one considers the operation of constitutional and political systems. To take the American example, the framers of the U.S. Constitution foresaw many of the problems that were to confront the new Republic and met them straight-on. But for the most part, they warned against the divisiveness and factionalism of political parties, as experienced in Europe, while at the same time requiring the election of officers of two of the three branches of government. Most state constitutions also failed to provide institutional means for bridging the gap between the citizen and the government, while they too were requiring the popular election of numerous public officials. The gap was closed by the advent of political parties. The party system, however, has never been accorded full constitutional or legal status, nor has it been helped much financially by governments at the state and federal levels until very recent years.

Of course, the Founding Fathers could not have foreseen all the developments that were to occur once the Republic began functioning. They could not have foreseen the rise of a highly competitive two-party system, nor the huge growth in the number of popularly elected officials, nor the direct election of U.S. senators, nor nomination campaigns, nor the democratization of the presidency, nor the advent of universal suffrage, nor the development of costly communications media—nor indeed the necessity for presidential contenders to spend literally millions of dollars on direct mail appeals designed to raise many millions more.

American history has witnessed an ever-expanding electorate, from the abolition of property qualifications through women's suffrage to civil rights legislation of the 1960s and the lowering of the voting age to 18 in the 1970s—all in addition to normal population growth. In 1919, for example, we doubled our voting potential by adopting the Nineteenth Amendment, granting nationwide suffrage to women. In the

1960s, big strides were taken to register blacks, with consequent increases in campaign costs, while the Twenty-Sixth Amendment added millions of voters 18 to 20 years old to the electorate.

COSTS OF MODERN ELECTIONS

Concurrent with the growth in the electorate has been the increase in the amount of money spent on reaching it in political campaigns: politics today has become a major industry. In 1972, for example, candidates and political parties spent about $425-million on political activity at all levels.

The 1972 expenditure total contrasts with estimated expenditures in 1968 of $300-million—a 42 per cent increase resulting from additional information made available in 1972 and an actual rise in spending, beyond the factor of inflation. The 1968 total itself represented a huge jump over previous totals. In 1952, the first presidential election year for which total political costs were calculated, it was estimated that $140-million was spent on elective and party politics at all levels of government, about one-third the total expenditure 20 years later.

Presidential Campaigns

Presidential campaigns, consisting of both the pursuit of the nomination and the general election, comprise the largest portion of the country's total political bill. The Citizens' Research Foundation has estimated that $138-million of the $425-million spent on the 1972 campaigns—33 per cent of the total—was in presidential campaign costs.[2] Of course, some presidential campaigns start a year or more before the election year and extend after the election year, cleaning up bills and debts.

In contrast, the total costs of congressional campaigning in 1972—involving all 435 House of Representatives seats and about a third of the 100 Senate seats—came to an estimated $98-million, or 23 per cent of the total bill. The remaining $190-million or so was split about evenly between the costs of

Figure 2-1 Total Political Spending in Presidential Election Years and Indexes of Total Spending, Total Votes Cast for President and the Consumer Price Index, 1952-1972.

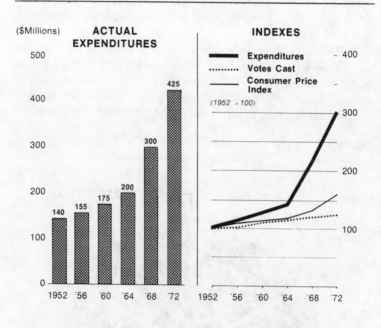

SOURCE: For 1952-72, Herbert E. Alexander, *Financing the 1972 Election* (Lexington, Mass.: Lexington Books, D.C. Heath and Company, 1976), pp. 77-78, derived in part from Alexander Heard, *The Costs of Democracy* (Chapel Hill, N.C.: The University of North Carolina Press, 1960), pp. 7-8.

state elections (governors, other statewide officials, state legislators, state ballot issues and constitutional amendments) and the costs of electing the hundreds of thousands of county and local public officials.

These costs should not escalate so dramatically in 1976, for several reasons: political money is scarce, because contribution limits are now in effect, and the recession and the scars of Watergate have reduced the willingness of some individuals to give as generously as before; spending in the presidential campaigns is limited by law (and partially provided by the federal government) in ways that will be explained later. Similar influences will keep political spending from continually increasing at the state and local levels. Accordingly, total spending at all levels in 1976 should be under $500-million.

Before 1972, it was more difficult to measure all the costs of presidential campaigns, since money traditionally was spent at the national, state and local levels by a multitude of committees and individuals (with no central accounting system necessary). Yet because of the prominence of presiden-

Figure 2-2   The Campaign Spending Dollar in 1972

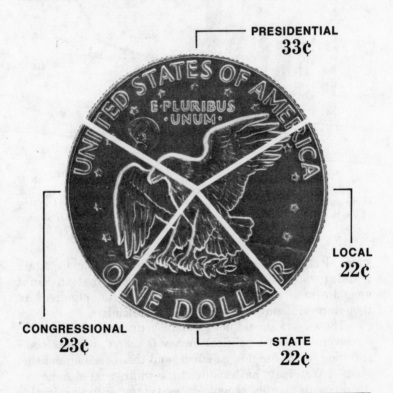

tial elections, more historical information is available about them than about most other categories of election campaigns.

John Quincy Adams, sixth President of the United States, argued that the presidency was an office which should neither be sought nor declined. "To pay money for securing it directly or indirectly," he asserted, was "incorrect in principle."[3] These were noble sentiments, but, in fact, all presidential candidates since George Washington have had to worry about campaign costs. From torchlight parade to "telethon," someone has had to pay expenses.

Table 2-1 shows the amounts spent by national-level committees on presidential candidates in the general elections since 1860, though the figures for years before 1912 are less reliable. A general upward movement in spending is revealed, with some startling differences in particularly intense contests. Much of the increase in expenditures over time is related to the growth in the size of the electorate and to general price increases. If expenditures are calculated on a per-vote basis, the sharp increase in costs is a recent phenomenon, beginning with the 1952 elections, the year, significantly, when the freeze on new television stations was ended; within the next four years, the number of commercial stations had quadrupled.[4]

Between 1912 and 1952, the nation's voting population expanded from 15 million to 62 million, and the value of the dollar shrank, yet in both years the "cost-per-vote" was 19 cents. There were wide variations in that 40-year period—from a low of 10½ cents per vote in 1944 to a high of almost 32 cents per vote in 1928—but after each rise the cost went down again. Thus in 1912 the cost-per-vote was just over 19 cents while in 1956 it was just under 21 cents.

By 1960, the cost-per-vote had risen to almost 29 cents, and in 1964 it set a record at more than 35 cents. But in 1968 even that record was shattered as the cost-per-vote jumped to 60 cents.

The 60-cent figure for 1968 includes spending for Alabama Gov. George C. Wallace beginning in February, normally the prenomination period. But Wallace's ticket, the American Independent Party, had no convention, so no distinction can

Table 2-1 Costs of Presidential General Elections, 1860-1972

Year		Republican		Democratic
1860	$ 100,000	Lincoln*	$ 50,000	Douglas
1864	125,000	Lincoln*	50,000	McClellan
1868	150,000	Grant*	75,000	Seymour
1872	250,000	Grant*	50,000	Greeley
1876	950,000	Hayes*	900,000	Tilden
1880	1,100,000	Garfield*	335,000	Hancock
1884	1,300,000	Blaine	1,400,000	Cleveland*
1888	1,350,000	Harrison*	855,000	Cleveland
1892	1,700,000	Harrison	2,350,000	Cleveland*
1896	3,350,000	McKinley*	675,000	Bryan
1900	3,000,000	McKinley*	425,000	Bryan
1904	2,096,000	T. Roosevelt*	700,000	Parker
1908	1,655,518	Taft*	629,341	Bryan
1912	1,071,549	Taft	1,134,848	Wilson*
1916	2,441,565	Hughes	2,284,590	Wilson*
1920	5,417,501	Harding*	1,470,371	Cox
1924	4,020,478	Coolidge*	1,108,836	Davis
1928	6,256,111	Hoover*	5,342,350	Smith
1932	2,900,052	Hoover	2,245,975	F. Roosevelt*
1936	8,892,972	Landon	5,194,741	F. Roosevelt*
1940	3,451,310	Willkie	2,783,654	F. Roosevelt*
1944	2,828,652	Dewey	2,169,077	F. Roosevelt*
1948	2,127,296	Dewey	2,736,334	Truman*
1952	6,608,623	Eisenhower*	5,032,926	Stevenson
1956	7,778,702	Eisenhower*	5,106,651	Stevenson
1960	10,128,000	Nixon	9,797,000	Kennedy*
1964	16,026,000	Goldwater	8,757,000	Johnson*
1968	25,402,000	Nixon*	11,594,000	Humphrey
1972	61,400,000	Nixon*	30,000,000	McGovern

* indicates winner

SOURCES: 1860-1888 Republican and 1860-1900 Democratic: The best available figures, although disputed, are from the *Congressional Record,* Vol. 45 (61st Congress, 2nd Session. April 18, 1910), p. 4931, as cited in Louise Overacker, *Money in Elections* (New York: The Macmillan Company, 1932), p. 71n; 1892-1924 Republican and 1904-1924 Democratic: Overacker, *op. cit.,* p. 73; 1928-1944: Louise Overacker, *Presidential Campaign Funds* (Boston: Boston University Press, 1946), p. 32; 1948: Alexander Heard, *The Costs of Democracy* (Chapel Hill: The University of North Carolina Press, 1960), p. 18, 20; 1952-1960: *Financing Presidential Campaigns.* Report of the President's Commission on Campaign Costs (Washington, D.C.: April, 1962), be made between primary and general election costs. If the Wallace component is excluded from the calculation, the 1968 cost-per-vote still was close to 51 cents.

Cost-per-vote in 1972 is difficult to calculate because the Nixon re-election campaign was geared from the start to the general election. The candidacies of Representatives Paul McCloskey and John Ashbrook, liberal and conservative Republicans respectively, seeking the Republican nomination against Nixon, posed only minor nuisances in Nixon's quest for nomination.

If one considers the full Nixon spending in 1971 and 1972, then adds in the McGovern general election campaign and national party spending oriented toward the presidential election, following the criteria used in the historical data presented above, $103.7-million was spent for general election purposes in 1972. With 76,025,000 voters in the presidential elections, some $1.36 per vote is indicated. If the Nixon expenditures before his nomination are excluded, the 1972 cost-per-vote would still be more than $1.

CAMPAIGN SPENDING: A GLANCE AT THE PAST

Where does the money go? Since the Republic's founding, printing has been the most basic campaign expense. In 1791, Thomas Jefferson asked Philip Freneau to come to Philadelphia, gave him a part-time clerkship for foreign languages in the State Department and made him editor of the *National Gazette,* the subsidized organ of the Anti-Federalists. The Federalists had been financing their own paper, the *Gazette of the United States,* with money from Alexander Hamilton, Rufus King and from public printing subsidies.[5]

---

p. 10; 1964: Herbert E. Alexander, *Financing the 1964 Election* (Princeton, N.J.: Citizen's Research Foundation, 1966); 1968: Herbert E. Alexander, *Financing the 1968 Election* (Lexington, Massachusetts: D.C. Heath and Company, 1971); 1972: Herbert E. Alexander, *Financing the 1972 Election* (Lexington, Massachusetts: D.C. Heath and Company, 1976).

Newspapers, Pamphlets, Books, Buttons

The system of a newspaper supporting, and being supported by, one or another political faction quickly developed. Editors' fortunes rose and fell with the political success of their patrons. Newspapers vilified candidates mercilessly, and various factions spun off their own papers.

Much early campaigning for the presidency took place in newspaper columns. As late as 1850, when a wealthy backer wanted to further the political ambitions of James Buchanan, he contributed $10,000 to help start a newspaper for Buchanan's support.[6] In 1860, Lincoln secretly bought a small German weekly in Illinois for $400 and turned it over to an editor who agreed to follow the policies of the Republican Party and to publish in both English and German.[7]

Not only newspapers were used to publicize views. In 1800, Thomas Jefferson contributed $50 for the publication of party pamphlets[8] and asked friendly congressmen to write letters favoring him to their constituents. In the campaign of 1832, when the fight between Jackson and the Bank of the United States was at its height, the bank spent some $80,000, an enormous sum in those days, on pamphlets attacking Jackson's veto of a bill to recharter and extend the life of the bank.[9]

During the early 1800s, books, pamphlets, and even newspapers were often handed from person to person until they were no longer readable. All that campaign publicity caused a reaction that seems quite modern. A letter writer to the *Charleston Gazette* complained that "We are so beset and run down by Federal republicans and their pamphlets that I begin to think for the first time that there is rottenness in the system they attempt to support, or why all this violent electioneering?"[10]

That present-day staple of presidential contests, the campaign biography, made its first appearance in 1824.[11] *The Life of Andrew Jackson,* written by John Henry Eaton, started the tradition of the man born in a log cabin who rose from humble origins to become a great statesman. During the 1844 campaign of Henry Clay, the Whig Party sold copies of his biography for three cents each.[12] In 1852, Nathaniel Hawthorne

wrote the authorized version of the life of his Bowdoin College classmate, Franklin Pierce—which was used to answer the Whig campaign slogan of that year, "Who is Franklin Pierce?"[13] When Abraham Lincoln was nominated by the Republican Party in 1860, he was not well-known outside Illinois, and party leaders saw the need for "a million copies of some cheap life (of Lincoln) to be put in the hands of indifferent, ill-informed and secluded voters."[14] One author of Lincoln's campaign biography, a young Ohio newspaperman named William Dean Howells, was rewarded by appointment as consul to Venice. Some biographies were sold and some were given away by the political parties, much as is done today.

By 1840, more than just the printed word was used to spread the story. Pictures, buttons, banners, and novelty items appeared. According to one observer, William Henry Harrison's campaign that year had "conventions and mass meetings, parades and processions with banners and floats, long speeches on the log-cabin theme, log-cabin songbooks and log-cabin newspapers, Harrison pictures, and Tippecanoe handkerchiefs and badges."[15] The main issue of the 1896 campaign, gold versus free silver, gave the Republicans an opportunity to use a gold theme—there were gold canes, gold glass lilies with McKinley's portrait, gold bug pins, gold neckties, and gold hatbands.[16]

The printing presses continued to grind out greater and greater amounts of material. It has been estimated that the Republican Party in 1896 sent out 120 million pamphlets at a cost of $80,000 for shipping alone[17] and a total cost of $500,000. There were 275 different pamphlets, and many were translated into foreign languages. In 1904, the Republican National Committee spent $30,000 on lithographs and buttons. Four years later, $160,000 was spent for all Republican advertising, including buttons, a news service, and lithographs.[18] By 1920, the Republicans were spending as much for billboards ($159,265)[19] as they had for all advertising in 1908. They also spent $200,000 to print and distribute 15 million lithographs[20] of their candidate that year, Warren G. Harding.

No one was ignored. Those who did not care to read could, in 1928, look at the cartoons in a pictorial life of Hoover, for which the Hoover for President Committee of New York paid $4,363.[21] The photographic plates and mats were distributed free to any interested newspapers. Twenty years later—124 years after the first campaign biography—the Democrats distributed three million copies of a comic book biography of Harry Truman.[22]

Active Campaigning

Active campaigning by the presidential candidates themselves is a fairly recent phenomenon. Andrew Jackson retired to the Hermitage after he was nominated, though his supporters did hold torchlight parades and hickory pole raisings. Political rallies came into their own in the mid-1800s. "Fifteen acres of men and 6,000 females"[23] were reported to have attended a rally for William Henry Harrison at Tippecanoe, Indiana, in 1840. A writer caught the flavor of the 1860 campaign when he wrote that the people did not seem to have much to occupy themselves with, besides attending meetings, listening to speeches, and participating in torchlight processions and rallies.[24] Political campaigns provided an opportunity for a widely scattered population to meet and socialize. Orators were judged by the length—not the content—of their speeches: a two- or three-hour speech was not uncommon.

Stephen A. Douglas decided to barnstorm the country in his 1860 campaign against Lincoln, a practice not really tried again until 1896 when William Jennings Bryan, the "Boy Orator," traveled 18,000 miles giving some 600 speeches to at least five million people.[25] His opponent, William McKinley, by contrast, sat on his front porch and let the people come to him; special trains were run to his hometown of Canton, Ohio, with the railroads cooperating by cutting fares. *The Plain Dealer* (Cleveland) reported that going to Canton was "cheaper than staying at home."[26] The costs of these early forays into personal campaigning by Douglas and Bryan are not known, but since both candidates lost, they probably were not considered worthwhile expenses.

The special campaign train used by the Democratic presidential candidate in 1920 was said to have cost $30,000,[27] and in 1956 a five-car campaign train cost $1,000 per day plus full fare for each passenger.[28]

COMPONENTS OF RISING COSTS

A more complete story of the role of money in modern campaigns is provided in Chapter 8, but it seems pertinent at this point to cite two reasons for the increasing costs of presidential contests.

One intangible component of the rising costs over the years relates to the role of the President. For many reasons—including the increased role of the United States in the world during the last decades, the power potential which the President holds, a growing view of the President as initiator as well as executor of the nation's policies, and the direct impact of federal policy on increasing numbers of people—the presidency has become more important today than ever before, and, therefore, the stakes for achieving it are greater.

Moreover, the scientific and technological advances which contributed to increased campaign costs in the 1960s, particularly in areas of travel, polling, computers and broadcasting, continued into the 1970s. Along with its notoriety as the "Watergate election," the 1972 contest may be cited by future historians for the culmination of a number of spending trends now seemingly impeded by the 1974 Amendments to the Federal Election Campaign Act of 1971 (FECA). The Amendments provided for public funding of presidential campaigns and set limits on spending.

Impact of TV and Radio Spending

The quantum jump in campaign spending that began in the 1950s can be attributed in considerable measure to the use of television in American politics. Between the 1948 and the 1952 elections enough Americans had bought television sets for the medium to figure seriously for the first time in campaign planning in the 1952 campaigns; by then, it was estimated that there were 19 million television sets and 58 million viewers.[29]

Candidates who choose to use broadcasting facilities pay dearly for the opportunity—talk on radio and television is not cheap. The only available systematic nationwide information on a single category of political expenditures is that for broadcasting, and it is provided by the Federal Communications Commission (FCC).[30] FCC figures show that political spending for television and radio combined in 1972 amounted to $59.6-million, or one out of every seven dollars of the total ($425-million) spent on politics at all levels in that year.

Radio. Campaign expenditures for broadcasting purposes go back well before television. Radio was first used in the 1924 election. In that campaign, the Republicans opened their own stations in their eastern campaign headquarters and broadcast every day from October 21 until election day, spending a total of $120,000 for air time (one-third the amount they spent on either pamphlets or speakers). The Democrats

Table 2-2 Radio Expenditures (or Time) for Presidential General Election Campaigns, 1928-1948, by Party

Year	Republicans	Democrats
1924	$120,000	$ 40,000
1928	435,000	650,000
1932	73 hours	51½ hours
	($1,250,000 total, with the Republicans spending more than half, and Socialist spending included)	
1936	97½ hours	70 hours
1940	$500,000	$ 500,000
1944	700,000	700,000
1948	500,000	6-700,000

SOURCE: Edward W. Chester, *Radio, Television and American Politics* (New York: Sheed and Ward, 1969), pp. 21(1924), 26(1928), 32(1932), 40(1936), 46(1940), 49(1944), 56(1948). Many figures are estimates.

Table 2-3 Radio and Television Expenditures for Presidential General Election Campaigns, 1952-1972, by Party

Year	Republican	Democratic
1952	$ 2,046,000	$1,530,000
1956	2,886,000	1,763,000
1960	1,865,000	1,142,000
1964	6,370,000	4,674,000
1968	12,598,000	6,143,000
1972	4,300,000	6,200,000

spent only $40,000 on air time in 1924. Four years later, the new medium was more fully utilized by both parties: the Democrats spent $650,000 and the Republicans, $435,000. Such levels of spending for radio were fairly constant for 20 years. In 1948, the Republicans spent about $500,000 and the Democrats in excess of $600,000 for radio time. A more detailed history of radio spending is shown in Tables 2-2 and 2-3.

Television. With television came sharp increases in purchases of broadcast time. When Adlai Stevenson was told that one television speech would cost $60,000, he said: "Now every time I start to put a word on paper, I'll wonder whether it's an expensive $10 word, or a little, unimportant word like 'is' or 'and' that costs only $1.75."[31] Abraham Lincoln's successful 1860 campaign cost $100,000. A century later, that much was spent for a single half-hour of television air time. Table 2-3 shows total radio and television spending for the presidential general election campaigns since 1952.

The highest level of broadcast spending came in 1968. That year Richard Nixon had a carefully programmed campaign calling for noncontroversial television spots and live regional broadcasts which featured the candidate answering prescribed questions from a panel of well-rehearsed supporters. The total of $58.9-million that FCC reports show was spent in 1968 by candidates at all levels was 70 per cent above the total spent only four years earlier ($34.6-million). On the presidential level, about \$12.6-million was spent on broadcasting for the Nixon campaign, and about \$6.1-million worth of broadcasting was devoted to the Humphrey campaign.

The 1972 broadcast spending totals were only slightly above the 1968 totals, representing an interruption of the trend of sharply rising broadcasting expenditures from one presidential election year to the next. Given the overall increase in all political spending from \$300- to \$425-million, broadcast spending declined as a proportion of the total from about 20 per cent in 1968 to 14 per cent in 1972. Among the reasons for this decline were the emergence in importance of nonbroadcast media of communications, such as direct mailing, and the provisions of the 1971 election law, which will be explained in Chapter 6. Nonetheless, at 14 per cent of the estimated total of expenditures, broadcast spending remains the largest single identifiable cost in political campaigns.

Production Costs. The broadcast figures represent only network and station charges and do not include related production or promotion costs. Generally, production costs of political advertising tend to be high. In normal commercial advertising, production work runs about 7 per cent of time and space charges, but 20 to 50 per cent production charges are not unusual in politics. There are several reasons for the high costs: the crash nature of campaigns, overtime, new issues that may emerge, the scrapping of undesirable spot announcements, and the need to revise materials to make regional or state references. For example, in Robert Kennedy's 1968 primary campaign, which was undertaken at very short notice, broadcast production costs were at least 50 per cent of the broadcast time costs. If all production costs were projected at that level, a comprehensive cost figure for broadcasting in the 1972 election, for example, could reach as high as \$90-million.

While much is said about the high cost of television in politics, usually little mention is made of the cost of radio. Actually, there has been a more rapid rise in the use of radio for political broadcasting in recent years than in the use of television. In the 1968 general election, radio costs were double what they had been in 1964, while TV costs were only 55 per cent higher. Between 1968 and 1972, TV costs in the general election declined $2.5-million while radio costs increased slightly by $200,000. Some candidates prefer radio to TV because it is much cheaper for an equivalent amount of time and for production and, therefore, much cheaper per message. They also like radio because of its potential for reaching "trapped" audiences, such as commuters traveling to and from work, or for its ability to pinpoint highly specialized groups, such as in the ethnic radio appeals made in 1972 by the Nixon forces.

With production costs for either television or radio high, the investment for a single spot is so great that it must be aired repeatedly to average down the initial investment. The more stations broadcasting the spot, the more copies that need to be duplicated—another production cost. When programs are broadcast, "tune-in" advertising in newspapers is desirable to ensure an audience. The related costs seem endless.

Drop in 1972 Broadcast Spending

The 1972 presidential campaigns witnessed a sharp drop in spending on broadcasting that is somewhat obscured in the comparisons of the overall spending totals—actually, only about half as much was spent on broadcasting by presidential and vice presidential candidates in 1972 as in 1968. Much of the decline is accounted for by a drop in Republican presidential broadcast spending—down from $15.6-million in 1968 to $4.4-million four years later.

Recognizing that what became known as the "selling of the presidency"[32] by TV in 1968 had in fact done little to bolster their candidate's showing in the polls, the Nixon campaign made a major shift in campaign strategy in 1972 to emphasize spending on direct mail aimed at particular groups in the electorate. When Nixon did appear on television, which was not until late in the campaign, the image that was emphasized was that of statesman and President at work, above the battle of a political campaign. Extensive use was made of film clips of his trips to China and the Soviet Union.

The McGovern strategy differed. It was designed to get the candidate before the public on the broadcast media as often as possible. Since he lacked national exposure, the Democrats had little choice but to spend funds this way. The effort was to try to overcome charges that McGovern was a radical while keeping his populist image intact. In the general election, the Democrats outspent Republicans $6.2-million to $4.3-million for air time purchases.

Table 2-4 illustrates both time and space advertising for the major presidential candidates in 1972, and it allows comparisons of purchases of time and space, as well as of production costs and advertising agency fees.

Table 2-4 National-Level Nixon and McGovern Advertising Expenditures for the 1972 General Election

	McGovern	*Nixon*
Time and Space		
TV		
Network	$2,251,088	$2,152,000
Regional Spot	1,820,000	1,125,000
Radio		
Network	120,000	333,000
Regional Spot	700,000	234,000
Ethnic Radio and TV	——	14,000
Subtotal	$4,891,088	$3,858,000
Adjustment	−80,000	——
Newspapers	962,273	670,000
TOTAL TIME AND SPACE:	$5,773,361	$4,528,000
Production		
Radio and TV	$ 792,596	NA
Newspapers	NA	NA
TOTAL PRODUCTION:	792,596	$1,500,000
Agency Fees	220,000	884,437
TOTALS:	$6,785,957	$6,912,437

NA Not Available

Given the limitations on the presidential campaigns of 1976, it is likely that 1976 broadcast spending will not be greatly increased from 1972. During the 1976 presidential prenomination campaigns, network television was used sparingly by the candidates, with the exception of Ronald Reagan who purchased prime air time for two half-hour programs, each costing about $80,000 for the time, with related production costs of about $20,000 bringing the total to about $100,000 per broadcast.

Approximately 40 per cent of Democratic nominee Jimmy Carter's budget for the general election period in 1976 was for media expenditures. His planning called for heavy use of television to establish the Carter identity as a national candidate. Five minute and 60-second spot announcements were featured. The Carter campaign budget emphasized TV time in target states and ads in national magazines to present Carter's views at length and contrast them with the positions of his opponent, President Ford.

Professionalizing Politics

Modern technology, as applied to politics, also requires candidates for major offices to purchase the services of political consultants—a new form of political spending which will continue growing well beyond the 1976 elections.

Many campaign consultants are prepared to run a candidate's entire campaign. Others will serve as advisers on basic strategy decisions, such as what issues the candidate should stress or how best to utilize his limited time and funds. Some firms specialize in polling, some in fund raising, some in assembling volunteer organizations and others in planning the most effective advertising for television and other media.

There are consultants who handle particular aspects of a campaign—putting voters' names on computer tapes, for example, for direct mail appeals, fund raising or election day get-out-and-vote reminders. Some firms provide automated telephone equipment and operators who can make thousands of calls to voters, play a message from the candidate or record responses.

The use of private professional pollsters is now common, with candidates at the state and sometimes even the local level employing the services of a polling firm.

The proliferation of political consulting firms points up the increasing professionalization of electoral politics. This trend is irreversible but has been criticized on the grounds that such profit-making firms have no base or interest in the candidate's constituency and often supplant established party organizations and traditional volunteer campaign staffs in the political process. Campaign managers, however, have often looked upon volunteers as of "marginal" help in campaigns. With the complexities of new regulations regarding disclosure and limitations, some campaign directors feel that the volunteer efforts are more often a burden than a boon.

Few party organizations are geared to provide these services with the competence and reliability that some of the professional consultants demonstrate. Fees for consultant services are usually a flat amount per month, plus expenses. For media consultants, a 15 per cent commission on the amounts spent for television and radio advertising is common. The commission is a payment for the consultant's skill in planning and scheduling actual broadcasts.

The reporting requirements of the new election laws—the FECA of 1971 and subsequent 1974 and 1976 Amendments—have proved to be something of a bonanza for lawyers and accountants; the FECA has been termed the "Lawyers and Accountants Full Employment Act!"

Tax attorneys have been called upon more and more by campaign organizations for advice on laws and IRS regulations relating to the gift tax, appreciated property, taxes on political committee earnings (if excess funds are invested) and other matters.

The responsibilities thrust upon campaign committee treasurers by the new laws have made it essential that persons accepting such positions be prepared to undergo thorough audits and be criminally liable for financial decisions that in earlier years would have gone unreported and unpublicized. Public accounting firms and computer consultants are often retained to assist campaign officials. More than one 1972 volunteer treasurer vowed never again to assume that role. Such positions in the future may be left more and more to paid professionals.

Joseph Cerrell, president of the political consulting firm Cerrell Associates Inc., has advised his clients to reserve at least 5 per cent and in some instances 10 per cent of their total campaign budgets for accounting, computer and legal cost.[33] An aide to Sen. Lloyd Bentsen (D Texas) estimated that at least $75,000 of the $763,000 spent during the first half of 1975 on Bentsen's presidential nomination quest went for accounting and reporting requirements.[34]

The 1976 Amendments take into account the money that must be spent in the "new politics" on accounting and legal services, by exempting from the definitions of contribution and expenditure any money paid by the regular employer of a person providing legal or accounting services to the national committee of a political party, or to a candidate or political committee, in order to comply with the FECA or Internal Revenue Code as it applies to political activity.

Fund-raising costs are also increasing as a proportion of campaign budgets as a result of the new laws. The contribution limits make it necessary for candidates to undertake broadly-based fund drives, which can be costly, in the search for more small contributors. Direct mail experts are being widely used. The 1974 law attempted to take fund-raising costs into account by allowing a 20 per cent overage beyond expenditure limits for spending on money-raising operations.

SUMMARY

Money is a tracer element in the study of political power, the common denominator in the shaping of many of the factors comprising political power. But in a democracy money is distributed unevenly, and one problem is how to hold to the "one man, one vote" principle in the face of unequal distribution of economic resources. The problem is now compounded by many factors unforeseen by the Founding Fathers: a competitive two-party system, a complex federal system, great numbers of elected officials, universal suffrage, costly communications media, and rapid technological and social changes.

Politics is now a major industry, with spending in 1972, at all levels, reaching $425-million. The largest portion of the bill—$138-million—was attributable to the presidential campaigns. Presidential campaign costs have risen from $100,000 for Lincoln in 1860 to more than $61-million for Nixon in 1972.

Printing is probably still the most basic campaign cost—a part of campaigning since the 18th century—but staff salaries, travel costs and electronic media expenses all mount up. One intangible catalyst affecting costs is the increased power of the modern presidency. The stakes are higher.

The quantum jump in campaign spending that began in the 1950s can be attributed in considerable measure to increases in the use of television, but radio costs are not inconsiderable, and in the 1970s cable television is being used more frequently by candidates. The major parties spent about $3.5-million on radio and TV in the 1952 presidential general election; by 1968, the comparable figure had grown to $18.7-million. However, broadcast spending dropped sharply in the 1972 presidential campaign, chiefly because of a shift in Republican strategy from broad TV exposure to direct mail efforts aimed at specific groups of voters.

Modern technology requires candidates to pay for political consultants, computerized voter mailings, polls and the latest know-how in record keeping. This is part of the trend toward professionalizing politics in which consultants, lawyers and accountants play important roles. Reform legislation has forced many candidates and political parties to pay for professional services to ensure compliance.

Chapter 3 takes up the questions of how wisely (or unwisely) money is spent on political campaigns in the United States and whether money usually makes the difference between winning and losing. It also illustrates the special value of money in primary or prenomination campaigns.

NOTES

1. Derived from Alexander Heard, "Political Financing," *International Encyclopedia of Social Sciences* (New York: The Macmillan Company and the Free Press, 1968), XII, 235-241.
2. Herbert E. Alexander, *Financing the 1972 Election* (Lexington, Mass.: Lexington Books, D.C. Heath and Company, 1976), pp. 77-83. Other information on 1972 throughout this book is drawn from the same source.
3. *Memoirs of John Quincy Adams,* (1875, VII, pp. 468-470, as quoted in Jasper B. Shannon, *Money and Politics* (New York: Random House, 1959), p. 15.
4. For a brief history of the uses of radio and television broadcasting in political campaigns see: Herbert E. Alexander, "Financing Presidential Campaigns," in *History of American Presidential Elections 1789-1968,* ed. Arthur M. Schlesinger Jr. (New York: Chelsea House Publishers in association with McGraw-Hill Book Company, 1971), pp. 3873-3875. Other historical information in this chapter is also drawn from the same source.
5. Eugene H. Roseboom, *A History of Presidential Elections* (New York: The Macmillan Company, 1957), p. 25.
6. Shannon, *op. cit.,* p. 21.
7. *Ibid.,* p. 23.
8. *Ibid.,* p. 14.
9. Louise Overacker, *Money in Elections* (New York: The Macmillan Company, 1932), p. 107.
10. Jules Abels, *The Degeneration of Our Presidential Election: A History and Analysis of an American Institution in Trouble* (New York: The Macmillan Company, 1968), p. 83.
11. James D. Hart, "They Were All Born in Log Cabins," *American Heritage,* vol. VII, no. 5 (August 1956), p. 32.
12. *Ibid.,* p. 105.
13. *Ibid.*
14. Allan Nevins, *The Emergence of Lincoln,* vol. II, *Prologue to Civil War, 1859-1861* (New York: Charles Scribner's Sons, 1950), p. 275.
15. Roseboom, *op. cit.,* p. 121.
16. Abels, *op. cit.,* p. 242.
17. James K. Pollock, *Party Campaign Funds* (New York: Alfred A. Knopf, 1926), p. 152.
18. *Ibid.,* p. 146.
19. *Ibid.,* p. 147.
20. *Ibid.,* p. 148.
21. Overacker, *op. cit.,* p. 26.

22. Robert Bendiner, *White House Fever* (New York: Harcourt, Brace and Company, 1960), p. 138.
23. Abels, *op. cit.,* p. 133.
24. Overacker, *op. cit.,* p. 99.
25. M. R. Werner, *Bryan* (New York: Harcourt, Brace and Company, 1929), p. 95.
26. Quoted in Abels, *op. cit.,* p. 242.
27. Pollock, *op. cit.,* p. 162.
28. Bendiner, *op. cit.,* p. 153.
29. Newton N. Minow, John Bartlow Martin and Lee Mitchell, *Presidential Television* (New York: Basic Books, Inc., 1973), p. 34.
30. See, for example, *Federal Election Campaign Act of 1973,* Appendix A, *Hearings* before the Subcommittee on Commerce, U.S. Senate, 93rd Cong., 1st sess. (1973); hereafter referred to as FCC, *Survey 1972,* the series was compiled from 1960-1972, for every federal election year.
31. Quoted in Robert Bendiner, *White House Fever* (New York: Harcourt, Brace and Company, 1960), p. 147n.
32. Joe McGinniss, *The Selling of the President 1968* (New York: Trident Press, 1969).
33. Barry E. Wagman, "Political Campaign Accounting—New Opportunities for the CPA," *The Journal of Accountancy,* March 1976, p. 36. Also see *Compliance with Federal Election Campaign Requirements: A Guide for Candidates,* compiled by the Federal Election Campaign Guide Task Force, American Institute of Certified Public Accountants, New York, 1976.
34. Bruce F. Freed, "This Time Everybody's Got a CREEP," *The Washington Monthly,* November 1975, p. 35.

3

The Pocketbook Advantage: Does Money Win Elections?

Popular lore has it that the candidate who spends the most wins the election and, on the surface, the record in recent elections would seem to bear this out. During the general election in 1972, the Nixon forces outspent the McGovern campaign by almost 2 to 1—some $60-million to $30-million—and in his successful battle for the Democratic nomination, McGovern himself was the top spender. The South Dakota Democrat spent some $12-million in the prenomination period; all 17 other Democratic contenders that year spent a total of about $21-million, with Sen. Edmund S. Muskie spending the second highest amount, $7-million.

The outcome of elections, however, usually depends upon much more than money. Clearly, Nixon's edge in campaign funds in 1972 was not the only reason he won; in fact the Committee to Re-Elect the President had excess monies available because Nixon's re-election was considered certain by many—a candidate who is likely to win is likely to attract strong financial support. And McGovern's capture of the Democratic nomination was as much a result of the hard work of his volunteers and skillful tactics with the new delegate selection process, as of his considerable fund-raising ability.

Voters sometimes refuse to respond favorably to frills, blitz campaigns or wealthy candidates. It is worth noting that despite the record spending on the presidential campaigns of 1972 the turnout of voters was the lowest since 1948. Survey data indicated that many persons did not vote simply because they were not interested or did not care for any of the candidates.[1]

A number of factors can compensate for a shortage of cash. A low-budget candidate may be campaigning in an area predominantly favorable to his party, or he may be a well-entrenched incumbent; he may be swept into office by a national trend or benefit from a presidential landslide. Any of these circumstances can bring victory if the candidate has sufficient resources to enable him to present his qualifications and positions—sometimes merely his name and face—to the voters.

In broad terms, money can be considered as a countervailing force to a natural majority, or to large aggregates of voters, with the minority party feeling compelled to spend more money than the party that otherwise would command the most votes. For the minority party to do so, however, is not always possible because the party out of power may have less money than the majority party if money, as is often the case, goes to those in power. As shown in Chapter 2, the McGovern campaign in 1972 felt compelled to concentrate a major share of its budget on expensive broadcast time because the candidate was relatively new to the national scene and was running against a highly visible incumbent President.

During the 20th century, at the national level, Republicans consistently have had more money at their disposal than the Democrats, even when independent labor funds are added to Democratic spending. Yet from the 1930s through the mid-1970s, the Democrats have been able to command a majority of voters more often than have Republicans. In his eight years in office, Dwight Eisenhower had a Republican-controlled Congress for only two years; Nixon and Ford from 1969 through 1976 faced large Democratic majorities in Congress.

In the 1936 presidential election, the Republican Party together with the wealthy Liberty League spent $9,411,095 (a total not topped until 1960) against the Democrats' $5,964,917. Yet despite this 3 to 2 financial advantage, the Republicans carried only two states for their nominee, Alfred

Landon. Some historians doubt that the results of a single presidential election in the 20th century would have been changed had the losing candidate been able to spend more money. Of course, the closer the election results, the greater the chance that any one factor could make a difference. For example, the Kennedy-Nixon contest in 1960 and the Nixon-Humphrey race in 1968 were won by such small margins—less than 1 per cent of the vote cast—that additional expenditures could well have made a difference.

The predisposition of voters, the issues of the moment, the advantages of incumbency and the support of various groups are always related to the final vote totals and are often more important than cash. Independent decisions by the news media—particularly TV—about what aspects of a campaign to cover can provide for more exposure than advertising purchased by the candidates. The McGovern campaign in 1972 spent substantial amounts of travel money to put its candidate at an event where free television coverage was certain. Campaign schedules are now drawn up with a view to obtaining media coverage, in time to make the morning or evening newspapers or to get on the evening newscasts. National nominating convention sessions are usually scheduled for prime viewing hours.

If not decisive, money at least is capable of reducing severe handicaps for most candidates. No candidate can make much of an impression without it, especially a maverick who contests the regulars or a candidate who challenges an incumbent.

How Much Is Enough?

One reason candidates seem to spend so lavishly is that little scientific evidence is available about the incremental value in votes of various levels of campaign spending and about the effectiveness of different campaign techniques. Traditionally, candidates spend as their supporters expect them to or as their opponents spend—and then some. New techniques win acceptance and to some extent displace older ones, but few candidates are willing to pioneer with unconventional methods alone; for example, although the electronic media are now widely used, the print media still comprise major expenditures in most campaigns. Indeed, new uses of old techniques develop. As an example, the print media have been enhanced by applications of computer technology, bringing increased use of direct mail that can be specially targeted to groups of potential voters or contributors. Contribution limits have produced pressures in the same direction, requiring candidates to attempt to reach a broader base of financial support by soliciting more small contributions. Matching fund plans have produced similar pressures. A provision in the 1974 Amendments to the FECA, for example, requires that, in order to qualify for public funds, a candidate for the presidential nomination must receive a minimum number of contributions in 20 states.

Other new pressures are at work; for example, statutory expenditure limits as well as contribution limits lead to less money available for spending, forcing campaigns to undertake vigorous "cost-benefit" budgeting of available resources. This may lead to the reduction or elimination of certain marginal campaign activities. Of course, there is no agreement on what activities are considered marginal, and, in fact, marginality differs for the various levels of campaigning. Neither social science nor market research has been able to tell candidates what kinds of spending achieve the most per dollar; indeed, the impact will be different in a national or statewide campaign than in a local one. Perhaps half of all campaign spending is wasted—but no one knows which half. In any case, political campaigns are not comparable to advertising campaigns selling products such as soap because of two important factors: the candidate's personality and unanticipated events both impinge on campaigns in ways that cannot be controlled as easily as can the environment for selling commercial products.

Significant spending also occurs from largely psychological motives: the candidate spends to quiet his anxieties (in most campaigns, plentiful), to stimulate workers or to show that he attracts money and is serious about winning. The high expenditures for President Nixon's 1972 re-election campaign grew in part from his need to build confidence in his ability as a vote-getter. Politicians often feel they must do something, anything, to keep the campaign going and morale high. The candidate's morale is bolstered when he sees his picture on posters or billboards along the route; some campaign managers spend a considerable amount of money just to keep the candidate happy and enthusiastic. Indeed, the costliest election is a lost election.

Relatively, the dollar price of U.S. elections is not high. The $425-million spent for campaigns in 1972 was less than the total of the advertising budgets for that year of the two largest corporate advertisers, Procter & Gamble and General Motors. It was a fraction of 1 per cent of the amounts spent by federal, state, county and municipal governments—and that is what politics is all about, gaining control of governments to decide policies on, among other things, how tax money will be spent. The $138-million spent to elect a President in 1972, including prenomination campaigns and minor party candidates, was just under half of what Americans spend in one year on clock and table radios. And compared with what is spent in other nations on elections, the U.S. total is not excessive—our average costs fall somewhere near the middle, clustered with costs in India and Japan. The cost per voter in Israel is far higher than in the United States.

Still, a high price is paid because of the irrational, irresponsible ways in which some money is raised and spent. There should be less concern with the actual costs of campaigning than with the need to raise and expend the money in ways conforming to democratic ideals.

Stanley Kelley has described at least four subcampaigns in the election process. One is to raise money; a second is to seek the support of party leaders; a third is to seek the support of interest group leaders and memberships, and a fourth is the public campaign directed to the electorate.[2] One might add the subcampaign directed to the party activists, to the people who volunteer to work and who thereby relieve some financial pressures on the campaign. Probably more expenditures are aimed at reinforcing potential workers and voters inclined to support the candidate than at converting voters not so inclined.

Political costs tend to be high because the political season is relatively short, and the intensity for each candidate is highest just before an election. Our system of elections creates a highly competitive political arena within a universe full of nonpolitical sights and sounds also seeking attention. Candidates and parties must compete not only with each other but also with commercial advertisers possessed of large budgets, advertising on a regular basis, often through popular entertainment programs on television and radio.

American politics is candidate-oriented. Over a four-year cycle, we elect more than 500,000 public officials, more elected officials per capita than in any other country in the world. Moreover, unlike most other democracies, where political parties choose the candidates, we have costly campaigns for nomination. Then too, as we have simultaneous federal, state and local elections in many jurisdictions, our ballots are long—and long ballots have important consequences with respect to the degree of competition for exposure in the media among the numerous candidates. In addition, we have ballot measures, bond issues, state constitutional amendments and other issues which attract money and spending to the political arena. And we seek to support the political party system, year in and year out, whether or not there is an election. Considering all these opportunities for political spending, there is no reason to be surprised at how much is spent on American politics.

IMPORTANCE OF PRENOMINATION SPENDING

Because of its ability to buy the kinds of services that produce name recognition and exposition of positions, money wields its greatest influence on campaigns—particularly presidential races—during the prenomination period. This is the period before the national nominating convention when the candidate's name and image must get national publicity, when a number of organizations, national and local level, must be created to win delegates, when the serious national candidate on the modern scene will probably need to contest a string of primary elections in states across the country. Moreover, the number of presidential primaries increased from 15 in 1968 to 23 in 1972 and to 30 in 1976.

The candidate traditionally has had to find money outside the party treasuries. The media and citizens groups watch that incumbents do not take special advantage of government or party help in their efforts to be nominated. Of course, the advantages of incumbency are many and subtle, based both on media exposure and the ability to utilize government staffs and decisions to attract support.

The primary campaigns of the early 20th century, congressional inquiries have revealed, could run into hundreds of thousands of dollars for an aspiring presidential candidate. In 1920, nearly $2-million was spent on the unsuccessful campaign of Leonard Wood for the Republican nomination.[3] In 1952, an estimated $2.5-million was spent on the campaign of Dwight D. Eisenhower; probably as much was spent for his opponent for the Republican nomination, Sen. Robert A. Taft.[4]

John F. Kennedy's prenomination campaign of 1960 reported spending $912,500; additional spending by state and local groups added unknown amounts to that total. In addition, Kennedy was able to threaten to spend enough money to discourage competition, as in California and Ohio. A California primary would have cost Kennedy, according to 1960 estimates, at least $750,000. By the time of the California primary in 1972, the McGovern campaign had spent more than $4-million in that state alone.

The 1964 Republican prenomination fight was essentially a battle between Nelson A. Rockefeller's personal wealth and Barry Goldwater's broad financial base consisting of many small contributions from his conservative supporters. The $10-million spent for the 1964 Republican nomination campaigns doubled the record $5-million spent in the Eisenhower-Taft contest of 1952.

These totals paled, however, in comparison with the sums spent on the 1968 nomination when, for the first time since 1952, there was serious rivalry in both parties. In all, about $45-million was spent before Nixon and Humphrey finally got the major party nominations. The combination of Robert F. Kennedy, Eugene J. McCarthy, Humphrey, George Romney and Rockefeller brought out more money from politically liberal sources than in any previous American campaign and demonstrated that the notion that political money comes mainly from wealthy conservatives is simplistic. (The fallacy in that theory, ironically, was first seen in the 1964 Goldwater campaign, which relied heavily on many small contributions.)

1968, 1972 Prenomination Campaigns

The 1968 prenomination totals for the Republicans amounted to about $20-million, with Nixon's campaign accounting for more than half of that in what was then the most expensive prenomination campaign in history. (McGovern's prenomination campaign four years later, with far stricter disclosure laws, cost $12-million.) Rockefeller, even without entering a primary in 1968, spent $8-million.

The Democrats in 1968 spent more than $25-million in the nomination campaigns. Eugene McCarthy's campaign cost an estimated $11-million, the 11-week campaign of Robert Kennedy about $9-million (with debt settlements following Kennedy's assassination, campaign costs were nearer $7-million). The campaigns of Lyndon Johnson, Hubert Humphrey and their Indiana and California stand-ins cost about $5-million, with Humphrey's spending accounting for about $4-million even though he did not contest in a single primary.

As noted in the previous chapter, the Republican prenomination spending in the 1972 presidential race is difficult to apportion because spending by the Committee to Re-Elect the President, from the time it first set up office in 1971 and with Nixon's nomination assured, was directed mainly toward the general election. His primary challengers, Rep. John M. Ashbrook of Ohio from the GOP conservative wing and Rep. Paul N. McCloskey Jr. of California from the liberal wing, spent $740,000 and $550,000 respectively on their activities, centered, for the most part, in only a few states.

The Democrats in 1972 topped the record $25-million they had reported spending four years earlier. A total of $33.1-

million was expended in the party's 1972 prenomination battle—a battle whose participants included George McGovern, the eventual nominee, and the 17 other candidates who at one time or another contested for the nomination. In addition, four avowed vice presidential candidates spent $328,000 in futile campaigns for that nomination. Combining the presidential and vice presidential totals for nomination in 1971-72, Democratic candidates spent more than $33.4-million.

The range of spending by candidates for nomination for President in 1976 will be shown in Chapter 10 in connection with discussion of 1971, 1974 and 1976 legislation which limited amounts candidates could spend and provided partial public funding for the first time in federal elections.

WEALTHY CANDIDATES

Although four of the last seven Chief Executives were considered wealthy men at the time they took office (Franklin D. Roosevelt, Dwight D. Eisenhower, John F. Kennedy and Lyndon B. Johnson), wealth was a factor only in the nomination of Kennedy. Adlai E. Stevenson and Barry Goldwater were considered wealthy, but their fortunes bore no relation to their nomination or subsequent defeats; at most, their wealth may have helped them to enter politics. George McGovern, Hubert H. Humphrey, Harry S Truman, Thomas E. Dewey, Richard M. Nixon (in 1960) and Gerald R. Ford were not even moderately wealthy when they became presidential candidates.

The Federal Election Campaign Act of 1971 (FECA) set limits on the amounts that a candidate and his immediate family could spend on his own campaign. Candidates for President and Vice President could spend on their own behalf from their own funds no more than $50,000 in the primary and general election campaigns combined; comparable figures for congressional campaigns were $35,000 for a candidate for the U.S. Senate and $25,000 for a candidate for the U.S. House of Representatives.

Buckley v. Valeo Decision

The 1976 Supreme Court decision, *Buckley v. Valeo,* removed these limits on a candidate's contributions to his own campaign. In the 1976 Amendments to the FECA, which Congress enacted to revise the law to conform to the Supreme Court ruling, the personal and family limits in presidential and vice presidential elections were re-enacted to apply if the candidate accepts government funding.

The *Buckley v. Valeo* decision re-opened the way for the candidacies of wealthy persons. In the 1976 campaigns for the Senate and the House of Representatives, the $35,000 and $25,000 limits no longer applied in any case because federal funding was not provided for those elections. Accordingly, there were several instances in 1976 of wealthy candidates spending considerable sums of their own money.

In Missouri, for example, Democratic Rep. Jerry Litton, a wealthy cattle rancher, sought his party's senatorial nomination to succeed retiring Sen. Stuart Symington, himself a self-made millionaire.[5] Litton's chief Democratic opponent was Symington's son, James, a Democratic member of the House of Representatives. Seeking the Senate seat for the Republicans was the state attorney general, John Danforth, an heir to the Ralston Purina fortune. Danforth offered to hold to the $35,000 limit voluntarily, but Litton refused to do so on grounds that Danforth had already used his family fortune to become known in earlier statewide political campaigns and that Symington had inherited a valuable family name from his retiring father. Litton said he would agree to spend no more money than the other candidates once his name and positions were as well-known as theirs.[6] (On August 3, Litton won the primary but was killed in the crash of a light plane while traveling to a victory celebration.)

In the 1976 Republican senatorial primary in Pennsylvania, Rep. H. John Heinz III financed almost 90 per cent of his successful campaign against former Philadelphia District Attorney Arlen Specter with loans from his personal fortune—$585,765 out of a total of $673,869. Specter spent only $224,105 on the primary, according to his campaign reports; of this total, Specter lent his campaign $38,744.

Even with the limitations that now obtain on spending by a wealthy presidential or vice presidential candidate accepting government funds, wealth would still seem to bring a candidate incalculable advantages. His name makes news, and items about his family draw attention—all part of the process of building valuable name recognition. The budding politician from a wealthy family is frequently able to enter the field near the top of the ticket, whereas men and women of less wealth (with the possible exception of actors, athletes and astronauts) usually must begin at lower elective levels and earn their way upward.

Other advantages for a wealthy candidate derive from his access to wealthy friends. Business associations are useful to him as a means of access to wealthy businessmen, suppliers and creditors. A well-connected person obtains credit with ease and can guarantee that loans or bills will be paid. His ability to pick up the tab at lunches and dinners, to phone long-distance without worrying about the cost, is helpful too.

Superficially, at least, a rich candidate does not need a political job and seems less likely to seek personal gain from public office. He may give the impression of being a dedicated man of principle who can be trusted. A wealthy candidate may, in fact, incur fewer obligations to contributors and thereby preserve more freedom of action than other candidates—and wealthy candidates have at times used just such an argument in their campaigns. In his first gubernatorial campaign in 1966, Milton Shapp in Pennsylvania freely acknowledged that he preferred to spend his own money and not be obligated to large contributors.[7] Republican Rep. Millicent Fenwick of New Jersey has repeatedly volunteered the information during her political campaigns that she has a net worth of more than $5-million.[8]

Even with the limitations imposed by federal law, potential candidates with their own wealth can still put task forces and experts to work on policy development and fact finding, insuring, among other benefits, that their names are in the news. This is not to say that wealthy candidates may not lose: they frequently do. But for many reasons, political realities continue to favor the wealthy candidate. Wealth propels, quickens and catalyzes. And it is only folklore that the average American admires the impecunious candidate who wins elections on a shoestring. The voter has often cast his ballot willingly for the man who is well-to-do with an expensive organization and a substantial war chest. American voters have been strongly drawn to the Roosevelts, Tafts, Kennedys and Rockefellers.

Two concerns are usually raised in discussions of wealthy candidates. One is that their personal resources give them too great an advantage over other candidates; the second is that the advantage they have gives the rich overrepresentation.

Most candidates spend some of their own money, and most probably receive some financial help from their families. The first concern is really where to draw the line?

Rockefeller Contributions

The most conspicuous examples of contributors on the record are the Rockefellers. When he appeared before the House Judiciary Committee in November 1974 as the Vice President-designate, Nelson Rockefeller said that in his 18 years in public office he and members of his family had spent more than $17-million on his various political campaigns. He noted that this family spending had been necessary because "it's very difficult for a Rockefeller to raise money for a campaign. The reaction of most people is, 'Why should we give money to a Rockefeller?' "[9]

Rockefeller submitted to the Senate Rules Committee a summary of his own political contributions during the years 1957-1974. He said his political spending since 1957 totaled $3,265,374, which included $1,000,228 in his own presidential campaigns, $80,599 in his New York gubernatorial campaigns, and $1,031,627 to New York State Republican Party and local committees and clubs. In addition, his brothers and sister had supported Nelson Rockefeller's political activities with contributions totaling $2,850,000, and his stepmother, the late Martha Baird Rockefeller, had added another $11-million or so. Adding in Rockefeller spending and family contributions to the campaigns of Nelson's brother, Winthrop, who was active in Republican politics in Arkansas and governor from

1967 to 1970, Nelson Rockefeller accounted for about $20-million spent by the family on the Rockefellers' own campaigns. Now younger members of the Rockefeller family, notably John D. (Jay) Rockefeller IV in West Virginia, are active in running for office and are adding to the Rockefeller totals.

As to the concern that the rich are overrepresented in politics, it is necessary to point out that wealthy candidates often are surrogates or in effect representatives of those who might not otherwise have strong voices in government. This tradition goes back to the Virginia squire who was the first President, and it carries up through such wealthy candidates as the late Robert Kennedy, with his appeal to the black and the poor voter. Kennedy's brother, Sen. Edward M. Kennedy, continued in early 1976 as the overwhelming choice for President of these two groups.

Contrary to the common assumption, wealthy candidates are not all conservatives who represent vested interests. A *New York Times* study in 1975 found that of the 100 U.S. senators, at least 22 were millionaires either in their own right or with their wives.[10] They cut across the political spectrum: among the liberals were Democrats Kennedy of Massachusetts, Claiborne Pell of Rhode Island, Philip A. Hart of Michigan, and Republicans Jacob K. Javits of New York and Charles H. Percy of Illinois; conservatives included Republicans Barry Goldwater of Arizona and Hiram L. Fong of Hawaii, Conservative-Republican James L. Buckley of New York, Democrats James O. Eastland of Mississippi and Russell B. Long of Louisiana, and Harry F. Byrd Jr., the independent from Virginia.

To the extent that these wealthy candidates help shore up the two-party system or give voice to minority interests, they contribute importantly to the political dialogue.

The main problem of wealth in elections may not be in the outcome of financially imbalanced contests but rather in depriving the voters of potential leaders who do not have the money to consider running for office because of the escalation, despite legal limitations, in election costs in recent years.

Three Case Histories

Three campaigns involving wealthy candidates—two for the Senate and one for governor—illustrate some of the advantages and pitfalls in the mixture of personal wealth and politics; they also demonstrate how at times the competition between wealthy candidates can drive up spending precipitously:

Richard L. Ottinger, New York. In 1970, Richard L. Ottinger, then a U.S. representative from the 25th District in Westchester County, N.Y., borrowed $3.1-million from his family to finance his primary and general election campaign for U.S. senator. Ottinger was victorious in the Democratic primary, spending $2-million with heavy emphasis on a television blitz; the other primary candidates reported spending a total of only $353,200. Ottinger reported spending another $2-million in the three-way general election campaign against the incumbent, Charles Goodell, a Republican, and the ultimate winner, James L. Buckley, a Conservative, also from a wealthy family. Spending in 1970 to elect one U.S. senator in New York State amounted to at least $7-million, and more than half that sum was spent by Ottinger.

Norton Simon, California. Also in 1970, Norton Simon, an industrialist and philanthropist, spent at least $2-million of his own fortune in an unsuccessful effort to defeat the incumbent, Sen. George Murphy, in the Republican senatorial primary in California; Murphy spent $637,761 in the primary and won it.

In the general election in California that fall, Murphy spent $1.9-million, but he was defeated by John V. Tunney, also from a wealthy family, who reported spending $568,180 in the primary and $1.3-million in the general election.

Milton J. Shapp, Pennsylvania. Milton J. Shapp, who had made a sizable fortune in a community television systems business, first ran for governor of Pennsylvania in 1966; he reported that he had spent $1.4-million in the primary to defeat the frontrunner and organization choice, Robert Casey, and $2.4-million in the general election when he lost to Republican Raymond Shafer. The campaign was marked by suits and countersuits involving Shapp's official financial reports. Shapp made no bones about not wanting to be obligated to contributors, and when charged with trying to buy an election, he responded that he was merely selling himself with his own money. Shafer won despite a Shapp claim that Shafer had actually spent more money in the campaign.

Four years later, Shapp again challenged Casey in the primary and again won, spending a reported $1.1-million. Less money was spent in 1970 than in the initial race because Shapp by then was better known, but again much of the money spent was his own. This time Shapp was victorious in the general election, on which he spent at least $1.6-million. Shapp publicly stated that his political spending and spending to oppose the Penn Central Railroad merger and on personal charities, coupled with adverse market conditions, had brought his personal fortune from $8-million to about half that amount. For Shapp, money made persistence both realistic and feasible.

In 1974, Shapp won a second term as governor without spending much money personally, because by then he was a well-known incumbent. Shapp became a contender for his party's presidential nomination in 1976. He withdrew from that race, however, in March 1976, noting that the FECA made it impossible for him, as a late starter, to become sufficiently well-known nationally to raise enough money to mount an effective campaign; he had entered the Massachusetts and Florida primaries and had finished well back in the running in each. Despite personal wealth and public funding, Shapp was unable to remain in the contest.

More Disclosures

The new disclosure laws becoming effective between the 1968 and 1972 elections made for a dramatic upsurge in the number of candidates who reported publicly that they had made a very large contribution—$10,000 or more—to their own campaigns.

From a more limited base of information in 1968, the Citizens' Research Foundation verified that nine political candidates contributed $10,000 or more to their own campaigns. Three of these were presidential contenders, all Republicans—Nelson Rockefeller, who reported he gave a total of $356,000 to his own campaign that year; George Romney, who gave $100,000; and Harold Stassen, who contributed $40,000 of his own money to his prenomination effort. Two candidates for governor in the Texas primary also reported contributions by themselves exceeding $10,000—Dolph Briscoe gave $460,000 to his own campaign, and Edward Whittenburg contributed $200,000 to his. There were also contributions exceeding $10,000 by the candidates themselves in such elections as a U.S. Senate race in Maryland and a U.S. House contest in Virginia in 1968.

In 1972, with the new reporting requirements of the Federal Election Campaign Act of 1971 in effect, a total of 247 candidates for federal and some state offices reported that they either contributed directly to their own campaigns or personally helped to pay off debts they incurred in amounts aggregating $10,000 or more. Nearly $3.6-million was in contributions (versus the $1.1-million reported in 1968), and $2.2-million was in loans (many never repaid).

The former Postmaster General in the Nixon administration, Winton M. Blount, an Alabama millionaire, belatedly paid $325,000 on his own 1972 campaign debt incurred in his unsuccessful race against Sen. John Sparkman.

Overall, Democratic candidates in 1972 contributed more to their own campaigns than Republican candidates. Contributions by Democratic candidates to their own campaigns in that year amounted to $1.8-million. Contributions by Republican candidates to their campaigns (including Blount's $325,000) totaled $1.2-million.

THE VALUE OF INCUMBENCY

Common Cause, the citizens' lobbying group formed in 1970, has played a leading role in seeking public disclosure of campaign funding, stressing the value of an open and competitive democratic system. In a number of its lobbying campaigns, Common Cause has sought to offset the advantages enjoyed by incumbents, contending that the two-party system as it now functions really means two classes of candidates—the incumbents and the challengers.

Scholars do not wholly agree with this basic thesis. Particularly in the area of fund raising, it is more accurate to say that money tends to be contributed to those who appear likely to *win*—whether or not an incumbent is involved—and this is most often the incumbent. In the four congressional elections from 1968 through 1974, the average percentage of incumbents seeking re-election who won ranged from 89.6 to 98.9.[11]

The disparity in political resources, including campaign funds, between opposing candidates and parties is often so great that competition is only nominal. Most important, candidates and parties in districts whose electoral balance is strongly in their favor usually are able to amass substantially more political resources than their opponents. More than three-fourths of the seats in the United States House of Representatives are filled from electorally noncompetitive districts, defined as those in which the incumbent won in the previous election by 55 per cent or more of the vote. Patterns in state, county and municipal legislatures vary, but most are characterized by one-party dominance.

A 1975 study by the liberal Americans for Democratic Action calculated that an incumbent congressman has a $488,505 edge on his challenger. The figure takes into account the value of salaries and office space, communications and travel allowances and other benefits that members receive and that help them stay in office.

Members of Congress, for example, get staff allowances that range upward from $200,000 annually. Each House member is permitted up to 18 paid employees, and a maximum staff allowance of $238,584 per year. In the Senate, staff allowances are based on the size of a senator's state; Alaska Sen. Ted Stevens, for example, was allotted $413,082 to hire staff in 1976, while California's Alan Cranston got $818,214, the Senate's highest staff allowance. Each senator is also authorized to spend up to $101,925 to hire three legislative aides to help with committee work.

Members receive free office space in Washington during their terms in office and allowances for offices in their home states or districts. Travel allowances also are provided. House members are allowed 26 free round trips each year to and from their home districts. Staff aides to each representative are permitted a total of six free trips a year. The travel allowance for Senate offices is based on the cost of 40 round trips a year for states with less than 10 million population and 44 round trips a year for states with more than 10 million population.

Senators and representatives have unlimited use of their mail franking privilege as long as the mailings are for "official," non-campaign purposes. Many candidates turned to direct mail campaigning in 1972 when the 1971 FECA placed limitations on media spending. Some incumbents took advantage of the then-vague wording in the law dealing with the franking privilege, which stated only that members may use the frank for correspondence "on official business."

In fiscal year 1972, members of Congress sent 308.9 million pieces of franked mail. About 326 million pieces were sent in fiscal 1973, and an estimated 354 million pieces, at a cost of $35.7-million, were sent in 1974. Studies have shown that members of Congress send nearly twice as much franked mail in an election year as they do in a nonelection year. The Post Office Department ceased supervising the frank in 1968, seeking to remain nonpolitical and presumably figuring that there was nothing to gain in trying to rule on when members of Congress—who pass on postal appropriations—abuse the privilege. Common Cause has undertaken a suit to diminish political uses of the franking privilege, and the 1974 Amendments prohibit use of the frank to send any "mass mailing" during the 28 days before a primary or general election.

The ADA study estimated that in 1974 an incumbent was able to raise an average of $23,340 more in campaign funds than his opponent. Senators and representatives also have traditionally put members of their staffs to work on their re-election bids, a legal practice although Common Cause and the Federal Election Commission have both brought it under question in recent years. Common Cause, in a lawsuit, has argued that the language in appropriations bills providing for staff salaries restricts funds to remuneration for legislative, not political duties. The FEC has been asked to consider whether pay given a White House staff aide involved in politicking duties should be counted against campaign spending limits.

A complication in apportioning such time is the difficulty of differentiating pure election work from legislative or representational work that is helpful to a re-election effort—in a broad sense, nearly everything a staff aide does is to advance his boss' career and, therefore, re-election.

And, of course, a basic advantage of incumbency can be that a member has a record in office. Incumbents can expect contributions from constituents or interests who simply approve of the member's views or performance.

SUMMARY

The candidate who spends the most often wins, but the outcome of an election depends upon much more than money.

In broad terms, money is a countervailing force to a majority. A minority party often feels compelled to spend more money than the party that otherwise commands more votes. During the 20th century, Republicans at the national level, the minority party for nearly half the century, have consistently had more money at their disposal than Democrats.

Little is known about whether candidates get more votes for each extra dollar spent above the minimum needed to reach the electorate effectively. There is pressure from many sources to spend. Much spending is done solely for psychological motives. Perhaps half of all spending is wasted—but no one knows which half.

Money wields its greatest influence in prenomination campaigns when candidates must gain name recognition and present their positions. Candidates traditionally must find this money outside party treasuries. When there is a serious rivalry, spending can be enormous—$45-million was spent in

1968 when both Democrats and Republicans had open races for their presidential nomination and more than $60-million in 1976.

The wealthy candidate will continue to play an important role in American politics, particularly in light of the 1976 Supreme Court decision permitting a candidate to spend as much as he wishes on his own campaign. A wealthy candidate has advantages other than his own money—a name that makes news, access to wealthy friends, the impression that he does not need a job, the ability to portray himself as a man of principle. Contrary to common assumption, rich candidates are not all conservatives representing vested interests—the 22 millionaire senators in the 94th Congress range across the political spectrum.

Money tends to be contributed to those who appear likely to win—and this is most often the incumbent. One study has suggested that an incumbent member of Congress has almost a half-million dollar edge on his challenger, thanks to various perquisites of his office—franking privilege, staff allowances, office space, and so on.

In the next chapter we begin to analyze the sources of campaign funds: the various ways in which money has been sought and given over the years.

NOTES

1. The Gallup Opinion Index, *Campaign '76* (Report No. 125) shows that nearly four of ten nonvoters in 1972 did not vote because of lack of interest in politics or because they did not like the candidates.
2. Stanley Kelley Jr., *Political Campaigning: Problems in Creating an Informed Electorate* (Washington, D.C.: The Brookings Institution, 1960), p. 5.
3. Louise Overacker, *Money in Elections* (New York: The Macmillan Company, 1932), pp. 69-70.
4. Alexander Heard, *The Costs of Democracy* (Chapel Hill, N.C.: University of North Carolina Press, 1960), pp. 334-335.
5. Richard D. Lyons, "Most Senators Get Political Advantage From Their Own Wealth," *The New York Times,* December 25, 1975.

6. "Candidates Find Money Still Matters in 1976," Congressional Quarterly *Weekly Report*, March 13, 1976, p. 555.
7. Herbert E. Alexander, *Money in Politics* (Washington, D.C.: Public Affairs Press, 1972), p. 44.
8. Richard D. Lyons, "Records Show 22 Millionaires in House, Despite Lack of Full Disclosure Law," *The New York Times*, January 4, 1976.
9. Reported by UPI in *The Trentonian*, November 22, 1974.
10. Lyons, *op. cit.*, December 25, 1975.
11. "Incumbent has $488,000 Edge," *The Washington Post*, August 26, 1975; also see Monty Hoyt, "$610,000: Annual Cost per Member of Congress," *The Christian Science Monitor*, January 29, 1975, and Monty Hoyt, "Valuable Extra Benefits for Congressmen," *The Christian Science Monitor*, January 30, 1975; and "State Population Determines Most Senate 'Perks'," Congressional Quarterly *Weekly Report*, July 3, 1976, p. 1700.

4

The Money Tree: Sources of Campaign Funds

The 1976 Supreme Court ruling on the new campaign finance laws capped a series of attempts in the late 1960s and first half of the 1970s to curb the role of the big contributor in U.S. politics, an effort accelerated by "Watergate." The court ruling left areas where "big money" still might influence campaigns—notably the unlimited spending permitted candidates in their own campaigns and the unlimited spending permitted the individual citizen as long as his effort is not coordinated with a candidate. On balance, however, the possibilities of a candidate's becoming beholden to large contributors were greatly reduced by a $1,000 gift limit in federal law.

If, as seems likely, the restrictions on large contributors work to expand the number of smaller donors, it would continue a trend noted over the past decade. The trend is discernible despite an emphasis upon large contributors in newspaper stories and scholarly analyses. With so much historical data available, the presidential campaigns are illuminating sources of information about "who gives how much to whom for what?"

THE AMERICAN EXPERIENCE

Money collected from the candidates themselves and assessments on officeholders were sufficient to finance some of the earliest American presidential campaigns. Yet the system was expensive for those participating, and only a few could afford to run for office. Even after election, the salary was low, there was entertaining to do and there were other demands on personal funds. Thomas Jefferson was almost insolvent when his last term of office as President was ended.[1]

By the 1830s, regular assessments were being levied on the government employees in the New York Custom House, and it was observed that those who refused to pay lost favor.[2] Soon, however, the money raised by collections and assessments was not enough.

✓ **Spoils System.** Andrew Jackson is generally credited with bringing in the "spoils system," rewarding with favors and government jobs those who had contributed to campaigns. The payoff, of course, might include favorable government policies as well as jobs and contracts.

When August Belmont, the American representative of the House of Rothschild, set up the Democratic National Committee in 1852, he did so to raise funds for the party's presidential candidate, Franklin Pierce. His solicitations apparently were not successful, for it was reported that "at the opportune moment Belmont stepped in and contributed a large sum to the national committee. Thus the matter of funds was taken care of."[3] He would not be the last chairman to contribute to the party from his own pocket.

Lincoln's Campaign. In 1860, 10 of Lincoln's friends pledged a minimum of $500 each to help cover his campaign expenses.[4] They thus contributed 5 per cent of the total the Republicans are believed to have spent in that campaign. Lincoln's opponent, Democrat Stephen A. Douglas, had no money. Belmont organized a finance committee, contributed $1,000 himself as a campaign kickoff and then turned to the New York Central Railroad for $100,000. Fearful of offending southern sympathies, the railroad men refused to contribute. Frantic appeals for money were made—each congressional district was assessed $100 for the cause—but to little avail. The wealthy interests in the North did not intend to aid a candidate who was hated in half the South.[5] Douglas ended the campaign with a personal debt of $80,000.[6]

With the end of the Civil War, the great corporations and individuals who had amassed fortunes from American industry began to pay a major share of presidential campaign costs. Grant is said to have entered office in 1869 more heavily mortgaged to wealth through campaign contributions than any candidate before him.[7] His $200,000 campaign (already double that spent for Lincoln's less than a decade earlier) was largely financed by such men as Commodore Vanderbilt, the Astors and Jay Cooke.[8] They represented the railroad and land grant interests which, along with major corporations, supplied most of the Republican money. The Democrats attracted funds from other interests, for example, from the ones represented by H. T. Helmbold, a manufacturer of patent medicines. Helmbold was the chief Democratic contributor in 1868. Then as later, however, only a small share of the wealthy were on the Democrats' side, but it included such individuals as Belmont, Cyrus H. McCormick and Samuel J. Tilden. Accordingly, the Democrats were only relatively disadvantaged.

Jay Cooke. Throughout the 1860s and 1870s, Jay Cooke held intimate fund-raising dinners in Washington, D.C., for the benefit of the Republican Party.[9] In 1864, Cooke supported Salmon P. Chase before Lincoln was renominated; then he gave $1,000 to Lincoln.[10] He contributed $20,000 to the Republicans' 1868 campaign and in 1872 increased his gift to $50,000.[11]

That businessmen should support the political party that most clearly favored their financial interests was accepted fact—"frying the fat" was a phrase used to describe the means of acquiring campaign contributions from Pennsylvania manufacturers.

The Democrats attempted to raise money in the same way. In 1868, eight Democrats (including Belmont, still chairman of the Democratic National Committee) signed a business contract with the treasurer of the party in which each agreed to give $10,000 "to defray the just and lawful expenses of circulating documents and newspapers, perfecting organizations, etc., to promote the election of Seymour and Blair."

In 1876, the Democrats nominated Samuel J. Tilden, a millionaire said by some to be worth as much as $10-million;[12] cartoonist Thomas Nast showed him supporting the Democratic campaign chest out of his own "barrel."[13] Actually, Tilden was notoriously tight-fisted and not at all interested in spending much of his own money. He may have lost the election to Rutherford B. Hayes (though he led the Republican contender in both popular and, initially, electoral votes) because he was unwilling to spend enough money to win over more electoral votes.

James A. Garfield, in his presidential campaign in 1880, appealed to his managers to assess government employees for the money he would need. That was the last election, however, in which that source could be legally tapped.[14] Reformers had launched a concerted attack on that system, and the Civil Service Reform Act of 1883 began to protect federal workers from the demands of the parties for tribute money.

Mark Hanna. The financing of campaigns found its genius in Mark Hanna, who rose from wholesale grocer in Cleveland to maker of Presidents because of his ability to raise funds for the Republican Party. In 1888, he raised more money than the Republican National Committee could spend; he returned the excess to the donors on a pro rata basis.[15]

In Hanna's view, there were few things that could not be bought with money; his battle to secure the Republican nomination for William McKinley in 1896 reportedly cost $100,000.[16] Hanna was named chairman of the Republican National Committee that year and proceeded to organize, on a scale never seen before, a campaign to elect McKinley. A well-known Wall Street figure took Hanna to meet the men of the East who could contribute the most to McKinley's campaign. In a style that foreshadowed the fund-raising techniques of a Maurice Stans or a Herbert Kalmbach 76 years later, quotas were set and contributions were determined by ability to pay. Banks were assessed at one-quarter of 1 per cent (.0025) of their capital. Life insurance companies, together with many other business organizations, contributed. For example, Standard Oil gave $250,000 in 1896,[17] $250,000 in 1900 (of which McKinley returned $50,000 because he felt Standard Oil had paid more than its fair share),[18] and $100,000 in 1904 (which Theodore Roosevelt told his campaign manager to reject).[19]

Hanna, in the words of his biographer, Herbert Croly, "always did his best to convert the practice from a matter of political begging on the one side and donating on the other, into a matter of systematic assessment according to the means of the individual and institution."[20] Hanna tried to make it clear that there were to be no favors in return for contributions; McKinley wanted to remain clean. In 1900, Hanna returned a $10,000 gift to a Wall Street brokerage firm which he believed was making a specific demand.[21]

The Republicans might not have had such easy access to large funds if the business community had not thought the stakes so large. The free silver issue threatened the existing economic policies of the United States and William Jennings Bryan and the people around him struck fear in many a Republican heart. These campaigns pitted the rich against the poor, the eastern establishment against western farmers.

William Jennings Bryan. Bryan never had access to funds in amounts the Republicans had. In 1896, he attempted to match the Republican campaign with resources of only $675,000, about 20 per cent of the GOP total. Bryan lost some wealthy "Gold Democrats" to McKinley; most of the contributions Bryan did receive came from a group of wealthy silver mine owners.[22]

Of the $3.5-million which the 1896 Republican campaign is said to have cost, about $3-million was said to have come from New York City and vicinity and the rest from Chicago.[23] Harold L. Ickes, who worked in that election for McKinley, later wrote: "I never doubted that if the Democrats had been able to raise enough money, even for legitimate purposes, Bryan would have been elected."[24]

The election of 1900 virtually repeated the election of 1896: the presidential candidates were the same, the issues similar, and the Hanna fund-raising system again functioned well. Once again, McKinley stayed home and Bryan toured the country. This time, Bryan was followed by Theodore Roosevelt, the Republican vice presidential candidate, who acted as a one-man "truth squad."

Theodore Roosevelt. "TR" succeeded to the presidency on the death of McKinley in 1901. For his campaign in 1904, Roosevelt turned down the suggestion of Lincoln Steffens that he depend on small gifts of from $1 to $5.[25] He solicited funds from two of the country's richest men, railroad magnate E. H. Harriman and Henry C. Frick, a partner of Andrew Carnegie. According to one account, Frick later reported: "He got down on his knees to us. We bought the son of a bitch and then he did not stay bought."[26] Despite the immense corporate and private contributions to his campaign, Roosevelt showed little appreciation for the "hand that had fed him" as he began to attack the trusts and the men who had given to his campaign. Harriman raised $250,000 for the Republicans with, he thought, the understanding from Roosevelt that Chauncey Depew would be appointed ambassador to France after the election. When Roosevelt did not appoint Depew, a long time spokesman for the Vanderbilt interests, Harriman refused, in 1906, to contribute to the Republican congressional candidates.[27]

Recalling free silver and Bryan, big business hesitated in 1904 to support the conservative Democratic candidacy of Alton B. Parker. But the Democrats managed somehow; it is thought that most of their funds came from two sources, August Belmont, who reportedly gave $250,000, and Thomas Fortune Ryan, who gave $450,000.[28]

It took a long time to recognize the need to avoid obligations to special interests, though as early as 1873 in a speech at the University of Wisconsin, Chief Justice Edward G. Ryan of the Wisconsin Supreme Court had said: "The question will arise... which shall rule—wealth or man; which shall lead—money or intellect; who shall fill public station—educated and patriotic free men, or the feudal serfs of corporate capital."[29] Charles P. Taft, the brother of William Howard Taft, contributed $250,000 to his brother's campaigns in 1908 and 1912 because he did not want him to have to go begging to the large corporations or be under obligation to anyone as President.[30] In 1907, Roosevelt made several proposals to Congress to improve the political finance system, including government funding of political campaigns; one

GOING — GOING

PRESIDENTIAL CHAIR

POLITICIAN

CAMPAIGN FUNDS

$

CAMPAIGN FUNDS

$

CAMPAIGN FUNDS

F.T. RICHARDS.

TO THE HIGHEST BIDDER

LIFE   July 8, 1920

proposal, prohibiting corporate contributions to federal campaigns, was adopted that year and remains the law today.

Thomas Fortune Ryan. Individuals, however, could still contribute, and Thomas Fortune Ryan continued to contribute large amounts to the Democrats. He is estimated to have given a total of $112,000 to two candidates in 1912 for preconvention spending. As Ryan was reported to be among the chief financial backers of Tammany Hall's "Boss" Richard Croker,[31] Woodrow Wilson refused to accept any contribution from him. Wilson wrote to Henry Morgenthau, chairman of the Democratic Finance Committee:

> I shall insist that no contributions whatever be even indirectly accepted from any corporation. I want especial attention paid to small contributors, and I want great care exercised over the

way money is spent...one thing more. There are three rich men in the Democratic Party whose political affiliations are so unworthy that I shall depend on you personally to see that none of their money is used in my campaign.[32]

The three rich men were Belmont, Morgan and Ryan.

In the 1920s, Ryan's money again became acceptable, and it is recorded that he gave $75,000 between January 1925 and the 1928 convention to help pay off Democratic debts.[33] He contributed $110,000 to the 1928 campaign itself.[34] That gift was smaller, however, than the donations by others to Alfred E. Smith—four individuals gave $360,000, $275,000, $260,000 and $150,000, respectively.[35] To put those gifts in perspective, all but the last were greater than the contribution to the Republicans by Standard Oil in either 1904 or 1908.

Franklin D. Roosevelt. Franklin D. Roosevelt had trouble raising money in his first campaign for the presidency in 1932; several times, his headquarters had no money at all. The conservative Democrats were alienated and would not contribute. It is reported that after the election a small, informal committee of persons close to Roosevelt was formed to consider federal appointments for some of those who were called the 34 original "investors" in Roosevelt's campaign. This group became known as "FRBC": "For Roosevelt Before Chicago" (site of the 1932 Democratic nominating convention). Said one of the members: "There was a more or less tacit understanding between the President-nominate and us that whenever possible they should be taken care of."[36]

The 1936 presidential campaign was one of the most expensive on record—the total was not exceeded until the 1960 race—and it gave birth to a new fund-raising technique that quickly became a staple, the $100-a-plate dinner. The technique is credited to Matthew McCloskey, a Philadelphia contractor and later treasurer and finance chairman of the Democratic National Committee, who arranged a dinner at the time of FDR's inauguration to raise money for the Democrats.[37] The idea spread quickly and widely; the $100-a-plate dinners, luncheons, breakfasts and brunches became common at all levels of the political system. With affluence and increased needs, the $500-a-plate and $1,000-a-plate affairs were held for more select groups. In 1968, Nixon held just one fund-raising dinner, but 22 cities were linked by closed-circuit television for that one event. The dinner grossed $6-million; the net profit, $4.6-million, was close to one-fifth the total cost of the campaign.

Big contributors continued to play a major part in the campaigns of the 1940s, 1950s and the 1960s. In 1948, for example, seven out of every 10 dollars (69 per cent) contributed to the Democrats' national-level committees came from donations of $500 or more. In 1956 the comparable proportion for the Republicans was 74 per cent. In 1964, 69 per cent of the Democrats' money came from large donors; four years later, the Democrats' national-level committees received 61 per cent of their funds from $500-plus donors.

The President's Club. The activities of the President's Club, formed of contributors of $1,000 each, produced a substantial amount of the Democrats' money in the 1960s. In 1964, the President's Club had as many as 4,000 members. By contrast, with Barry Goldwater as their candidate, the Republicans had notable success in 1964 in attracting small contributions. By means of mail drives and television appeals, they received about 651,000 contributions in small sums (under $100). Through all of their fund-raising programs that year, the Republicans received 10,000 individual contributions of from $100 to $999 and 1,500 that were $1,000 and over.

1968 Campaign

In 1968, much more information about large contributors, both on and off the record, was available than ever before. That was especially the case in the prenomination period. Nixon, Eugene McCarthy and Robert F. Kennedy are believed to have had at least one $500,000 donor in their prenomination campaigns. One political contributor, Stewart R. Mott, divided $300,000 between Nelson Rockefeller and McCarthy. Initially, Mott spent $100,000 trying to persuade Rockefeller to run as an anti-Vietnam War candidate; then he turned to McCarthy. Possibly two $500,000 donors are believed to have contributed to McCarthy. Five other individual donors are known to have contributed to him in amounts ranging from $100,000 to $300,000. Both the Kennedy and Rockefeller campaigns also received single contributions of $100,000 or more from donors outside those candidates' immediate families.

One of the largest known contributions in 1968, just under $1.5-million, was given by and went to a Rockefeller. It came to light very unexpectedly. Until 1972, no federal law required disclosure of campaign funds in the prenomination period, and most campaign committees were legally set up in a state (such as Delaware) that had no disclosure laws. As a result, only a few of the scores of McCarthy committees reported, and not one major Nixon, Romney, Humphrey or Kennedy committee reported under any state law. But for an unknown reason, one major Rockefeller committee was set up in New York which did have a reporting law. The committee received $1,482,625 from Mrs. John D. Rockefeller Jr., Nelson Rockefeller's stepmother.

Mrs. Rockefeller's contribution was an unusual one in American politics in that she subsequently was required to pay gift taxes of $854,483. A normal practice of large contributors was to take advantage of an Internal Revenue Service policy of some years' standing that permitted them to escape gift taxes. As gift taxes applied only to contributions in excess of $3,000, the larger donor would split up his gift into numerous smaller contributions made to multiple paper committees, all supporting the same candidate and established expressly for the purpose of tax avoidance.

The largest single contributor in the 1968 election was W. Clement Stone, chairman of the Combined Insurance Co. of America. Stone gave more than $2.8-million to the Republicans—all but $39,000 of that amount to Nixon to aid both his nomination and general election campaigns. At least 14 individual contributors are known to have given $50,000 or more to Republican causes. Humphrey, the Democratic presidential nominee in 1968, had seven contributors of $50,-000 or more. His largest single contributor was Mrs. Rella Factor, wife of wealthy California real estate investor John Factor, who gave him $100,000; her husband also provided an additional $240,000 in unsecured loans to the Humphrey campaign. In important measure, the Humphrey campaign relied on large loans. Forty-three persons were reported to have loaned the campaign at least $3.1-million. Only partial repayments were made by the Democratic National Committee after it assumed responsibility for the debts.

In terms of both numbers of individuals and amounts given, very large donors reached what seems almost certain to stand as their highest level of participation in campaign financing in the 1972 election. The information available about those largest of donors—contributors of $10,000 or more—indicates that they bankrolled the 1972 campaigns to an extraordinary degree. Just 1,254 individuals contributed a total of $51.3-million.[38] An analysis of their giving will follow a description of how the information became available.

BROADER DATA BASE IN 1972

By broadening the coverage of required disclosure, the Federal Election Campaign Act of 1971 (FECA) changed the data base of information about the financing of federal campaigns. Beginning with the 1972 election, much more than was ever known previously about sources of funds and categories of expenditures came to light, providing data for a more systematic analysis.

The Corrupt Practices Act of 1925 did not apply to primary candidates, and it required reporting only by committees operating in two or more states. The adoption of the FECA brought primaries and runoffs under coverage of the law. It also brought under coverage of the law any committee raising or spending in excess of $1,000 and seeking to influence federal elections. These provisions led to geometric increases in information about both contributions and expenditures. Although welcomed by students of campaign finance and other political observers, the vastly increased information made comparisons with data from earlier years perilous.

In the 1972 election, the General Accounting Office (GAO), the Clerk of the House, and the Secretary of the

Senate each began to receive thousands of detailed reports: for the period covering April 7 (when the law took effect) to Dec. 31, 1972, the GAO had some 83,000 pages of reports, the clerk, 117,000, and the secretary, 69,500—a total of well over a quarter-million pages of data, excluding instruction pages and audit notices.

Unfortunately, the reporting arrangement meant considerable overlap and duplication in the filings. A single committee supporting candidates for President, for the Senate and for the House, for example, was required to file reports containing the same information with the Comptroller General of the United States (head of the GAO), the Clerk of the House and the Secretary of the Senate. More than 1,000 committees—about a fifth of the 4,744 separate committees registered under the FECA—filed with two or three of those supervisory officers. Consequently, the problem confronting the student of campaign finance was to distinguish the discrete from the overlapping information.

Nevertheless, the massive amounts of data meant that journalists and scholars could study and report campaign practices in greater detail and with greater certainty than ever before. Selected information from the 1972 filings was widely published; in the future, such information should serve as the basis for a better-informed electorate on the matter of political funding. Major newspapers ran lists of the larger contributors in 1972 and assigned reporters to dig into major reports. At least two national political reporters spent all of 1972 writing exclusively on the subject of political funding.

Voluntary Disclosure

Spurred on by the new law and seeing a strategic campaign advantage, several of the presidential candidates voluntarily disclosed some of their contributions prior to April 7, 1972, adding considerably to the data base. Sen. George McGovern, a Democratic contender, and Rep. Paul N. McCloskey Jr., a Republican challenger to incumbent President Nixon, made full disclosure of all contributions their central campaigns received. With varying scope and for varying times, partial disclosures were also made by four other

Democrats—Sen. Hubert Humphrey, John Lindsay, then mayor of New York City, Sen. Edmund S. Muskie and Gov. George C. Wallace. In all, almost 1,500 contributions in sums of $500 or more were disclosed voluntarily by the six candidates. They totaled almost $4-million.[39] The other candidates flatly refused to make voluntary disclosures, though some data were subsequently collected and made public by the Citizens' Research Foundation from filings in states requiring disclosure where presidential primaries were held. Common Cause sued to force disclosure of the pre-April 7 receipts and expenditures of the Nixon re-election campaign. The legal action resulted in partial disclosure by court stipulation just before the November election; full disclosure was agreed upon and complied with in September 1973. Ironically, full disclosure meant that a campaign otherwise noted for its secret funds and undercover operations became the first presidential campaign in history fully on the record as far as its financing was concerned. The McGovern voluntary disclosures put that campaign mostly on the record. But McGovern's committees were so widely decentralized, with spontaneous grass-roots organizations not accounted for, that the national campaign headquarters did not know about some spending in the period before April 7.

BIG CONTRIBUTORS

The 10 largest contributors in 1972 gave a total of $7.4-million, the bulk of it to the presidential campaigns; names and amounts are shown in Table 4-1.

W. Clement Stone. The largest single contributor was again W. Clement Stone of Chicago, who donated a total of $2,141,655.94. Stone, who began his insurance office with $100 and a rented desk and developed it into the Combined Insurance Co., contributed $2-million of the total to the Nixon re-election campaign in the pre-April period and $51,643.45 after disclosure became mandatory; the true dimensions of his support only became known later. He also made contributions ranging down from $11,500 to $500 to a number of congressional candidates and various committees. All but one were Republicans or Republican causes (the exception was an $8,411.54 donation to the re-election campaign of Democratic Sen. Jennings Randolph of West Virginia). From 1968 to 1972, Stone and his wife, Jessie, contributed a total of $7-million to political candidates and committees. All but a small amount—about $25,000—of this money went to the Republicans, and most of it—more than $4.8-million—went to Nixon's 1968 and 1972 campaigns. These contributions may make Stone the largest contributor in American history.

Richard Mellon Scaife. The second largest contributor in 1972 was Richard Mellon Scaife, heir to the Mellon oil (Gulf), aluminum (Alcoa) and banking fortune, who gave the Republicans $1,068,000, most of it—$1-million—as a contribution to the Nixon campaign. As details of the Watergate scandal came to light, Scaife repudiated Nixon. In a May 1974 editorial in the *Greensburg* (Pa.) *Tribune-Review,* which he publishes, he called for Nixon's impeachment.[40]

Stewart R. Mott. The third largest 1972 contributor, Stewart R. Mott, heir to a General Motors fortune, was a McGovern supporter. As Table 4-2 shows, Mott gave a total of $822,592 in 1972 (not including some $25,200 in investment-loss deductions) to liberal and mainly anti-Vietnam policy candidates and causes. Most of Mott's contributions went to the Democrats. Nearly half ($400,000) went to McGovern.

Table 4-1 Ten Largest Contributors to 1972 Election Campaigns[a]

W. Clement and Jessie V. Stone	$2,141,665.94
Richard Mellon Scaife	1,068,000.00
Stewart Mott	830,339.50
Anne and Frank Forsyth	703,000.00
John A. and Naomi Mulcahy	681,558.97
Leon Hess	481,000.00
Meshulam Riklis	449,000.00
Max Palevsky	377,190.00
Martin and Anne Peretz	343,968.47
Dwayne Andreas	342,994.11

[a] Includes 1970-71 gifts to 1972 presidential campaigns.

Missing from the list of top givers in 1972, with the exception of Richard Mellon Scaife, are the names of the owners of the great American fortunes—the Fords, Rockefellers, Whitneys and Astors, whose support had been crucial in earlier political campaigns, particularly those of Republicans. In 1972, those families were displaced by donors such as Stone, John A. Mulcahy, Anthony Rossi and Abe Plough. All of the latter could boast of Horatio Alger success stories: Mulcahy, a poor Irish immigrant in the 1920s who rose to the presidency of a steel industry equipment supplier and then became a major stockholder in a drug firm merger (Pfizer Inc.), gave Nixon close to $625,000; Rossi, a former bricklayer and tomato farmer, born in Sicily, who built Tropicana Products into a major company, contributed $103,000; Plough, chairman of the drug firm (Schering-Plough Corp.) that makes, among other products, St. Joseph's aspirin, who began his career in 1908 as a door-to-door medicine oil salesman, gave Nixon $56,002.

Others. Along with Mott on the Democratic side was Max Palevsky—at one time the largest stockholder in the Xerox Corp. Palevsky contributed $377,190, of which $319,365 went to McGovern. (A Republican, Rep. Paul McCloskey, who was challenging Nixon for the nomination, received $9,825 from Palevsky.) Martin Peretz—a member of the Harvard faculty whose wife, Anne, is a Singer Co. heiress—contributed jointly with his wife $343,968, almost all to Democratic causes. Dr. Alejandro Zaffaroni—the Uruguayan-born president of Alza Corp., a California drug research firm —contributed $231,753, almost all to Democrats ($206,753 to McGovern). All of these were among McGovern's top 10 contributors, replacing the traditional Democratic supporters, such as the Lehmans, the Harrimans and others of earlier years.

Several of the very largest contributors gave to both Republican and Democratic presidential campaigns. Leon Hess, chairman of the board of Amerada Hess Oil Co., who was in Nixon's "Top 25" in 1972 with a gift of $250,000, also gave $225,000 to the presidential prenomination campaign of Sen. Henry M. Jackson. Another so-called "split contributor" was Meshulam Riklis, chairman of the board of Rapid-American Corp., who contributed $188,000 to Nixon, $100,000 to Jackson and $125,000 to Humphrey. Riklis also lent Humphrey $550,000, most of which was not repaid. Riklis was among a group of Democratic businessmen who met with McGovern in a New York hotel in January 1970. At the meeting he asked McGovern about his position on Israel (Riklis was an Israeli immigrant). McGovern answered that lasting peace in the Middle East could only be achieved by a negotiated settlement worked out by the United Nations. This position, not acceptable to Zionists, cost McGovern the support of some members of the Jewish community. It even diverted unprecedented sources to Nixon from Hess, Riklis and others.[41]

Part of the gift of another of the largest split contributors, Minnesota soybean millionaire Dwayne O. Andreas, figured in the early unraveling of the Watergate affair. Andreas' check for $25,000, made out to the Nixon re-election campaign, was discovered in the Miami bank account of Watergate burglar Bernard Barker, a revelation that triggered an audit of the Finance Committee to Re-Elect the President by the General Accounting Office. In all, Andreas gave $144,000 to Nixon in 1972, $161,000 to Humphrey and $25,000 to Jackson.

One of the very largest contributors in 1972 was Anne R. Forsyth, a tobacco and textile heiress from Winston-Salem, N.C., who was the financial mainstay of the presidential nomination campaign of Terry Sanford, president of Duke University and former governor of North Carolina. Sanford's campaign, which was concentrated in North Carolina, is known to have cost about $850,000, and Mrs. Forsyth's contribution totaled $701,000. She made an initial gift of $1,000, then loaned the Sanford campaign $700,000, and subsequently forgave the entire amount of the loan.

THE VERY RICH

The dominant allegiance to the Republican Party of wealthy persons—a fact of U.S. political history for

Table 4-2 Political Contributions of Stewart R. Mott in 1972

Presidential

Shirley Chisholm	$ 2,100
John Lindsay	6,000
Eugene McCarthy	5,000
Paul N. McCloskey Jr.	6,000
George McGovern	400,000
Anti-Edmund S. Muskie, negative research and advertisements	39,000
	$458,100

Senate

James Abourezk, S.D.	$ 1,000
Edward W. Brooke, Mass.	200
Lee Metcalf, Mont.	200
Walter F. Mondale, Minn.	200
Claiborne Pell, R.I.	500
Floyd K. Haskell, Colo.	500
	$ 2,600

House

Herman Badillo, N.Y.	$ 1,100
James Burch, Va.	1,000
Phillip Burton, Calif.	100
John Conyers Jr., Mich.	100
Ronald V. Dellums, Calif.	100
Charles C. Diggs Jr., Mich.	100
John Dow, N.Y.	100
Don Edwards, Calif.	100
Walter Fauntroy, delegate, D.C.	100
William J. Green, Pa.	500
Ken Hechler, W.Va.	500
Robert W. Kastenmeier, Wis.	100
John Kerry, Mass.	1,000
Edward I. Koch, N.Y.	400
Howard Lee, N.C.	1,000
Allard Lowenstein, N.Y.	1,000
Paul N. McCloskey Jr., Calif.	1,000
Parren J. Mitchell, Md.	500
Alberta Murphy, Ala.	500
Richard L. Ottinger, N.Y.	100
David Pryor, Ark.	2,500

Charles B. Rangel, N.Y.		200
Ogden Reid, N.Y.		100
Henry S. Reuss, Wis.		100
Donald W. Reigle Jr., Mich.		100
Frank Smith, Miss.		500
Gerry E. Studds, Mass.		1,000
Yancy White, Texas		500
Charles Wilson, Texas		500
Senate and House candidates (unspecified)—amounts given directly, plus expenses		5,000
Senate and House Candidates (unspecified)—amounts given through National Committee for an Effective Congress		13,992
		$ 33,892

Miscellaneous

Albert Blumenthal, N.Y.	$	500
Tony Olivieri, N.Y.		500
Sissy Farenthold (gov.), Texas		1,000
Dan Walker (gov.), Ill.		1,000
Center for Political Reform		66,000
Democratic Planning Group		6,000
October 9 mini-campaign—Vietnam		80,000
Opposition to DNC telethon		6,000
People Politics (fund-raising cost)		22,000
Vote for Peace (TV program)		75,000
		$258,000

Administrative expenses

Presidential campaigns	$	40,000
Party reform and delegate selection		10,000
Miscellaneous issues (including some not specified above)		20,000
		$ 70,000
GRAND TOTAL		**$822,592**

Investment-loss deductions (not included in hard money total)

The Informed Delegate (newsletter)	$	17,000
New Democrat Magazine		5,200
The Reliable Source (publication)		3,000
		$ 25,200

decades—was never more apparent than in 1972. An analysis of the contribution patterns of the nation's centimillionaires (those with fortunes of $150-million or more) shows that Republican money "outnumbered" Democratic money by better than 10 to 1 (Table 4-3). The Republican advantage was even more marked in 1972 than it had been in 1968 when centimillionaires also were studied.[42]

Centimillionaires

There were 66 centimillionaires on the 1968 *Fortune* list, each with wealth amounting to at least $150,000,000. Forty six of them (70 per cent) were recorded as political contributors in 1968,[43] with total gifts of $3,705,000. Four years later, 63 of those centimillionaires were still living and 51 of them (81 per cent) made contributions to a political candidate or committee. Their contributions reported in 1972 amounted to $6.1-million, more than their gifts reported in 1968, when contribution disclosure laws were less stringent.

Twenty four of the 51 centimillionaire contributors in 1972 gave only to Republicans. Five gave only to Democrats. Among the major Republicans-only supporters were: Richard Mellon Scaife of Pittsburgh ($1,068,000); Joan Whitney Payson ($149,000); J. Paul Getty of Los Angeles ($128,000); Winthrop Rockefeller ($115,700); and Peter Kiewit of Omaha ($100,912).

The five contributing only to Democrats were: former Sen. William Benton ($32,250); Iphigene Sulzberger of the family that publishes *The New York Times* ($24,500); Daniel K. Ludwig of New York City ($2,500); James S. Abercrombie of Houston ($1,000); and Jacob Blaustein of Baltimore ($1,000).

Seventeen of the centimillionaires split their contributions, giving to both sides, though often only a nominal amount to one. But the largest Democratic contributor, Leon Hess, gave $228,500 to Democrats (accounting for more than half of the total contributions of the centimillionaires to Democrats) and $252,500 to Republicans. Hess's donations to Republicans made him the second-largest contributor to Republicans in the centimillionaire group.

Table 4-3 American Centimillionaires' Contributions in 1972 and 1968 Campaigns

	1972	*1968*
No. of Contributors	51	46
To Republicans	$5,550,896	$3,584,000
To Democrats	496,522	121,000
Miscellaneous	23,600	11,000
Totals	$6,071,018	$3,705,000

The Newly Rich

In 1973, *Fortune* compiled and published a list of 39 persons who had amassed the bulk of their wealth since the 1968 list was put together and who possessed fortunes of at least $50-million.[44] The new list did not include persons who had become wealthy entirely through inheritance.

Of those who were named, 28 (72 per cent) contributed in 1972 to a political campaign or committee. Although the Republican contributions among this group in 1972 heavily outweighed the Democratic gifts, the advantage was not as overwhelming as it had been with the older, more established wealthy—about 3 to 1 Republicans compared with 10 to 1 on the earlier list. From the newly rich, the Republicans received $1,118,754 and the Democrats $321,865 ($4,000 fell in the miscellaneous category). Sixteen of the 28 gave only to the Republicans and two gave only to the Democrats.

Both the 1968 and 1972 elections have become known for disillusionment with candidates and the political process on the part of large segments of the electorate. At the same time, the techniques of fund raising—television, sophisticated direct mail appeals and other means—have been used to seek out broader audiences. Indeed, while new fund-raising techniques are reaching more people, the proportion that is contributing seems to be declining.

Still, the probability that there is a reservoir of untapped potential for campaign funds is suggested by other survey findings. From time to time, the Gallup Poll has asked people whether they would contribute $5 to a party campaign fund if they were asked. Throughout the 1940s and 1950s, approximately one-third of those surveyed said that they would be willing to contribute; in the 1960s this segment increased to more than 40 per cent. Even with the enormous costs of today's presidential elections, only a small portion of potential of this kind would have to be tapped to eliminate many of the financial problems of the parties.

In both the centimillionaire and new rich groups, the percentages of those contributing are very high—ranging from 46 per cent to 72 per cent—compared with percentages of financial participation in politics by other groups in society or by the rest of the population. For example, surveys indicate that from 8 to 12 per cent of the total adult population contributes to politics at some level in presidential election years.

Survey results compiled by the Gallup Poll and the Survey Research Center of the University of Michigan over the last quarter-century show a large increase in the number of contributors during the 1950s. As shown below, the number remained relatively steady in 1960 and 1964, fell off in the 1968 election, and in 1972 climbed back to about the level of eight years earlier. Applying survey percentages to the adult, noninstitutionalized population suggests that there were:

>3 million contributors in 1952,
>8 million contributors in 1956,
>10 million contributors in 1960,
>12 million contributors in 1964,
>8.7 million contributors in 1968, and
>11.7 million contributors in 1972.

Another long-term pattern that the survey figures suggest is that of a declining return on investment in a broad-based solicitation effort. Such a pattern is shown by the percentage of individuals solicited who contributed in recent years: 50 per cent in 1956; 70 per cent in 1960; 77 per cent in 1964; 40 per cent in 1968; and 33 per cent in 1972.

Table 4-4 Percentage of National Adult Population Solicited and Making Contributions, 1952-1972

Year	Organization	Solicited by: Rep.	Dem.	Total[a]	Contributed to: Rep.	Dem.	Total[a]
1952	SRC				3	1	4
1956	Gallup	8	11	19	3	6	9
1956	SRC				5	5	10
1960	Gallup	9	8	15	4	4	9
1960	Gallup						12
1960	SRC				7	4	11
1964	Gallup				6	4	12
1964	SRC	8	4	15	6	4	11
1968	SRC	8	6	20[b]	3	3	8[c]
1972	SRC	9	13	30[d]	4	5	10[e]

[a] The total percentage may add to a different total than the total of Democrats and Republicans because of individuals solicited by or contributing to both major parties, other parties, nonparty groups, or combinations of these.
[b] Includes 3.5 per cent who were solicited by both major parties and 1 per cent who were solicited by Wallace's American Independent Party (AIP).
[c] Includes 0.6 per cent who contributed to Wallace's AIP.
[d] Includes 8 per cent who were solicited by both parties.
[e] Includes contributors to American Independent Party.

SOURCES: Survey Research Center, University of Michigan; data direct from center or from Angus Campbell, Philip E. Converse, Warren E. Miller, Donald E. Stokes, *The American Voter* (New York: John Wiley and Sons, 1960), p. 91; Gallup data direct or from Roper Opinion Research Center, Williams College.

Family Groups

The patterns of political contributions by members of 12 prominent American families have been analyzed in each presidential election year since 1956. Initially, the analyses were done in connection with the investigations of a Senate committee headed by then Sen. Albert Gore of Tennessee. In subsequent election years, they were carried out by the Citizens' Research Foundation. The families studied were the Du Ponts, Fields, Fords, Harrimans, Lehmans, Mellons, Olins, Pews, Reynolds, Rockefellers, Vanderbilts and Whitneys. Considered in the study were only persons known to be family members, including members by marriage. Husbands and wives were counted separately, and divorced spouses were not included. The contribution patterns of the families are shown in Table 4-5.

In an election campaign marked generally by the increased numbers of contributors that were publicly disclosed, it is noteworthy that numbers of contributors, but not size of contributions, declined among these families in 1972. Four years earlier, 122 members were recorded as making a gift to a political campaign or committee; in 1972 that figure dropped to 88. But the total amount of 1972 support was substantially greater—about $3.7-million compared with about $2.7-million in 1968.

The family that gave the most in 1972 was the Mellon family. The principal reason for that fact, however, was the contribution of Richard Mellon Scaife of Pittsburgh, who has been mentioned above. Scaife's donations, totaling $1,068,000, to the Republicans amounted to 83 per cent of the Mellon family's total.

Contributions by the Rockefeller family in 1972 were considerably smaller than they had been four years earlier (Nelson Rockefeller was not a candidate). In 1968, as has been noted, Mrs. John D. Rockefeller Jr. had contributed at least $1,482,625 to her stepson Nelson's presidential campaign, while Rockefeller himself, as noted, contributed $356,000. Counting the latter, the Rockefeller total on the record in 1968 was $2,070,375. Four years later, the donations of the 19 members of the family who contributed amounted to only about a quarter of that—$521,360. Nelson Rockefeller and his wife contributed $82,500 to the Republicans in 1972.

A trend toward Democratic contributions in these formerly all Republican groups, observable since 1956, continued in 1972. The Rockefellers, for example, gave $33,210 to the Democrats in 1972, with the bulk of that coming from three younger members of the family, Sandra Ferry of Cambridge, Massachusetts ($15,600), and Mr. and Mrs. John D. (Jay) Rockefeller IV of West Virginia ($9,610). Mrs. Rockefeller is the former Sharon Percy, daughter of Republican Sen. Charles H. Percy of Illinois.

Table 4-5 Pattern of Giving by 12 Prominent Families in 1956, 1960, 1964, 1968 and 1972

	Rep.	*Dem.*	*Misc.*	*Totals*
1956	$1,040,526	107,109	6,100	$1,153,735
1960	548,510	78,850	22,000	649,360
1964	445,280	133,500	24,146	602,926
1968	2,580,785	149,700	35,651	2,766,136
1972	3,453,140	199,206	39,400	3,691,746

In 1956, the first study of these 12 family groups found that the Du Ponts, Fords, Mellons, Olins, Pews, Rockefellers and Whitneys were all exclusively Republican contributors. By 1968, only the Olin and Pew money continued to show up as "Republican-only"; in 1972, the Olins were the sole remaining family in this category.

In the 1968 election, there were only two families whose Democratic contributions exceeded Republican gifts—the Fields and the Lehmans—although giving from the Ford family was fairly evenly divided ($57,750 Republican, $52,000 Democratic). In 1972, four families gave more to Democrats than to Republicans—the Fields, the Lehmans, the Reynolds and the Vanderbilts. The Ford family donations, meanwhile, swung heavily back into the Republican camp—$159,026 to $35,620.

Along with the gifts of the Rockefellers, contributions of the Fields and the Lehmans, the two traditionally Democratic families in the group, also declined. The remaining nine families made substantially larger contributions in 1972 than in 1968.

Gifts of $10,000 or More

Because of the expansion of information as well as particular interest in the election events of that year, Citizens' Research Foundation prepared a list of contributors whose aggregate contributions totaled $10,000 or more in 1972. The list was drawn from both governmental and nongovernmental sources.[45] This compilation shows that $51.3-million was raised from such contributors—more than four times the amount recorded in this gift category in 1968 when reporting requirements were less stringent.

The data show that 64 per cent of the money given by these very large donors came from contributors who gave to only one party, so-called "straight party givers." The remainder is accounted for by individuals who, for various reasons, chose to give to candidates of both parties; their giving patterns will be discussed shortly.

Straight-Party Giving

Nearly half of the straight party money came from 82 individuals, each of whom gave an aggregate of $100,000 or more—some $14.3-million of the $33-million in straight party gifts.

Straight party contributions from the large donors to Republican candidates and party organizations amounted to more than twice the sum given to Democratic candidates and party organizations—$23.3-million to $9.4-million. The major beneficiary of large contributions was Nixon, who received $19.8-million in gifts from straight party contributions from these sources. More than half of that sum (52 per cent) was in gifts made before the April 7 disclosure deadline. In contrast, George McGovern's straight party contributors in the $10,000 and over category gave him a total of $4.1-million. In McGovern's case, 96 per cent of that amount came after April 7th.

Split Contributions

Large contributors who split their gifts made political donations totaling $18.2-million in 1972. The split contributors tended to divide their gifts among different levels—giving, for example, to a presidential candidate of one party and a senatorial candidate of another. Or they supported the candidate of one party in the primary and then shifted their financial allegiance to the other party's candidate in the general election—in most cases, when their original primary candidate had lost the nomination.

There were exceptions, even at the presidential level. In 14 instances, contributors of $10,000 or more gave to both Nixon and McGovern—Nixon won in dollar amounts in this contest, but by a small margin—$213,445 to $191,746.

A number of split contributors gave to three or more presidential candidates, and one donor, Charles E. Smith, a Washington, D.C., realtor, divided his presidential contributions of $30,350 among no less than six candidates—Nixon, McGovern, Jackson, Humphrey, Muskie and Vance Hartke.

In the 1972 election campaigns, 284 individuals made loans of at least $10,000. A total of $11.8-million was lent, $9.9-million to the Democrats by 202 lenders and $1.9-million to the Republicans by 82 lenders.

Table 4-6 Individuals Contributing $500 and Over, $10,000 and Over, and Amount, 1952-1972

Year [a]	No. of Individuals Contributing $500 and Over	No. of Individuals Contributing $10,000 and Over	Amounts Contributed by Individuals Contributing $10,000 and Over
1952	9,500	110	$ 1,936,870
1956	8,100	111	2,300,000
1960	5,300	95	1,552,009
1964	10,000	130	2,161,905
1968	15,000	424	12,187,863+
1972	51,230 [b]	1,254 [c]	51,320,154

[a] The filings and listing which provided data about individual contributors of $500 or more were not the same for each of these six years. Data for 1952 and 1956 are from Alexander Heard, *The Costs of Democracy* (Chapel Hill: The University of North Carolina Press, 1960), p. 53, note 37. For subsequent years, see Alexander, *Financing the...Election.*
[b] This figure is derived from the same ratio used for the 1968 figure, when reporting conditions were somewhat different, and may be inflated.
[c] Includes individuals who contributed an aggregate of $10,000 or more to candidates and/or committees. Does not include: candidates who contributed to their own campaigns, loans, contributions which if combined with loans add to $10,000 or more, or returned contributions.

Table 4-6 shows the dramatic increases that have taken place in the number of persons making political contributions of $500 or more and of persons making contributions of $10,000 or more during the 20-year period, 1952 to 1972. The data are derived from reported information on federal elections and from smaller and varying amounts of information made public under state disclosure laws. The notable increase in information in 1972 reflects, for the most part, the comprehensiveness of the reporting requirements of the Federal Election Campaign Act of 1971. Some 1972 information, however, resulted from voluntary disclosures by some candidates and from Watergate-related disclosures.

AMBASSADORIAL POSTS

The reward of ambassadorial posts to large contributors has been a common practice in U.S. politics. Beginning in 1956, the Gore Committee compared lists of contributors with the names of the chiefs of foreign missions and special missions, both career officers and political appointees. The chiefs of foreign missions and special missions comprised one of 13 groups whose contribution patterns have been studied in subsequent presidential years.

During the 1972 election campaigns, there were 116 such posts, 80 held by career foreign service officers and 36 held by others. Among the 116 were 23 large contributors ($500 or more), 20 of whom were not career officers. The 23 gave a total of $1,117,964, and 99 per cent of it went to Republicans.

The average individual contribution from this group was far larger than that of any of the officers or directors of the other 13 groups analyzed (including such special interest groups as the American Petroleum Institute, National Association of Manufacturers (NAM), and the U.S. Chamber of Commerce). The mean size gift from the foreign service group was $48,400, compared, for example, to the NAM's $4,160 or the Chamber of Commerce's $2,100.

Six chiefs of mission, all of them already serving as ambassadors in 1972 by appointment of President Nixon, made contributions of $100,000 or more to the Nixon re-election campaign. They were: Walter H. Annenberg, Great Britain, $254,000; Arthur K. Watson, France, $303,000; Kingdon Gould Jr., Luxembourg, $100,900; Vincent de Roulet, Jamaica, $103,000; Shelby Cullum Davis, Switzerland, $100,000; John P. Humes, Austria, $100,000.

The practice of rewarding large contributors with federal jobs became the focus of one set of investigations by the special Watergate prosecutor, Leon Jaworski, following the 1972 election. Herbert W. Kalmbach, President Nixon's personal lawyer, was sentenced to a prison term for having promised an ambassadorship in 1970 as well as for his role in raising a fund of $3.9-million from incumbent ambassadors, among others, for use in the 1970 congressional campaigns without creating a proper committee structure for the purpose.

In the months following his re-election, Nixon sent to the Senate the names of 319 persons whose appointments to various high level federal positions (including ambassadorships) were subsequently confirmed. Fifty-two of these appointees, or 17 per cent, were recorded as having made a large contribution ($100 or more) to the Republicans; their gifts totaled $772,224. Of that amount, $703,654 (91 per cent), went to the Nixon campaign, with 36.7 per cent of that flowing in during the predisclosure period. Several of these Nixon appointees also contributed to the Democrats (eight gifts totaling $5,973). Three Nixon appointees gave in excess of $50,000: John N. Irwin II gave $53,000, of which $50,000 went to Nixon; Kingdon Gould Jr. gave $112,900, of which $100,900 went to Nixon; and Dr. Ruth Farkas gave $300,000 to Nixon.

Dr. Farkas was subsequently appointed ambassador to Luxembourg, a move that generated by far the most controversy and produced the most impact of any of Nixon's ambassadorial appointments. A sociologist and a director of Alexander's, a New York department store, Dr. Farkas testified in her confirmation hearings before the Senate Foreign Relations Committee that more than half of the $300,-000 contribution that she and her husband had promised to the Nixon campaign was delayed until January 1973, by prearrangement, to await a more favorable market for stocks. She denied any connection between her contribution and her appointment, stating that she made the gift because of her respect for Nixon's actions as President.

She told the committee that New Hampshire Republican Rep. Louis C. Wyman arranged a meeting for her in Washington, D.C., with Maurice Stans. At that meeting Stans explained how a contribution of $300,000, to be legal, must be split up into gifts to individual committees not exceeding $5,000 each, and he said he would provide her with a list of committees; she and her husband subsequently wrote a total of 76 checks to some 31 committees.

When Kalmbach appeared under oath before the House Judiciary Committee's impeachment inquiry in July 1974, he told a different and expanded story. He testified that White House aide Peter Flanigan had told him that he should contact Dr. Farkas regarding a campaign contribution in exchange for the ambassadorship to Costa Rica; the arrangements for that meeting were also made by Rep. Wyman. At the session, Mrs. Farkas reportedly balked at the Costa Rica offer, saying, according to Kalmbach, that she was interested in Europe and "isn't $250,000 an awful lot of money for Costa Rica?"[46]

Several individuals felt the repercussions of the Farkas affair. Kalmbach was imprisoned for fund-raising activities relating in part to "ambassadorial auctions"—a promise of a federal job in return for financial support is a violation of federal law. Peter Flanigan's nomination as ambassador to Spain drew strong opposition during confirmation hearings, and he asked President Ford not to renew the nomination in the 94th Congress. Rep. Wyman, who began as a heavy favorite to move up to the U.S. Senate seat vacated by Norris Cotton, emerged from the election with only a razor-slim lead over Democrat John A. Durkin. After a lengthy recount battle, the election was run again, and Durkin was elected.

In the wake of the Farkas appointment, both the Senate and the House considered possible restrictions on the process of "ambassadorial auction."[47] The House Foreign Affairs

Committee proposed that nominees to ambassadorial posts be required to report all campaign contributions for the four preceding years before their names could be submitted to the Senate for confirmation. The Senate prepared draft rules on ambassadorial nominations: one called for the Foreign Relations Committee to oppose confirmation if a *prima facie* qualification for a nominee were a large contribution; a second would limit the number of noncareer ambassadors to 15 per cent of the total, or about half the present ratio. The Department of State objected to such restrictions, however, and major contributors continued to be named to ambassadorial posts after routine, almost perfunctory, screening by the Foreign Relations Committee. But the listing of contributions remained a requirement for confirmation.

DIRECT MAIL APPEALS

The direct mail approach to raising campaign funds—essentially an appeal for a great many individual contributions, however modest—has been used in politics for a number of years, but it was raised to something of a high art form in the 1972 contests.

McGovern Campaign

This was particularly true in the case of the McGovern campaign in which direct mail was the key to the financial success and to some extent the preconvention political success of McGovern's presidential drive; McGovern attracted at least 600,000 donors. McGovern's massive direct mail drive was begun in early 1971; during that year, when McGovern was the choice of fewer than 10 per cent of Democrats responding to the national opinion polls, $600,000 was raised by this means. Between the New Hampshire primary in March 1972 and the convention in the summer, an additional $2.4-million was raised through direct mail; that spring, some three million pieces were mailed. Thus, McGovern raised some $3-million in the prenomination period, at a cost of over $1-million. That sum was largely received in contributions of

$100 or less. In the general election campaign, $12-million was brought in through direct mail, with 15 million pieces mailed, at a cost of about $3.5-million to the national headquarters alone; some state groups mailed their own appeals in competition with the central campaign.

The direct mail method of fund raising used by McGovern had its beginnings in South Dakota politics. McGovern was a compulsive list-keeper as he crisscrossed the traditionally Republican state; he added to those lists when he moved into the national spotlight with anti-Vietnam War activities in 1970, and he obtained still more names from a massive national direct mail appeal for a 1970 campaign fund on behalf of some of his fellow Democratic senators.

Three days before McGovern formally announced, in January 1971, that he was seeking the presidency, 300,000 letters went into the mail, timed to arrive on the day he announced. The seven-page letter had been drafted in consultation with Morris Dees, a millionaire civil rights lawyer and direct mail expert, and Thomas Collins of Rapp and Collins, a New York mail firm. The letter discussed in detail McGovern's reasons for seeking the nomination, and it appealed for funds to help the cause. The strategy subsequently proved to be the most successful effort using this approach in American political history. It more than tripled the Goldwater results of 1964. Dees, who had also lent the McGovern campaign an aggregate of $190,000, which was partially repaid, donated his services.

Throughout the campaign, Dees and others on the McGovern staff generated new strategies for direct mail. Contributors were asked for additional contributions before key primaries; some contributors gave on a monthly basis. In one letter before the California primary, Mott promised to match each contribution, dollar for dollar, up to a specified amount; it was claimed the letter netted $600,000, exceeding both expectations and Mott's matching agreement.

A major appeal of McGovern fund raisers was for loans from wealthy persons to serve as "seed money" for the direct mail drive. This money made it possible to reach out continually to the thousands of potential small contributors, whose gifts, in turn, helped repay the loans. This practice of lending large sums of money is no longer possible since the contribution limits of $1,000 per candidate per election include loans within the definition of contribution.

McGovern mailings averaged about 16 cents a piece, broken down as follows:

Postage	$0.080
Letter	0.015
Envelope	0.008
Return envelope	0.005
Mailing house fee	0.015
Lists and record keeping	0.030
Agency fee	0.010
Total	$0.163

The increase in postage costs since 1972—which by the 1976 election brought the cost per first-class letter to between 20 and 25 cents—raises a question about the future use of direct mail. Except for lists with a proven return, direct mail may well become too expensive to use in future political campaigns—especially in contests where spending limits apply.

McGovern invariably appealed for funds at the conclusion of his television broadcasts; some five-minute broadcasts were designed essentially as fund raisers. Such appeals brought in an estimated $3-million. Broadcasts were timed to coincide with direct mail appeals that were already on their way. The intention was to have the appeal arrive in the mail about the time of the broadcast.

Nixon Direct Mail

Although direct mail did not have the importance in the 1972 Nixon campaign that it had in McGovern's campaign, the Nixon campaign did make use of it. A gross of $9-million was realized from mailings of 30 million pieces. Before July 1972, the appeals to small contributors were conducted chiefly by the Republican National Committee (RNC). In the months before Nixon's renomination, the RNC raised $5.3-million through its sustaining membership program. The contributions averaged $20. A telephone drive during that period brought in more than $500,000. In that drive, the contributions averaged $30. Direct mail drives conducted by the RNC alone and conducted jointly with the Committee to Re-Elect the President after Nixon's renomination brought in $14.3-million. Combined telephone drives raised $2.5-million.

A number of claims were made regarding the number of Republican contributors in 1972. About 250,000 persons contributed to the RNC. About 600,000 contributors were claimed by national and state affiliates of the Committee to Re-Elect the President. Eliminating duplications and repeat contributors, probably 600,000 gave some money to the RNC in its annual program, in response to its combined Nixon mailings after his nomination, or to some level of the CRP or of Democrats for Nixon.

Thanks in large part to direct mail, the McGovern general election campaign, launched with a reported $280,000 debt, managed to end the race with the first Democratic presidential surplus since the campaigns of Franklin D. Roosevelt. McGovern was the third presidential candidate in as many elections to rely successfully on the direct mail approach to voters' pocketbooks. All three, McGovern, Goldwater and Wallace, were considered factional or fringe candidates, not men of the center. Like Barry Goldwater in 1964 and George Wallace in 1968, McGovern succeeded in getting financial support from large numbers of small contributors though, in the end, he badly lost the election.

Goldwater's campaign in 1964 raised some $5.8-million from about 651,000 contributors. It thereby disproved the widely held notion (up to that point) that large amounts of money could not be raised from a great many small contributors. Still, as the Republican presidential candidate, Goldwater carried only six states and won only 38.5 per cent of the total popular vote.

The Wallace campaign in 1968, the costliest third party campaign on record, achieved a level of grass-roots participation never previously reached by the major parties in this country. It was estimated that some 750,000 small (under $100) contributors helped the Wallace effort, giving just over $5-million or 76 per cent of the income received by the campaign. The Alabama governor received 13.5 per cent of the popular vote and carried five states of the Deep South.

ADVENT OF TELETHONS

The 1972 campaign witnessed the conversion, by the Democrats, of the nonstop continuous telecast—a device previously used mainly to benefit health-related charities—into an effective political fund-raising tool for the party. That success came, however, only after a wracking fight within the Democratic Party as to where the proceeds from the first telethon should go. The Democratic National Committee (DNC) had initially conceived of the telethon as a way to help retire the $9.3-million debt largely left over from Humphrey's 1968 campaign. But when it came to be produced on the eve of the party's Miami Beach convention, the McGovern forces argued that the proceeds should be used to benefit the 1972 campaign, then in need of funds, and not a previous election.

The DNC officials had negotiated a trust agreement requiring that the funds raised by the telethon be spent to settle the party's debts and to pay production costs. They contended that without settling debts with the airlines, telephone companies and other industries, the Democrats would have difficulty carrying on the fall campaign. Although unhappy with the arrangement, McGovern, then the frontrunner for the party's nomination, finally accepted it. Stewart Mott, a major McGovern contributor, for a time threatened to go to court unless part of the telethon proceeds went to the 1972 presidential nominee. The proceeds, however, were never used in the 1972 campaign.

The first telethon, held in Miami Beach the day before the convention opened in July 1972, was a star-studded 19-hour show broadcast nationally over ABC-TV. John Y. Brown, then board chairman of Kentucky Fried Chicken, organized the affair. He underwrote it by guaranteeing—jointly, with several others—all of its costs. The goal of the telethon was $5-million, and the final tabulation showed that about 300,000 contributors had made pledges of $4,461,755. In addition, several hundred thousand dollars was raised at a $1,000-a-plate dinner held in Miami Beach in connection with the telethon. Production costs of the telethon were about $1.9-million. The net amount realized by the DNC was about $2-million, as about 15 per cent of the pledges were not honored. Thus, the costs of this kind of fund raising proved to be very high, virtually costing a dollar to net a dollar.

The first telethon was also beset by both political and technical problems. Actor Warren Beatty refused to produce it because the proceeds were not going to McGovern, and other stars refused to participate. Mayor Richard Daley of Chicago canceled a phone bank when his convention delegates were not seated, video transmissions were occasionally "garbled," audio lines crossed, and a water main break disrupted the New York City phone bank for eight hours. Undaunted, and with the Democrats now more united as the Watergate scandals were surfacing, Brown went ahead with another such production in September 1973. The second telethon was a deliberately shortened seven-hour event that aimed for prime time nationally on NBC-TV. It netted just over $1.9-million (from $4.2-million received). A third Democratic telethon was held in June 1974, in an atmosphere charged with the issues of honesty in government and the manner in which campaign funds were raised; the 21-hour show, aired on CBS-TV, cost about $2.5-million and netted about $2.7-million. As with the 1973 telethon, the net was distributed one-third to the national committee, two-thirds to the state committees. A state's share was determined by the amount that contributors in the state had provided.

Determined to learn from Democratic telethon success, the Republicans scheduled a regional pilot telethon for the West Coast to be held in August 1974. It was canceled at the last minute—another Republican casualty of Watergate—because of President Nixon's resignation.

By the time of the Democrats' 1975 telethon, provisions of the 1974 Amendments raised an issue for the newly created Federal Election Commission (FEC): would an individual who guaranteed or endorsed a bank loan to the Democratic

National Committee to absorb telethon production costs be subject to the new individual contribution limits? John Y. Brown, for example, had personally guaranteed the first telethon to what turned out to be $1.9-million, the second one to an amount that turned out to be $2.2-million. The FEC ruled that such individuals would now be under the ceiling imposed—and that guaranteeing a loan under these circumstances would count against the $25,000 overall ceiling on individual contributions to federal candidates. Whether the full amount would be counted, however, was left unclear. If the loan were repaid could the lender then still contribute up to the $25,000 limit within a calendar year? The FEC thus opened debate on a controversial area of the 1974 Amendments.

A slightly different combination of television and fund raising was used by the Democrats at their 1976 convention in New York City. In a strategy devised by the Democratic National Chairman Robert S. Strauss, some $250,000 worth of television time during the convention was bought by the Democratic National Committee; the time was used in 30- and 60-second spots that included appeals for contributions. Strauss had originally planned to film spots in advance, making use of the various Democratic contenders in fund-raising appeals. But with the nomination all but wrapped up in early June by former Georgia Gov. Jimmy Carter, the Democratic TV effort was able to concentrate on presenting the party's presidential nominee to the broad audiences that watch the conventions.

Fund raising by television was successfully carried out in the 1976 primaries by the Republican contender, Ronald Reagan. Reagan bought a half-hour of network prime time in late March, at a cost of $80,000, for an appeal for funds for his campaign. The appeal brought in more than $1-million.

SUMMARY

Since as early as 1852, when August Belmont, the representative in America of the European banking and commercial empire of the Rothschild family, stepped in to help the flagging presidential campaign of Franklin Pierce with a large contribution, big donors have played a major role in U.S. election campaigns. Their role has been curbed by law over the last decade, with an accompanying trend of expanding numbers of small donors.

More is known about the financial record of the 1972 presidential campaigns than any other in history, thanks to the Federal Election Campaign Act of 1971 (which took effect midway in the campaigns), voluntary disclosures by some candidates, and information that emerged from Watergate investigations.

The ten largest individual contributors in 1972 gave a total of $7.4-million. Largely missing from the list are the names of the great American families of wealth, whose support was crucial to Republicans in earlier campaigns, and many of the names of wealthy, traditionally Democratic contributors. Their support was replaced by money from the "new rich," many in the "self made" category. Overall, the dominant allegiance to the Republican Party among the wealthy continued, although the pattern among prominent families has been less clear cut in recent years.

The wealthy are more likely to make political contributions. About 8 to 12 per cent of the total U.S. adult population contributes to political campaigns, compared with between 46 and 72 per cent of the individuals in various wealthy groups analyzed.

The campaign contribution is one of a number of forms of political participation that range from the simple act of voting to actually running for office. The contributor tends to be higher on the socio-economic and educational ladder than the noncontributor and more active in community affairs.

There was continuing evidence in 1972 of the reward of ambassadorial posts to large contributors. There were 36 "non-career" ambassadors in 1972; 20 of them made contributions of $500 or more. Three career ambassadors also contributed on this scale. The average contribution from this group was far larger than for most other special interest groups studied.

The direct mail approach to campaign fund raising reached a high art form in 1972, particularly in the McGovern campaign; McGovern raised $3-million in the prenomination period in this fashion and $12-million in the general election. Nixon's several direct mail drives brought in almost as much. The telethon was also turned into an effective political fund-raising tool in 1972 by the Democratic National Committee.

Chapter 5 concludes our examination of the sources of campaign funds by assessing the nature and impact of giving by special interest groups.

NOTES

1. Jasper B. Shannon, *Money and Politics* (New York: Random House, 1959), p. 14.
2. Louise Overacker, *Money in Elections* (New York: The Macmillan Company, 1932), p. 102.
3. Roy Franklin Nicholas, *The Democratic Machine 1850-1852*, as quoted in Shannon, *op. cit.*, p. 21.
4. Shannon, *op. cit.*, p. 23.
5. Allan Nevins, *The Emergence of Lincoln*, vol. II, *Prologue to Civil War, 1859-1861* (New York: Charles Scribner's Sons, 1950), p. 292.
6. Overacker, *op. cit.*, p. 71.
7. Wilfred E. Binkley, *American Political Parties* (4th ed.; New York: Alfred A. Knopf, 1962), p. 279.
8. Edwin P. Hoyt Jr., *Jumbos and Jackasses, A Popular History of the Political Wars* (Garden City: Doubleday & Company Inc., 1960), p. 77.
9. Alexander Heard, *The Costs of Democracy* (Chapel Hill, N.C.; University of North Carolina Press, 1960), p. 233.
10. Shannon, *op. cit.*, pp. 24, 25.
11. *Ibid.*, pp. 25, 26.
12. John Bigelow, ed., *Letters and Literary Memorials of Samuel J. Tilden, 1908*, p. 245, as quoted in Shannon, *op. cit.*, p. 26.
13. Eugene H. Roseboom, *A History of Presidential Elections* (New York: The Macmillan Company, 1957), p. 242.
14. Shannon, *op. cit.*, p. 27.
15. Hoyt, *op. cit.*, p. 189.
16. Roseboom, *op. cit.*, p. 304.
17. *Ibid.*, p. 314.

18. Shannon, *op. cit.,* p. 33.
19. *Ibid.,* p. 36.
20. Herbert Croly, *Marcus Alonzo Hanna, His Life and Work* (New York: Macmillan, 1912), as quoted in M. R. Werner, *Bryan* (New York: Harcourt, Brace and Company, 1929), p. 101.
21. Shannon, *op. cit.,* p. 33.
22. Roseboom, *op. cit.,* p. 316.
23. M. R. Werner, *Bryan* (New York: Harcourt, Brace and Company, 1929), p. 101.
24. *Robert M. LaFollette, Autobiography,* (Madison, Wisconsin: *LaFollete's Magazine,* 1913), pp. 23-24, as quoted in Shannon, *op. cit.,* p. 35.
25. Shannon, *op. cit.,* p. 35.
26. O. G. Villard, *Fighting Years, 1939,* pp. 179-181, as quoted in Shannon, *op. cit.,* p. 35.
27. George Kennan, *E. H. Harriman: A Biography,* vol. II, p. 193, as cited in Overacker, *Money in Elections,* p. 171.
28. *Ibid.,* pp. 141, 152.
29. *Robert M. LaFollette, Autobiography,* pp. 23-24, as quoted in Shannon, *op. cit.,* p. 35.
30. Overacker, *op. cit.,* p. 180.
31. Gustavus Myers, *History of the Great American Fortunes* (New York: The Modern Library, 1936), p. 380.
32. Ray S. Baker, *Woodrow Wilson,* as quoted in Shannon, *op. cit.,* pp. 41-42.
33. Overacker, *op. cit.,* p. 153.
34. *Ibid.,* p. 158.
35. *Ibid.,* p. 155.
36. Edward J. Flynn, *You're the Boss* (New York: Viking Press, 1947), p. 123.
37. Arthur M. Schlesinger Jr., *The Politics of Upheaval* ("The Age of Roosevelt," vol. III, 1960 [Boston: Houghton Mifflin Company]), pp. 594-595.
38. CRF Listing of: *Political Contributors and Lenders of $10,000 or More in 1972* (Princeton, N.J.: Citizens' Research Foundation, 1975).
39. CRF Listing of: *Political Contributors of $500 or More Voluntarily Disclosed by 1972 Presidential Candidates* (Princeton, N.J.: Citizens' Research Foundation, 1972), Introduction, unpaged.
40. Christopher Lydon, "Big Donor Wants Nixon Impeached," *The New York Times,* May 15, 1974.
41. Stephen D. Isaacs, *Jews and American Politics* (Garden City, N.Y.: Doubleday & Company Inc., 1974), pp. 1-6.
42. For the listing of centimillionaires see: Arthur M. Louis, "America's Centimillionaires," *Fortune,* May 1968, pp. 152-157; 192-196.

43. The analysis of the 1968 contribution patterns is contained in Herbert E. Alexander, *Financing the 1968 Election* (Lexington, Mass.: Lexington Books, D.C. Heath and Company, 1971), pp. 187-188. Other information on 1968 throughout this book is drawn from the same source.

44. Arthur M. Louis, "The Rich of the Seventies," *Fortune* (September 1973), pp. 170-175, 230, 232, 236, 238, 242.

45. CRF Listing of: *Political Contributors and Lenders of $10,000 or More in 1972* (Princeton, N.J.: Citizens' Research Foundation, 1975).

46. *Final Report of the Senate Select Committee on Presidential Campaign Activities*, 93rd Cong. 2d sess. (Washington, D.C.: U.S. Government Printing Office, 1974), p. 904.

47. For a discussion of the process of "ambassadorial auction," see Charles W. Yost, "Ambassadorships for the Highest Bidders," *The Washington Post*, November 29, 1972. Also see Gordon Strachan's memo to H. R. Haldeman, containing references to "commitments" to large contributors seeking ambassadorships, in Political Matters Memoranda, December 16, 1971, "House Committee on the Judiciary, *Statement of Information: Appendix IV*, 93rd Cong., 2d sess. (Washington, D.C.: U.S. Government Printing Office, May-June 1974), pp. 69-70.

5

Special Interests: Contributions by Organizations

While reducing the role of the large individual contributor in American politics, the 1974 campaign finance legislation at the same time increased the roles that could be played by corporations, labor unions and other special interests. But even before the 1974 legislation, their roles in the political arena could hardly be overstated; they were among the largest institutions in the country both in numbers of people and economic resources.

The Federal Election Campaign Act Amendments of 1974 limited to $1,000 the amount an individual may contribute to any federal candidate in one election. However, a committee of either a business or labor union (usually called a political action committee), under the right conditions, may make a $5,000 contribution.[1] This provision gives new emphasis to the roles of business and labor in relation to individual donors.

CORPORATIONS

Even before the Federal Election Campaign Act of 1971 (FECA) provided that companies may spend their own funds on the administration of their own political action committees, the corporate role in the electoral process was considerable. It reached a new level in the 1972 election, chiefly in the interest of re-electing President Nixon and often in response to fund-raising appeals that some of those solicited thought bordered on extortion. In funneling their money into the campaign, as will be discussed in more detail, some companies "laundered" cash abroad, disguised it in Swiss bank transactions or purchased nonexistent equipment in order to move cash from where it was available to where it was needed for political purposes.

Although generally tamer than these subterfuges disclosed by the Senate select committee investigating Watergate, or the Watergate special prosecutor, there have traditionally been a number of ways by which corporate funds could percolate into partisan politics. One has been the use of expense accounts to reimburse employees for political spending. Federal law has prohibited corporate contributions since 1907. Companies have gotten around the prohibition by giving employees pay raises or bonuses with the understanding that the employee will make political contributions with the extra money. That was the device used by the American Ship Building Co. in 1972 to raise $25,000 as a Nixon gift (the company chairman, George Steinbrenner III, an owner of the New York Yankees, was later found guilty and fined for his role). The bonuses were scaled higher than the expected contributions so the employee could pay his taxes at no personal loss.

Another way has been to provide free use of company goods, services and equipment, ranging from furniture and typewriters to airplanes or office suites or storefronts. Complimentary travel in company autos and airplanes has been common even when no campaigns are going on. Corporations also have kept executives and their secretaries on the payroll while they work full-time in a campaign. In the aftermath of the abuses brought to light in the 1972 election, the laws against such corporate practices are now being more vigorously enforced and corporations generally are far more cautious.

Payments to public relations firms, lawyers, and advertising agencies have been used by companies in an attempt to charge off to "business-as-usual" what are really political contributions. During the last year of the Johnson administration and the first year of the Nixon administration—1968 and 1969—there was a series of federal prosecutions of corporations for illegal practices. The Justice Department obtained 15 indictments and 14 convictions of businesses, many of them in southern California, for deducting, as legitimate business expenses, payments that were in effect political contributions; the cases had been uncovered initially by the Internal Revenue Service and referred to the Justice Department.

Institutional advertising also can serve as a means of using corporate funds to convey a political message.

Paying for Political Conventions

A fund-raising innovation in 1936 was aimed at circumventing the legal bar on direct contributions by corporations. At their national nominating convention that year, the Democrats produced a *Book of the Democratic Convention of 1936;* it contained pictures of the Democratic leaders, articles about various branches of the national government written by party figures and other information. Advertising space in the book was sold to national corporations. The book was sold in various editions, ranging in price from $2.50 to a $100 deluxe edition that was bound in leather and autographed by President Roosevelt. The sale of the book and advertising revenue from it raised $250,000 for the campaign.[2]

Convention program books became more and more elaborate and the advertising rates went up accordingly, but after 1936 the money was used to pay for convention costs, not campaign costs. At the local level, program books were often used to raise money for party organizations.

The major parties continued to publish the convention books every four years, with ads costing about $5,000 per page, until 1964. That year, the Democrats published their convention book as a memorial to President Kennedy. Ads were $15,000 per page, producing an estimated profit of $1-million. The success prompted the Republicans to publish a program in 1965 called *Congress: The Heartbeat of Government,* which charged $10,000 per page for ads and raised about $250,000.

Not to be outdone, the Democrats came back in late 1965 with *Toward an Age of Greatness*. Ads again cost $15,000 per page, and they produced a profit of at least $600,000. This edition had been prepared for distribution at fund-raising movie premieres for Democratic congressional candidates in 1966.

Matters had gone too far, and reaction in Congress and the press was instant and hostile. The result was an amendment in 1966 which required the Internal Revenue Service to disallow corporate tax deductions for advertisements in political program books, which previously had been construed as legitimate business expenses. Congress backed off a bit in 1968, however, changing the law to permit such tax deductions, but only in connection with the national nominating conventions. For many years, hotels, restaurants and transportation lines servicing the host city made contributions,

In addition to advertising in program books, business firms also directly helped cities pay the costs of nominating conventions. For many years, hotels, restaurants and transportation lines servicing the host city made contributions, considered as legitimate business expenses, to nonpartisan committees established to guarantee bids for bringing the convention to the city. Such funds helped pay for hosting the political convention. In 1972, the reported pledge of the International Telephone and Telegraph Co. (ITT) of $100,000 or more to the Republican Party for its convention was one example, though the amount was greater than previously known; the subsequent uproar was not so much about the propriety of the pledge itself as about an alleged connection between the pledge and the terms of the government's settlement of an antitrust suit against ITT.

In addition to money for bid guarantees, many companies provided free goods or services, forms of indirect contributions, to the national conventions—car dealers provided fleets of autos, soft drink companies gave away drinks. However, many such practices became illegal for the 1976 and future national conventions under new guidelines set down by the Federal Election Commission. The 1976 conventions, it should be noted, marked the first time that these quadrennial gatherings could use government funds to cover some of their costs. The federal law now provides grants of up to $2.2-million to each of the major parties to arrange for and run their national conventions. It provides lesser amounts for qualifying minor party conventions. While the government funds will not cover some of the goods or services corporations previously provided, public dollars at least have partially taken the place of corporate dollars, thereby presumably decreasing the potential for corporate access or influence.

LABOR UNIONS

Labor union funds became significant in national politics in 1936 and ever since have provided an important resource to the Democratic Party. With a great infusion of labor support in 1968, Humphrey in the end nearly defeated Nixon. With labor badly divided in 1972, presidential nominee George McGovern went down to the worst Democratic defeat in history.

In their early years, unions were not important political contributors. Union funds were used only for such expenses as postage, leaflets and speakers and were not contributed directly to candidates. In 1936, however, unions are estimated to have contributed $770,000 to help re-elect Franklin D. Roosevelt. The biggest contributor was the United Mine Workers, which gave $469,000.[3] John L. Lewis, the union president, wanted to show up at the White House during the campaign with a check for $250,000 and a photographer, but Roosevelt vetoed the idea.[4]

Like corporations, unions learned ways to get around the law against direct contributions. They formed political auxiliaries, such as the AFL-CIO's Committee on Political Education (COPE), which collect voluntary contributions from union members for political purposes. In 1944, the first year in which there was a union-affiliated political committee, more than $1.4-million was raised.[5] That was the campaign in which the Republicans charged that everything the Democrats did had to be "cleared with Sidney"—referring to Sidney Hillman, then head of the CIO.[6]

Although the union members' contributions to these committees are voluntary, a strong union may use various means, not the least of which is simple social pressure, to persuade members to "volunteer." The funds thus gathered can be used legally for direct assistance to candidates.

Besides these "free funds," which are voluntary, there are three other channels by which labor money can flow into campaigns:

1. Nonfederal Contributions. These are sums spent where state laws permit contributions by labor unions to election campaigns for state and local office. As will be seen later, more states prohibit or limit corporate contributions than they do labor contributions. Studies have shown that labor consistently provides 10 to 20 per cent of the funds of major Democratic candidates in some states and often is the largest single organized group in Democratic circles. In some places, labor support helps keep the two-party system alive.

2. 'Educational' Expenditures. Funds taken directly from union treasuries to be used for such technically "nonpolitical" purposes as registration drives, get-out-the-vote campaigns, or the printing of voting records of legislators are considered "educational" expenditures. Labor's registration drives may be of more value to Democratic candidates than direct money contributions. In recent presidential election years, COPE has spent more than $1-million on registration alone, concentrating on marginal congressional districts. Nationally, the registration drives are carried out selectively in heavily Democratic areas.

3. Public service activities. Union newspapers, radio programs and the like, financed directly from union treasuries, express a sharply partisan, pro-labor point of view. Such expressions of opinion are, of course, constitutionally protected.

Although labor was badly split over the McGovern candidacy in 1972, the unions' reported gross disbursements at the federal level continued to rise—up from $7.1-million in 1968 to $8.5-million in 1972. The increase, however, resulted almost entirely from requirements for more comprehensive reporting. The reporting disclosed: (1) previously unreported

AFL-CIO spending from dues money for COPE staff and fixed operational costs, which was legal but had never been disclosed before; and (2) the first-time filings of scores of state and local union political committees whose activities fell under the FECA because they involved federal elections.

The 1972 campaigns were no exception to the rule that at the national level labor spends relatively less on presidential campaigns ($1.2-million) than on senatorial and House campaigns ($5-million).

Many political observers contend that labor's true strength lies not in its campaign war chests but in the volunteers it can muster to handle the strenuous precinct work, with all the drudgery of registering voters and getting them to the polls. In 1968, when the labor effort almost put Humphrey over the top in the closing weeks of the campaign (he had been trailing Nixon badly in the polls), unions registered 4.6 million voters, printed and distributed over 100 million pamphlets and leaflets from Washington, D.C. Local chapters deployed nearly 100,000 telephone callers or house-to-house canvassers and, on election day, put 94,457 volunteers to work as poll watchers and telephone callers, and in other jobs designed to get "their people" to the polls.[7] When labor concentrated the same sort of effort, though on a smaller scale, on the special U.S. Senate election in New Hampshire in September 1975, the Democrat, John Durkin—who had virtually tied with Republican Louis Wyman the previous November—won handily in the rerun.

The money limits set by the 1974 legislation work to place an even greater value on the ability of labor to mobilize large numbers of volunteers. There are no limitations on the use of "person power," and labor has an enormous pool of manpower. A similar advantage accrues to any other organization that can draw on the services of large numbers of people.

ANALYSES OF SELECTED GROUPS

In an effort to trace the contribution patterns of various segments of American business, analyses have been made over the years of the political gifts of officers and directors of trade associations, special-interest groups and large corporations.

Beginning in 1956, a U.S. Senate committee compared its lists of contributors with lists of the officers and directors of 13 selected groups—among them the American Bar Association, the American Medical Association, the Business Council, the National Association of Manufacturers and the U.S. Chamber of Commerce. Citizens' Research Foundation has continued to analyze the giving of these groups in subsequent presidential elections. (One of the groups studied, the chiefs of foreign missions and special missions, was discussed in detail in the previous chapter.)

Political giving by individual officers and members of these groups generally has been heavily Republican (with the exception of 1964 when a financial switch to President Johnson occurred). In the 1972 election, 90 per cent of their total contributions went to the Republicans, the bulk to the Nixon campaign ($2.6-million of $3.3-million). McGovern, in contrast, received only $1,250, or less than 1 per cent of the far

Table 5-1 Total Contributions of 13 Selected Groups:[a] 1956, 1960, 1964, 1968, and 1972

Year	Republicans	Democrats	Miscellaneous	Total [b]
1972	$3,323,283+	$339,950+	$32,206	$3,695,440+
1968	1,132,982+	136,106	11,967	1,281,055+
1964	200,310	225,790	4,618	468,218 [b]
1960	425,710	62,225	2,500	493,465 [b]
1956	741,189	8,000	2,725	751,914

[a]The groups are: The American Bar Association, American Medical Association, American Petroleum Institute, American Iron & Steel Institute, Association of American Railroads, Business Council, chiefs of foreign missions and special missions, Manufacturing Chemists Association, National Association of Electric Companies, National Association of Manufacturers, National Association of Real Estate Boards, National Coal Association and U.S. Chamber of Commerce.

[b]Republican, Democratic and Miscellaneous columns do not equal the totals shown because some contributors belonged to more than one of the 13 groups, and duplicated amounts have been subtracted in the overall totals.

smaller Democratic total derived from these 13 groups.

The same heavy Republican preponderance holds as one goes down the list, looking at the same patterns of each group in 1972. A comparison over the years is shown in Table 5-1. More than 80 per cent of the money contributed by 10 of the groups went to Republicans. The National Coal Association records no Democratic contributions; three others—the chiefs of foreign and special missions, the Manufacturing Chemists Association and the National Association of Manufacturers—gave over 90 per cent of their political funds to Republican candidates and committees.

The one exception to this pattern in the 1972 campaigns was seen among the officers and delegates of the American Bar Association (ABA), who gave more to the Democrats than to the Republicans—$33,473 to $28,450. This was a sharp turnabout from 1968 when the contributions of ABA officers and delegates had split 80-20 in favor of the Republicans. It should be noted, however, that nearly half ($15,000) of their 1972 Democratic total was a contribution by one individual, E. Smythe Gambrell of Atlanta, Ga., to his son's senatorial campaign.

The Petroleum Lobby

The energy crisis in the winter of 1973, together with revealed instances of illegal corporate political gifts here and abroad, created new concern over the alleged influence of the oil and gas interests on national policy. The contribution patterns of officers and directors of five petroleum organizations were analyzed both in 1968 and 1972. They included the American Petroleum Institute, American Gas Association, National Petroleum Refiners Association, Independent Natural Gas Association of America (INGAA) and Independent Petroleum Association of America (IPAA).

Contributions by these groups were more diversified and less "Republican" than those by a number of other groups examined. About 52 per cent of their contributions in 1972, for example, went to the Nixon re-election campaign, compared with some 70 per cent to that cause from the 13 selected groups whose giving patterns have been discussed. Participation was about at the same level as that of the 13 groups—31 per cent. Of the $1.6-million in gifts of petroleum organization members and officers, about 30 per cent in 1972 was contributed by one individual, Leon Hess, chairman of the executive committee of Amerada Hess Corp. His contribution of $250,000 to the Nixon campaign was nearly matched by the amount he gave ($225,000) to the presidential prenomination campaign of Democratic Sen. Henry M. Jackson.

Largest Defense, Industrial Firms

Citizens' Research Foundation also analyzed large contributions ($500 or more) in 1972 by the officers and directors of companies that were among the top 25 contractors for the Defense Department (DOD), Atomic Energy Commission (AEC) and the National Aeronautics and Space Administration (NASA).[8] The three agencies are the federal government's largest buyers of military and other hardware, with the Defense Department alone spending more than $20-billion a year on weapons systems and equipment. As a control group, large contributions from similar officials of the 25 largest industrial companies on the *"Fortune* 500" list also were studied. The results are shown in Table 5-2.

Again, the percentage making a large contribution was about three times the national average—a figure perhaps as attributable to their wealth as to any special interest. Support for Republicans dominated. Of a total of $3.1-million contributed by officers and directors of the 72 companies represented in the study (there was overlapping on the lists), $2.6-million (85 per cent) went to Republican candidates or committees.

Among the largest contributors from the defense segment of the business community was the late multimillionaire recluse Howard Hughes, whose Hughes Aircraft Co. was the 10th largest Pentagon contractor in fiscal 1972 and the 20th largest NASA contractor. Completely apart from the $100,000 which Hughes gave to Charles G. (Bebe) Rebozo, Nixon's longtime friend who said he kept it in a strongbox for three years and then returned it, Hughes gave $197,000 to the Republicans in 1972 and $3,000 to the Democrats. Two other

Table 5-2 Contributions from Officers and Directors of the 25 Leading Contractors for Three Governmental Agencies and of the 25 Largest Companies on the *Fortune* Industrial List, 1972.[a]

	DOD	AEC	NASA	Fortune Industrial
Total number of officers and directors	998	632	772	1,073
Number of individual contributors	364	184	236	402
Total contributions	$2,107,677	$674,535	$1,276,705	$1,757,251
Republican				
Number of contributors [b]	306	140	173	329
Amount of contributions	$1,852,694	$616,570	$1,082,203	$1,516,374
Democratic				
Number of contributors [b]	54	18	39	58
Amount of contributions	$216,613	$25,965	$163,821	$202,429
Miscellaneous				
Number of contributors [b]	57	52	52	55
Amount of contributions	$38,370	$32,001	$30,681	$38,449

[a]For each of the four groups, certain individuals were officials of more than one company within that group. They and their contributions have been counted only once.

[b]Due to the presence of individuals who gave to more than one party or cause, the number of Republican, Democratic and miscellaneous contributors is larger than the total number of individual contributors given at the top of each column. The first total gives the actual number of individuals.

executives of his company gave $1,000 to the Republicans and $1,700 to the Democrats.

The analysis did not include illegal corporate contributions. Only three of the 72 companies in the study—Goodyear Tire & Rubber, Gulf Oil and Northrop—are among those named as making illegal contributions.

A new focus is provided to the charge, heard frequently in the aftermath of the 1972 election, that certain segments of industry made block contributions in return for government contract favoritism. A breakdown of the officers and directors shows that the bulk of the contributions (about 66 per cent) came from directors who were outside the company. Such directors may have a smaller direct interest in the company's well-being than others. They were men (no women were on the list), many from the financial or legal worlds, who because of position and wealth were serving on a number of corporate boards. They also were the kind of men likely to be tapped in major fund drives. A case in point was John McCone, former director of central intelligence, who was included in the study because of his membership on the boards of directors of Standard Oil of California and International Telephone & Telegraph and because of his contribution of $14,000 to the Nixon campaign. However, McCone at that time was also on the boards of Pacific Mutual Life Insurance and the United California Bank, companies not included in this study. McCone's interests must be considered as typically diverse for someone of his wealth, and they cannot fairly be attributed to any one company.

ILLEGAL CONTRIBUTIONS

One of the disturbing aspects of election financing in 1972, brought to light by Watergate-related investigations, was the string of illegal corporate contributions made by a number of the most prestigious firms in American industry. That some businesses had engaged in such practices in the past was suspected; what was particularly startling about the roster of illegal corporate contributors in 1972 was its "blue chip" quality and the amounts involved. Moreover, these disclosures unlocked the door on a multitude of unethical practices by American industry, both within the country and abroad.

The story began in the fall of 1973 when the Watergate special prosecutor filed suit in U.S. District Court in the District of Columbia against American Airlines, Goodyear Tire & Rubber Co., and Minnesota Mining & Manufacturing Co., alleging violations of federal laws in making illegal contributions of corporate funds to Nixon and other presidential candidates in the 1972 campaign. Over the next two years, 21 companies pleaded guilty to this charge. The companies, their contributions and disposition of the cases are shown in Table 5-3.

In all, the 21 companies were charged with contributing almost $968,000 illegally, with the bulk of it, $842,500, going to the Nixon campaign. Democrats receiving illegal corporate contributions included McGovern, Humphrey, Wilbur D. Mills, Jackson and Edmund S. Muskie. As the case developed, a deliberate pattern of devious activity by the corporations designed to mask the sources of contributions became apparent.

'Laundered' Money

A new phrase entered the American political lexicon in 1972—the "laundering" of money, the description given the process by which corporations sought to hide the fact that the contributions had originated in their company treasuries and were thus illegal. The laundering of money took many forms. For example, American Airlines Inc. sent money from one U.S. bank to an agent in Lebanon for supposed purchase of aircraft; it came back to a second U.S. bank and then on to the Finance Committee to Re-Elect the President.

In seeking to hide the fact that their political contributions came from company treasuries, firms drew on secret slush funds, sold bogus airline tickets and created fictitious bonus schemes for employees. The employees then contributed the bonus to a campaign.

Although there had been sporadic federal prosecutions of corporate political practices in past elections, the picture that unfolded from 1973 to 1975 suggested illegal corporate giving on a scale unlike anything previously imagined. Many of the corporate officials convicted of involvement in the effort said they had contributed illegally because the fund raising had been carried on by high officials such as Maurice Stans, former Secretary of Commerce, and by persons close to the President, such as Herbert Kalmbach, Nixon's personal at-

Table 5-3 Illegal Corporate Contributions in the 1972 Presidential Campaigns

Corporation	Campaign	Amount of Contribution	Plea (Date)	Court Action
American Airlines	Nixon	$55,000 (refunded by FCRP)	Guilty (10/17/73)	$5,000 fine
American Ship Building Co. George M. Steinbrenner III, Chrm. John H. Melcher Jr., Exec. Vice Pres., Counsel	Nixon	$25,000	Guilty (8/23/74) Guilty (8/23/74) Guilty (4/11/74)	$20,000 fine $15,000 fine $2,500 fine
Ashland Petroleum Gabon, Inc. Orin E. Atkins, Chrm. Bd., Ashland Oil Inc.	Nixon	$100,000 (refunded by FCRP)	Guilty (11/13/73) No contest (11/13/73)	$5,000 fine $1,000 fine
Associated Milk Producers Inc. (AMPI)	Nixon Mills Humphrey	$100,000 5,000 50,000	Guilty (8/1/74)	$35,000 fine
Harold S. Nelson, Gen. Mgr. David E. Parr, Spec. Counsel			Guilty (7/31/74) Guilty (7/23/74)	3 yr. sent. susp.-4 mo., $10,000.
Braniff Airways Harding L. Lawrence, Chrm. Bd.	Nixon	$40,000 (refunded by FCRP)	Guilty (11/12/73) Guilty (11/12/73)	$5,000 fine $1,000 fine
Carnation Company H. Everett Olson, Chrm. Bd.	Nixon	$7,900	Guilty (12/19/73) Guilty (12/19/73)	$5,000 fine $1,000 fine
Diamond International Corp.	Nixon	$5,000	Guilty (3/7/74)	$5,000 fine

Ray Dubrowin, Vice Pres.	Muskie	1,000	Guilty (3/7/74)	$1,000 fine
Greyhound Corporation	Nixon McGovern	total $16,040 to both candidates' committees	Guilty (10/8/74)	$5,000 fine
Goodyear Tire & Rubber Co. Russell DeYoung, Chrm. Bd.	Nixon	$40,000 (refunded by FCRP)	Guilty (10/17/73) Guilty (10/17/73)	$5,000 fine $1,000 fine
Gulf Oil Corporation	Nixon Mills Jackson	$100,000 (refunded by FCRP) 15,000 (refunded) 10,000 (refunded)	Guilty (11/13/73)	$5,000 fine
Claude C. Wild Jr., Vice Pres.			Guilty (11/13/73)	$1,000 fine
HMS Electric Corp. Charles N. Huseman, President	Nixon	$5,000	Guilty (12/3/74)	$1,000 fine
LBC & W, Inc. architecture firm William Lyles Sr., Pres. & Chrm.	Nixon	$10,000	Guilty (9/17/74) Guilty (9/17/74)	$5,000 fine $2,000 fine
Lehigh Valley Cooperative Farmers Richard L. Allison, Pres. Francis X. Carroll, Lobbyist	Nixon	$50,000	Guilty (5/6/74) Guilty (5/17/74) Guilty (5/28/74)	$5,000 fine $1,000 susp. $1,000 susp.
Minnesota Mining & Mfg. Co. (3M) Harry Heltzer, Chrm. Bd.	Nixon Humphrey Mills	$30,000 (refunded by FCRP) 1,000 1,000	Guilty (10/17/73) Guilty (10/17/73)	$3,000 fine $500 fine
National By-Products Inc.	Nixon	$3,000	Guilty (6/24/74)	$1,000 fine
Northrop Corporation Thomas V. Jones, Chrm. Bd.	Nixon	$150,000	Guilty (5/1/74) Guilty (5/1/74)	$5,000 fine $5,000 fine

Table 5-3 Cont.

Corporation	Campaign	Amount of Contribution	Plea(Date)	Court Action
James Allen, Vice Pres.			Guilty (5/1/74)	$1,000 fine
Phillips Petroleum Co. William W. Keeler, Chrm. Bd.	Nixon	$100,000 (refunded by FCRP)	Guilty (12/4/73) Guilty (12/4/73)	$5,000 fine $1,000 fine
Ratrie, Robbins & Schweitzer, Inc. Harrie Ratrie, President Augustus Robins, III, Exec. V.P.	Nixon	$5,000	Guilty (1/28/75) Guilty (1/28/75) Guilty (1/28/75)	$2,500 fine
Singer Company* Raymond A. Long; M.A. Leader	Nixon	$10,000	Guilty (6/11/75)	$2,500 fine
Time Oil Co. (Seattle)	Nixon Jackson	$6,600 1,000	Guilty (10/23/74)	$5,000 fine
Raymond Abendroth, President			Guilty (10/23/74)	$2,000 fine
Valentine, Sherman & Associates Norman Sherman John Valentine	Humphrey	$25,000 worth of computer services, paid by AMPI	Guilty (8/12/74) Guilty (8/12/74)	$500 fine $500 fine
TOTAL CONTRIBUTIONS: Nixon Others		$967,540 842,500 (excluding Greyhound amount) 109,000 (excluding Greyhound amount)		

* Prosecuted by the Attorney General

torney. They claimed their concern was not to obtain favors but to avoid possible government discrimination against them if they did not contribute. Some said that the Nixon fund-raising effort differed from earlier campaign fund raising in the amounts of money involved and the unquestioning acceptance of cash. In the words of the Senate Select Watergate Committee, "there is evidence that a number of them (the solicitors) either were indifferent to the source of the money or, at the very least, made no effort whatsoever to see to it that the source of the funds was private rather than corporate.... [T]here is no evidence that any fund raiser who was involved in these contributions sought or obtained assurances that the contribution was legal at the time it was made."[9]

Certain companies reportedly flatly refused when they were asked for large amounts. Among them were American Motors Corp.[10], Union Oil Co. and Allied Chemical Corp.[11]

Most of the prime defense contractors, a *New York Times* survey disclosed, had been solicited by fund raisers from the Finance Committee to Re-Elect the President. The customary amount suggested for the major corporations was $100,000; requests were scaled down for the smaller firms. A distinct pattern of high pressure was discerned by some.[12] Ironically, the image of the greedy businessman as the corrupter, seeking favors from the politician, underwent change in the minds of some observers as reports of the kind of pressures applied came to light. Instead, the businessman became the victim, not the perpetrator, of what some saw as extortion. American Airlines' chief executive officer, George Spater, told the Senate Watergate Committee that he was motivated by "fear of the unknown," likening his state of mind to "those medieval maps that show the known world and then around it, Terra Incognita, with fierce animals." Gulf's Claude Wild said he decided to arrange the contribution so that his company "would not be on a blacklist or at the bottom of the totem pole" and so that somebody in Washington would answer his telephone calls.[13] How much of this was rationalization, remains for the reader to determine.

The Finance Committee to Re-Elect the President maintained that it never solicited corporate contributions—that it only asked corporate executives to take responsibility to raise money from among other executives for the campaign. Target amounts were proposed, it was admitted, but no quotas imposed. Yet targets by their very nature suggest quotas that, if unmet, pose problems for those not complying. And because the Nixon campaign represented an incumbent administration, requests for funds were taken seriously. The pattern of pressure was reported by so many corporate executives that they all could not have misjudged the zeal of some fund raisers in an atmosphere that seemed to exploit incumbency, with its implied (and inferred) power.

Dairy Contributions

A classic illustration of how money may "talk" when special interests deal with the government was provided by the dairy industry in the first Nixon administration. The story included the so-called "milk deal"—the sudden increase in the government subsidy to the milk industry in what seemed to be a response to campaign contributions and congressional pressure. The story included a criminal antitrust investigation of one dairy co-op allegedly thwarted by an Attorney General who was also the President's de facto campaign manager and alleged efforts by the co-op to buy its way out of a civil antitrust suit. However, none of these charges was proved.

The deep involvement of dairymen in politics flows from their great stake in federal policy. An almost direct connection exists between government decisions and the prices of dairy products. The dairy lobby in 1972 essentially consisted of the three largest milk co-ops in the country: Associated Milk Producers Inc. (AMPI) with 40,000 members and headquarters in San Antonio, Texas; Mid-America Dairymen Inc. (Mid-Am) of Springfield, Missouri, with about 20,000 members; and Dairymen Inc. (DI) of Louisville, Kentucky, with about 10,000 members. Together, the three co-ops came in the late 1960s to constitute the richest new source of political money in years.

After supporting the presidential candidacy of Hubert Humphrey with over $150,000 in 1968, AMPI faced a problem in 1969 with Nixon in power. Feeling it was imperative to win friends in the Nixon administration, its leaders gave a secret $100,000 contribution (in $100 bills) in August 1969 to Kalmbach, the President's chief fund raiser. The illegal gift, which was concealed by an elaborate laundering scheme involving exaggerated payments to lawyers and public relations men, came from the co-op's treasury. In addition to its illegality on that count alone, the gift also violated by its size the $5,000 limit on campaign contributions.

Reportedly disappointed with the lack of influence the $100,000 contribution had produced, the three co-ops then offered, some time before Sept. 9, 1970, $2-million to the Nixon re-election effort. That same fall AMPI contributed about $135,000 to Republican candidates in the congressional elections through a special fund—also a violation of the law.

The central event in the dairy scandal was the alleged "milk deal" of March 1971, in which Nixon played a leading role—the question was whether he had raised milk price supports in return for the campaign contributions. Less than two weeks after Secretary of Agriculture Clifford Hardin had declined to raise the subsidy level, the dairy industry had persuaded the administration to increase the subsidy, with Nixon himself reversing the Secretary's decision. The reversal meant a windfall variously estimated at from $300-million to $700-million for dairy farmers. The bill was paid by consumers in higher milk prices and by taxpayers in the larger subsidies.

After the initial announcement that price supports would not be raised, the dairy industry put on a lobbying campaign that climaxed on March 23, 1971, with an "audience" at the White House for 16 dairy executives. Although Nixon made no reference to any pledges of campaign contributions, he agreed in a follow-up meeting with administration officials to support higher parity. And later that day, the White House passed word to the dairy officials that it expected a reaffirmation of their $2-million campaign commitment in light of the forthcoming hike in price supports. The next day, March 24, the dairymen renewed their pledge and made a contribution of $25,000 as evidence of their intentions. The price support boost was announced by the Department of Agriculture on March 25.

The co-ops contributed another $45,000 two weeks later and an additional $247,500 by the end of 1971. Altogether, dairy co-ops contributed a total of $682,500 to Nixon's 1972 re-election. Most, but not all, of the money came from the three biggest co-ops. In 1972 the Lehigh Valley Cooperative Farmers, a Northeastern farm group, secretly gave $50,000 in $100 bills toward Nixon's re-election. The Lehigh group subsequently admitted the money was an illegal contribution and was fined $5,000; its president received a suspended fine of $1,000.

While the co-ops were dealing on a large scale with the Nixon administration, they did not neglect the Democrats in 1972. Their strongest support went to the presidential campaign of Rep. Wilbur D. Mills, one of the dairymen's chief allies in Congress, who wielded immense power as chairman of the House Ways and Means Committee. In all, Mills received nearly $200,000 from the dairymen. Some $55,600 of that amount was on the public record; the remainder was given before the April 7 date disclosure laws took effect. Although Mills said he was unaware of it, some of the unrevealed donations were in illegal corporate contributions.

Minnesota Sen. Humphrey, a supporter of legislation favorable to the dairy industry since 1949, received more than $40,000 in contributions from the dairy cooperatives in 1971 and 1972. When the financing of Humphrey's presidential campaign came under scrutiny during the Watergate investigations, the Senate committee raised a question about an illegal corporate contribution-in-kind of $25,000 from AMPI. The co-op had used corporate funds to pay for computer services from a political firm working in Humphrey's campaign; those funds represented part of a total of $137,000 in corporate funds paid by AMPI to the firm, Valentine, Sherman and Associates, for services to Democratic candidates in several states during 1971-72.

Some Case Histories

There were a number of instances relating to campaign contributions in 1972 in which the questions raised were often a matter of the ethics as well as of the legality of gifts.

Moreover, with respect to these contributions, it was conjecture as to whether the subsequent treatment accorded the giver resulted from the gift. A problem area troubles many observers of political finance. It arises from the fact that it is difficult to draw the line between the contribution given to a candidate as a signal of support for his positions and that given in expectation of influencing or changing his positions. The former has been found "entirely proper and legal" in a court of law[14] and is indeed to be encouraged as a desirable aspect of citizen participation, whereas the latter either is, or verges on, bribery.

Howard Hughes. Perhaps the most widely publicized case in this category—one of Watergate's remaining mysteries—was the matter of the $100,000 gift from the late Howard Hughes to the Nixon campaign, which Rebozo, Nixon's close friend, said he kept intact, in $100 bills, before returning them to the millionaire recluse in 1973.

The mystery is replete with conflicting evidence as to when the $100,000 was delivered to Rebozo, where it was delivered, and for what purpose. It may have helped gain Hughes a number of things, among them federal approval to purchase the airline, Air West, a new reading on a Justice Department prohibition against a Las Vegas casino purchase, or even a CIA contract for his ship, *The Glomar Explorer,* in an attempt to salvage a sunken Russian submarine. Such is the degree of mystery about the Hughes-Nixon involvement that Watergate investigators have speculated that somewhere in the relationship may be hidden the real reason for the break-in at the Democratic National Committee headquarters on June 17, 1972.

The Hughes gift, whether or not it purchased anything from the Nixon administration, was clearly a matter of great concern to the White House. When it first became public, in August 1971, there was apparently consternation. Reportedly, there was something akin to panic when, several months later, Hank Greenspun, editor of the *Las Vegas Sun,* asked whether the Hughes contribution had been used to help buy Nixon's estate at San Clemente, Calif. The Nixon forces subsequently heard—from Robert Bennett, a Republican fund raiser and the president of a Washington public relations firm which both represented Hughes and served as a CIA cover—that Greenspun could well have hard evidence in his possession about long-term connections between Hughes and the Nixon family. When John Mitchell heard Gordon Liddy outline his plans for campaign espionage, the day after *The New York Times* reported it had evidence of a Hughes-Rebozo connection, he was apparently interested in using the Liddy project to break into Greenspun's office in Nevada as well as into Lawrence O'Brien's office in Washington. (The Democratic National Chairman also had previously handled public relations for Hughes.)

Two phones were tapped by the team of Cuban-Americans that broke into the party headquarters, O'Brien's (unsuccessfully) and that of R. Spencer Oliver Jr., chairman of the Association of Democratic State Chairmen who had offices at the Democratic National Committee. His father, Robert Oliver, was employed by Bennett's public relations firm and was in fact the man who specifically represented the Hughes interests there. Somewhere in this mix, investigators have postulated, may lie the ultimate reason for the Watergate break-in. Perhaps it was a hunt for evidence relating to the Hughes $100,000, thought to be in the Democrats' possession.

Foreign Money. Some cases drew the attention of the Watergate investigators, others did not. Investigations, for example, were made into foreign money given to the Committee to Re-Elect the President, an ironic twist in light of the fact that one early "cover story" of the Watergate burglars was that they were looking for evidence of money from Fidel Castro's government allegedly given to support the Democrats. The ensuing investigation brought to light sizable gifts to the Nixon campaign from representatives of Philippine interests ($30,000 of the Philippine money was given by Ernesto Lagdameo, along with two associates). He was a former Philippine ambassador to the United States and later a Philippine businessman; the $30,000, however, was subsequently returned because of doubts over the legality of accepting it.[15] Another contribution, for $25,000, came from

Raymon Nolan, a roving representative for Philippine sugar interests. The Philippines had the largest foreign share of the U.S. sugar market in 1972, a quota set by the American government at twice the level allocated to any other nation.

A number of Greek nationals were contributors to the Nixon campaign in 1972. The late Nikos J. Vardinoyiannis contributed $27,500; of that amount, $12,500 was donated after a Greek company he headed was chosen to supply fuel to the U.S. Sixth Fleet.[16] Thomas A. Pappas, a Greek-born industrialist from Boston, who holds dual citizenship in his native country and the United States, gave the Nixon re-election campaign $101,673, all but $1,000 of it in pre-April 7 contributions. Pappas' name came up in March 1973 when the White House was looking for cash to pay the Watergate defendants; in the round of phone calls and meetings that followed E. Howard Hunt's demand for $130,000 and the possibility of having to find an eventual sum of $1-million, the President and his men, John Dean, John Ehrlichman, H. R. Haldeman and Mitchell, all made references to Pappas as a possible source of funds.

There were also allegations, though no proof, that money from the Swiss bank account of the Shah of Iran, perhaps amounting to $1-million or more, found its way to the Nixon campaign after being transferred to a bank in Mexico.[17] Watergate investigators also probed extensively into reports that money from Arab states went to the Committee to Re-Elect the President. The multimillionaire Italian financier Michele Sindona confirmed reports that he had made an offer of $1-million to the Committee to Re-Elect the President;[18] it was turned down by Maurice Stans, Nixon's chief fund raiser, because Sindona did not want the contribution made public, which would have violated the law then in effect.

Under federal law in 1972,[19] it was a felony to solicit, accept or receive a political contribution from a foreign principal or an agent of a foreign principal. The law also prohibited an agent of a foreign principal from making a political contribution on behalf of his principal or in his capacity as agent of the principal. The legality of political contributions by foreign nationals hinged on the definition of the term "foreign principal." The Justice Department held that the term connoted an agency relationship within the United States. The term "foreign principal" included governments of foreign countries, foreign political parties and various kinds of businesses organized under the laws of, or having their principal place of business in, a foreign country. A direct contribution from a foreign national, without an agent or other connection with a "foreign principal," was considered legal—even though that had the effect of permitting political contributions from individuals who neither resided in the United States nor had the right to vote in U.S. elections. The FECA Amendments of 1974, however, revised the law to apply directly to foreign nationals. Under the 1974 Amendments, any individual who is not a citizen of the United States and who is not lawfully admitted for permanent residence (as defined in the Foreign Agents Registration Act of 1938) is prohibited from contributing.

A number of other instances came to light that involved alleged relationships between money contributed in 1971-72 and possible favored treatment. While none of these allegations was proved and some may be completely unfounded, they do suggest the climate that led reformers and others to be suspicious about many large campaign gifts.

1. In a series of meetings of trucking executives, held at a time when the industry was fighting a government proposal that would have created more competition among various modes of freight transportation, more than $600,000 was raised in campaign contributions for the Nixon re-election effort.[20] The executives of at least nine trucking firms met a goal of $25,000 per company. The money represented the largest centrally organized single-industry collection apart from the dairy industry gifts; moreover, while the latter was spread out over a period of years, the trucking contributions were concentrated in the several months before the November election.

2. A gift of $18,000 was made by the two top officials of Overseas National Airways Inc., a jetliner charter company carrying both military and civilian groups, four months after the 1972 election.[21] At the time the contribution was received, the Committee to Re-Elect the President was reporting a $5-million surplus.

3. A letter was written to then Attorney General John Mitchell by a major figure in the pharmaceutical industry, Elmer H. Bobst, honorary chairman and a director of Warner-Lambert. Bobst told Mitchell he had a close friend with a $100,000 gift if the Federal Trade Commission acted as the industry wished in a merger challenge between Warner-Lambert Co. and Parke, Davis & Co.[22] The contribution was never made.

4. A $30,000 contribution was made to the Nixon campaign by Calvin Kovens, indicted and found guilty with James Hoffa, former Teamsters president, of conspiracy and mail fraud. Kovens was paroled unexpectedly shortly after Charles Colson was asked to see what Nixon could do to help.[23]

5. The head of a black management consulting firm in Washington, Samuel E. Harris, said he learned that he needed to make a second $1,000 contribution to Nixon to get on the Finance Committee to Re-Elect the President "white list" and be considered a "fully recognized contributor."[24] The FCRP claimed it had no "white list."

6. McDonald's Corp., whose chairman, Ray A. Kroc, contributed $250,000 to the Nixon campaign, won a subsequent favorable ruling from the government. This permitted McDonald's to raise prices while price controls were in effect. There were mitigating circumstances in that the approval followed agreement to put on an extra slice of cheese, permitting treatment of the claim as a new product. McDonald's also benefited after the election from efforts by the Nixon administration, which were successful, to establish a lower teenage minimum wage.[25] No relationships were proved.

7. Sen. Warren G. Magnuson, chairman of the Senate Commerce Committee, publicly charged that the Nixon administration had promised to postpone effective federal regulation of the flammability of carpeting in order to get campaign contributions from carpet manufacturers. He alleged that Maurice Stans set up a secret White House meeting with industry and government representatives for that purpose. Stans and other participants denied any favors had been sought or given or that contributions had been solicited. Several carpet manufacturers were very large contributors to the Nixon campaign.[26]

None of the actors in the foregoing seven cases was officially charged with improper actions. Such allegations reflected an atmosphere of suspicion; the suspicion was triggered by day after day of new disclosures. The climate created pressures for new legislation by dramatizing the potential for abuses among large contributors, special interests and campaign fund raisers.

INCREASE IN SPECIAL INTEREST GIVING

A dramatic increase in political contributions by special interest groups—as they rushed to fill the void left by the sharply restricted individual giver—could be clearly charted both in the 1974 off-year congressional elections and the 1976 election campaigns.

Some $12.5-million in contributions came from special interest groups in the 1974 congressional campaigns. Similar groups reported spending $11-million on the 1970 elections. Part of the increase could be attributed to the stricter reporting requirements of the FECA of 1971. But also apparent was the proliferation of new political action committees. Teachers, for example, contributed through new political action committees—PACs—and were numbered among the top spenders in 1974.

By the beginning of the 1976 presidential election year, the political war chests of the various political action groups were filling again.[27] By January 1976, special interest committees had accumulated $16.4-million for the year's political campaigns—an increase of more than 40 per cent over the $11.7-million held by interest groups at a similar point in the 1974 races. Some 242 new committees—30 per cent of all interest group committees registered under the federal law—had been formed for the presidential campaign year.

About three out of four of the new committees had been formed by business-related interests, with 107 corporations and 22 banks having set up political action committees during 1975. They thereby more than doubled the number of corporations and banks with registered PACs prior to the 1974 elections. Seventeen oil companies registered PACs for the first time, along with eight steel companies, four aerospace companies, and a "blue chip" list of others in industry, including American Express Co., Bristol-Myers, Dow Chemical, Litton, Pepsico and R. J. Reynolds Industries.

There were also 36 newly registered labor-related political committees, most of them new committees of unions which already had one or more political action committees prior to the 1974 elections. The Communications Workers of America, for example, registered 12 additional committees.

With the presidential campaigns in 1976 financed partly by government funds, the interests of the newly formed political action groups centered on the congressional races—where the impact of a $5,000 contribution can be far greater than it would be in a presidential campaign. A presidential race over the past few campaigns costs tens of millions of dollars, whereas a Senate campaign that exceeds $1-million usually occurs only in larger states, and a House race that costs more than $100,000 is quite unusual. The full effects of the newly organized political action committees may not be felt until elections in 1978 or later, when more corporate political action committees are activated.

SUMMARY

The limits imposed on the individual contributor by the 1974 Amendments to the Federal Election Campaign Act of 1971 have served to give new emphasis to the role of campaign contributions by business and labor—their political action committees may make donations up to $5,000 each while individual contributions are held to $1,000 per candidate per election.

Corporate funding of American political campaigns has long played a major role in the electoral process, but it reached a new level in 1972, chiefly in the interest of re-electing President Nixon. Fund-raising appeals for the Nixon campaign in 1972 often appeared to border on extortion.

Corporate funds have percolated into politics in various ways—establishing expense accounts for political spending, providing company goods and services in the form of in-kind contributions, keeping officials on the payroll while they are working in a campaign. Corporations have helped foot the costs of conventions through advertising in program books and free services to conventioneers. Republicans were embarrassed in 1972 by the I.T.T. affair. Federal and some state laws now prohibit many of these forms of corporate political activity.

Labor union funds became significant in national politics in 1936 and have been an important Democratic resource ever since. As corporations had, unions learned ways to get around laws prohibiting direct contributions. Labor's true strength may lie not in its campaign war chests (it spent $8.5-million on federal campaigns in 1972) but in the volunteers it can muster for precinct work.

Analysis of the patterns of political contributions by various segments of American business shows political giving among company officers and directors to be heavily Republican at both the presidential and congressional levels—with some exceptions, such as in the 1964 presidential election when major elements of the business community switched to President Johnson.

The 1972 campaign spawned a string of illegal corporate contributions, involving a "blue chip" list of American companies. These contributions brought the phrase "laundered money" into the political lexicon. In seeking to hide the true origins of their political contributions, firms drew on secret slush funds, sold bogus airline tickets and created fictitious bonus schemes for employees who then contributed the bonus to a campaign. In defense of their actions some companies maintained that their concern was not to obtain favors but to avoid the unknown consequences of not giving.

An increase in special interest giving could be clearly charted in 1976, as various groups sought to fill the void left by the new restrictions on individual contributions.

In the following chapter, we discuss the history of regulation of political finance, and the issues raised by recent reform.

NOTES

1. The 1974 Amendments to the FECA specify that in order to make a gift up to $5,000 the political action committee must have received contributions from 50 individuals, have been in existence six months and have contributed to five separate campaigns. Unless such conditions are met, it has the same $1,000 ceiling on contributions as an individual.
2. Louise Overacker, *Presidential Campaign Funds* (Boston: Boston University Press, 1946), p. 29.
3. *Ibid.,* p. 50.
4. Jasper B. Shannon, *Money and Politics* (New York: Random House, 1959), p. 54.
5. Eugene H. Roseboom, *A History of Presidential Elections* (New York: The Macmillan Company, 1957), p. 487.
6. Overacker, *op. cit.,* p. 49.
7. Theodore H. White, *The Making of the President 1968* (New York: Atheneum, 1969), p. 365.
8. For an independent analysis of these data, see Congressional Quarterly *Weekly Report,* October 5, 1974, pp. 2668-2674.
9. *Final Report of the Senate Select Committee on Presidential Campaign Activities,* 93rd Cong., 2d sess. (Washington, D.C.: U.S. Government Printing Office, 1974), pp. 446-447.
10. Morton Mintz and Nick Kotz, "Automen Rejected Nixon Fund Bid," *The Washington Post,* November 17, 1972.
11. Michael C. Jensen, "The Corporate Political Squeeze," *The New York Times,* September 16, 1973.
12. Ben A. Franklin, "Inquiries Into Nixon's Re-election Funds Turning Up a Pattern of High Pressure," *The New York Times,* July 15, 1973.
13. *Final Report, op. cit.,* p. 470.
14. U.S. District Judge George L. Hart Jr. in his instructions to the jury in the bribery case against Sen. Daniel B. Brewster of Maryland in 1972. For a discussion of this, see Lawrence Meyer, "The Fine Line Between Contributions and Bribes," *The Washington Post,* March 17, 1973; and Brooks Jackson, "Bribery and Contributions," *The New Republic,* December 21, 1974. On the question of political temptation Lincoln Steffens once observed that Adam blames Eve who in turn blamed the Serpent, whereas the real fault, in Steffens' view, was and continued to be with the apple.

15. James R. Polk, "Philippine Cash Surfaces," "Sugar Envoy Mum on Donation" and "Nixon Donation From Second Filipino Revealed," *The Washington Star*, June 11, 12 and 13, 1973.

16. Rowland Evans and Robert Novak, "Greek Gifts for President," *The Washington Post*, July 20, 1972; and Seth Kantor, "Jaworski Eyes Probing Foreign '72 Gifts," *The Washington Post*, January 25, 1974.

17. Columnist Jack Anderson made the allegations, which he said came from the report of a former Justice Department official to Watergate investigators. See Anderson, "Kissinger to Press Shah on Oil Costs," *The Washington Post*, November 1, 1974. The story was later denied by the Committee to Re-Elect the President. But if such money had been given it could have gone to the Rebozo fund and not been passed to the CRP. The Office of the Special Prosecutor probed these matters, with no findings at this writing.

18. "Sindona Said to Vow to Save Franklin," *The New York Times*, July 2, 1974.

19. 18 U.S.C. § 613.

20. James R. Polk, "$600,000 From Truckers Led Nixon's Industry Gifts," *The Washington Star*, November 6, 1973. In 1974 a bill allowing heavier trucks on the interstate highway system passed Congress after a lobbying drive that included some last-minute election contributions to some 117 House members. Earlier the House had rejected the weight increase but reversed itself, and President Ford signed the legislation. ("Successful Truck-Bill Lobbying Included Campaign Fund Drive," *The New York Times*, January 7, 1975.)

21. James R. Polk, "Post-Election Gift Solicited," *The Washington Star*, July 29, 1973.

22. The case is mentioned in "Special Report: Nixon and Big Business," *FACT*, vol. III, no. 13 (June 23, 1972), p. 5.

23. James R. Polk, "Mitchell Handled Cash From Miamian Paroled Early," *The Washington Star*, June 15, 1974.

24. Richard M. Cohen, "Candidates' Accounts of Gifts Differ," *The Washington Post*, June 8, 1974.

25. Nick Kotz, "Politics Enters Teens' Pay Scale," *The Washington Post*, October 6, 1972; and "McDonald's Price Increase Linked to Donation," *The Washington Post*, November 3, 1972.

26. Morton Mintz and William Chapman, "Carpet Lobby Said to Pay GOP for Aid," *The Washington Post*, October 7, 1972; Mintz, "Campaign Giver Denies Return Aid," *The Washington Post*, July 21, 1973.

27. See Common Cause press release of March 10, 1976, on study by its Campaign Finance Monitoring Project.

6

The Drive for Reform:
Pre- and Post-Watergate

For decades, official apathy toward serious reform of political finance was a Washington habit. The federal and state laws that were enacted tended to be predominantly negative—their chief purposes were to prohibit and restrict various ways of getting, giving and spending political money.

From the early 20th century, when President Theodore Roosevelt proposed disclosure laws, a prohibition on corporate political giving and government subsidies, until 1961, several Presidents went on record in favor of reform, but none took vigorous action.[1] President Kennedy was the first president in modern times to consider campaign financing a critical problem, and he showed this concern in 1961 by appointing a bipartisan Commission on Campaign Costs. This started a chain of events which began to falter in the late 1960s. Then, in the short space of two months, efforts to reform our antiquated system of political finance came to a sudden climax when Congress passed two measures—the Federal Election Campaign Act of 1971 (FECA),[2] which replaced the 1925 Federal Corrupt Practices Act, and the Revenue Act of 1971.

Until the time the Kennedy Commission was appointed, most of the laws affecting political finance were devised to remedy or prevent flagrant abuses. It was evidently assumed that honest politicans could afford to pay their campaign expenses with their own money or with "untainted" gifts. Efforts to free candidates from dependence upon any one person or interest group usually took the form of restricting or prohibiting contributions from presumably dubious sources. Moreover, arbitrary ceilings were set to prevent excessive spending. The rationale was that ceilings would prevent dollars from dominating and unwisely influencing elections and would tend to reduce undue advantages held by wealthy candidates or the party with the most funds.

As restrictive laws were passed, however, new methods of raising and spending money were soon devised. When the assessment of government employees was prohibited, attention swung to corporate contributions. When they in turn were barred, gifts from wealthy individuals—including many stockholders or officers in corporations—were sought. When direct contributions from the wealthy were limited by law, ways to circumvent the limitations were shortly found.

EARLY EFFORTS AT REGULATION

After the 1904 election—during which it was charged that corporations were pouring millions of dollars into the Republican campaign to elect Theodore Roosevelt—a move for federal legislation that would force disclosure of campaign spending led to the formation of the National Publicity Law Association (NPLA). Under the banner of the NPLA were gathered such prominent figures as Charles Evans Hughes (later Chief Justice), William Jennings Bryan, Harvard President Charles William Eliot and American Federation of Labor President Samuel Gompers.

The first federal prohibition of corporate contributions was enacted in 1907. The first federal campaign fund disclosure law was passed in 1910; the following year, an amendment required primary, convention and pre-election financial statements and limited the amounts that could be spent by candidates for the House and Senate. The law was contested in a famous case in 1921 in which the U.S. Supreme Court overturned the conviction of Truman Newberry—a candidate for the Senate in 1918 who defeated Henry Ford in the Republican primary in Michigan—for excessive campaign spending.[3] The court held that congressional authority to regulate elections did not extend to primaries and nomination activities (most of the questionable expenses in Newberry's campaign had preceded the Republican primary). This narrow interpretation of congressional authority was rejected in 1941 in another Supreme Court case relating to federal-state powers,[4] but Congress did not reassert its power to require disclosure of campaign funds for prenomination campaigns until 1972.

Corrupt Practices Act

Relevant federal legislation was codified and revised, though without substantial change, in the Federal Corrupt Practices Act of 1925. That act remained the basic law until 1972. Essentially, the law required disclosure of receipts and expenditures by candidates for the Senate and House (not for President or Vice President) and by political committees which sought to influence federal elections in two or more states. The Hatch Act of 1940 also limited to $5,000 the amount an individual could contribute to a federal candidate or to a political committee in a single year and set a $3-million limit on committee expenditures. The former provision, however was interpreted to mean that an individual could give up to $5,000 to numerous committees, all supporting the same candidate. A more significant factor in limiting individual contributions was the federal gift tax which imposed progressive tax rates on contributions of more than $3,000 to a single committee in any year. But again, individuals could give up to that amount to multiple committees working for the same candidate. Thus, $25,000 or $100,000 or larger gifts from one individual to one candidate were legally acceptable. The bar on corporate giving that had been on the books since 1907 was temporarily extended to labor unions in the Smith-Connally Act of 1944 and then reimposed in the Taft-Hartley Act of 1947.

The post-World War II years witnessed a series of congressional gestures, usually no more than congressional committee reports, toward reform. In 1948 and again in 1951, special House committees on campaign expenditures recommended that substantial revisions be made in the Corrupt Practices and Hatch Acts. But no legislation passed. In 1953 the Elections Subcommittee of the Senate Committee on Rules and Administration proposed that the limit on spending for national political committees be increased from $3-million to $10-million a year. It also proposed increases in permissible spending for congressional campaigns. The Senate did not act. In 1955, a comprehensive bill requiring all committees active in campaigns for federal office to file financial reports, even if their activities were confined to one state, was introduced and reported out of committee, but it never was called up for debate on the Senate floor.

The 1956 disclosure by Sen. Francis Case of South Dakota that he had been offered a $2,500 campaign gift if he would vote for the Harris-Fulbright natural gas bill led to three congressional investigations. None of them produced reform legislation. President Eisenhower, however, vetoed the gas bill on the grounds that "arrogant lobbying" had been exercised on its behalf.

Post-World War II

Presidents Truman, Eisenhower, Kennedy and Johnson all voiced concern about the methods used to raise money to pay for political campaigns. Truman favored government subsidies. He and Eisenhower both endorsed the recommendations of the Kennedy Commission on Campaign Costs.

COMMISSION ON CAMPAIGN COSTS

Kennedy had expressed much concern about campaign finance before he became President. He was sensitive to the advantages wealth gave a candidate. Having himself been accused of buying public office, he was aware of the public's cynicism. Before his inauguration, he set in motion the activities which led to the creation of the Commission on Campaign Costs.

Kennedy asked the commission to recommend suitable ways to finance presidential general election campaigns and to reduce the costs of running for the presidency. When he submitted legislative proposals based on the commission's report, he invited Congress to extend the proposals to all federal offices. Among those endorsing the report[5] were the chairmen of the Republican and Democratic national committees, former Presidents Truman and Eisenhower and Richard Nixon, Adlai Stevenson, and Thomas Dewey—all the living presidential candidates of both major parties in the preceding quarter century.

Taken as a whole, the report presented a model and comprehensive program for reforming the financing of the political system, covering not only federal legislative remedies but also bipartisan activities, certain party practices and state actions. Few innovations were included in the report's recommendations; most of the proposals had been suggested before. An exception was one alternative presented for the first time: matching funds (or matching incentives). The proposals were not to be adopted for more than 12 years, but the report's purpose was more immediate: to get things moving in the field by detailing a comprehensive program for reform of political finance, covering all aspects of regulation—disclosure, publicity, limitations, corrupt practices, tax incentives and political broadcasting.

One of the commission's recommendations was carried out promptly by the Treasury Department. The Internal Revenue Service authorized taxpayers to deduct from income their expenditures in connection with federal, state or local elections, if the money was used for the following purposes: buying advertising to encourage the public to register and vote and to contribute to a political party or campaign fund; sponsoring a political debate among candidates for a particular office; granting employees time off with pay for registration and voting; and maintaining a payroll deduction plan for employees wishing to make political contributions.

The recommendations were less than enthusiastically received on Capitol Hill, where certain members of Congress were distrustful of a presidential initiative in a field traditionally considered a legislative prerogative. Nor was there applause from such groups as the U.S. Chamber of Commerce, which was concerned that the tax incentive features would erode the tax base, and the labor movement, which objected to proposals on public reporting and tax incentives. Press comments, however, were favorable.

Johnson Administration

Understandably, the new Johnson administration had other priorities. During his first two years in office, President Johnson failed to support any legislative reform of political finance and ignored representations to act made by former members of the commission. The program was one of the few Kennedy creations to suffer seriously in the transition that followed his death. Publicity about Texas oil money and the Bobby Baker case may have turned Johnson against opening the political financing issue in the 1964 election. The White House gave the subject no public attention until 1966 when reports of criticism about the President's Club (a group composed of contributors of $1,000 or more, including some government contractors) and other political fund-raising activities moved Johnson to act. In his State of the Union address in 1966, he stated his intention to submit an election reform program. His proposals, however, were not transmitted until too late for passage by the 89th Congress. During this period, 1962-66, the cause of campaign finance reform had also been dormant on Capitol Hill.

Ashmore-Goodell Bill

In 1966, the censure of Sen. Thomas Dodd of Connecticut for using political funds for personal purposes helped spark new interest in reform, and the House subcommittee on elections produced the bipartisan Ashmore-Goodell bill, the most comprehensive bill considered in Congress up until then. The bill was a mixture of the stronger portions of the Johnson and Kennedy proposals and of other bills and proposals. Most importantly, it called for a bipartisan Federal Election Commission (FEC) to receive, analyze, audit and publicize spending reports by all candidates and committees in federal elections. A weakened version of the bill, eliminating the FEC as the single repository, passed the Senate the following year by a surprising 87-0 vote.

Both the Baker and Dodd cases no doubt contributed to the Senate's major step forward. Another factor was pressure growing out of extended debate over the Long Act.

Long Act

The Long Act was enacted by the Congress in 1966 largely as the result of the persuasion and parliamentary skill of its sponsor, Sen. Russell Long of Louisiana, chairman of the Senate Finance Committee. The bill provided a federal subsidy for presidential elections, a scheme contrasting sharply with the Johnson administration's plan to provide tax incentives for political contributors who were taxpayers. The bill passed on the last day of the second session of the 89th Congress without drawing much attention from the public, press or opinion leaders. It caught the Johnson administration off guard but, at the last hour, the White House chose to support it, shelving its own recommendation for tax incentives.

In the spring of 1967, Sen. Albert Gore of Tennessee and Sen. John Williams of Delaware cosponsored an amendment to repeal the Long Act. Passage of the bill had met with a negative reaction. One of the leaders of the floor fight for repeal was Sen. Robert Kennedy, who argued that the subsidy put a dangerous amount of power into the hands of the national party chairmen. Through promises of distribution of money in the general election, Kennedy argued, the chairmen would be able to influence the delegations of the large states to support the presidential candidate of the chairmen's choice. The Long Act was not formally repealed, but its provisions were no longer in force after May 1967.

FEDERAL ELECTION CAMPAIGN ACT OF 1971

But the Long Act and the Ashmore-Goodell bill might be termed the parents of the two pieces of legislation passed by Congress four years later that constituted a major turning point in the history of campaign finance reform: the Federal Election Campaign Act of 1971 (FECA), which replaced the Federal Corrupt Practices Act of 1925, and the Revenue Act of 1971. The latter provided tax credits, or, alternatively, tax deductions for political contributions at all levels and also a tax checkoff to subsidize presidential campaigns during general elections. The FECA of 1971,[6] which passed in January 1972, a month after the Revenue Act, required fuller disclosure of political funding than ever before—a factor that was to play a key role in the Watergate affair. Among its provisions, the FECA:

● Set limits on communications media expenditures for candidates for federal office during primary, runoff, special or general election campaigns. This provision was replaced in the 1974 Amendments[7] with candidate expenditure limitations on total spending (which were then in part declared unconstitutional by the Supreme Court in 1976).

● Placed a ceiling on contributions by any candidate or his immediate family to his own campaign of $50,000 for President or Vice President, $35,000 for senator and $25,000 for representative, delegate or resident commissioner. This provision was later ruled unconstitutional by the Supreme Court, but it was reinstated in the 1976 Amendments[8] for presidential elections because public funding is provided.

● Stipulated that the appropriate federal supervisory officer to oversee election campaign practices, reporting and disclosure was the Clerk of the House for House candidates, the Secretary of the Senate for Senate candidates, and the Comptroller General for presidential candidates and miscellaneous other committees. This provision was partially changed by the 1974 Amendments which established the Federal Election Commission (FEC).

● Required candidates and their committees for the Senate and House to file duplicate copies of reports with the secretary of state, or a comparable officer in each state, for local inspection. This provision was designed to help provide information about the funding of campaigns to local voters.

● Required each political committee and candidate to report total expenditures, as well as to itemize the full name, mailing address, and occupation and principal place of business of each contributor, plus date, amount and purpose of each expenditure in excess of $100; to itemize similarly each expenditure for personal services, salaries and reimbursed expenses in excess of $100.

● Required candidates and committees to file reports of contributions and expenditures the 10th day of March, June and September every year, on the 15th and fifth days preceding the date on which an election is held and on the 31st day of January. Any contribution of $5,000 or more was to be reported within 48 hours if received after the last preelection report. The dates of these filings were changed in the 1974 Amendments to include quarterly disclosures as well as one 10 days before an election and 30 days after an election.

● Required a full and complete financial statement of the costs of a presidential nominating convention within 60 days of the convention.

Revenue Act of 1971

The Revenue Act of 1971 provided that political contributors could claim a tax credit against federal income tax for 50 per cent of their contributions (to candidates for federal, state or local office and to some political committees), up to a maximum of $12.50 on a single return and $25 on a joint return (increased to $25 and $50 in the 1974 Amendments). Alternatively, the taxpayer could claim a deduction for the full amount of contributions up to a maximum of $50 on a single return and $100 on a joint return (increased to $100 and $200 in the 1974 Amendments).

The tax credits and deductions had an easy passage, but the accompanying tax checkoff provisions have had a long and stormy history. The checkoff represented a revival of a provision of the Long Act of 1966 but was revised to provide money directly to presidential candidates, not to the political party committees on their behalf. The checkoff provided that every individual whose tax liability for any calendar year was $1 or more could designate on his federal income tax form that $1 of his tax money be paid to the Presidential Election Campaign Fund; married individuals filing jointly could designate $2. The money it raised was to be paid directly to the candidates, not the parties.

The Watergate events brought new pressures for reform. In May 1973, President Nixon proposed creation of a nonpartisan commission to study campaign reform. Nixon was by no means "out in front" on the issue. A week earlier, a House Republican leader, John B. Anderson of Illinois, had introduced a bill that he cosponsored with Democrat Morris K. Udall of Arizona calling for an independent Federal Election Commission. Nonetheless, it was almost two years before a new election law became fully operative. This happened in April 1975, when President Ford swore in the six members of the FEC established by the 1974 Amendments. Less than a year would pass before their method of selection (some by Congress, others by the President) would be declared unconstitutional by the U.S. Supreme Court.

1974 AMENDMENTS

Along with creation of the commission, the other major "firsts" in the 1974 Amendments were the establishment of overall limitations on how much could be spent on political campaigning and the extension of public funding to campaigns for the presidential nomination and to the national conventions.

Despite impetus given reform by the Watergate scandals, consideration of the measure was drawn out. Movement toward enactment in 1973 came only in the Senate where, on July 30, a reform bill designed to improve the FECA was adopted by an overwhelming 82-8 margin. As has been the pattern with most campaign finance legislation in the Senate in the past decade, the version reported out of committee was then strengthened on the floor of the Senate.

In the fall, the scene had moved to the House, where the greater frequency with which its members must face reelection has traditionally made it a more conservative body when dealing with campaign reform. There the bill faced Rep. Wayne L. Hays of Ohio, chairman of the Committee on

House Administration, a vocal opponent of reform and of public financing of elections. Referred to his committee's Subcommittee on Elections, it remained there throughout the remainder of the first session of the 93rd Congress.

When the 93rd Congress reconvened in January 1974, campaign reform was a major item on its agenda. In his State of the Union message, President Nixon noted the congressional delay on reform and announced he would submit an administration proposal. When the Nixon proposals arrived, they pleased almost no one in Congress, and members of his own party made that clear publicly. The Nixon proposals were viewed by many as combining "safe" reforms with others that were unpassable. Nixon called public finance "taxation without representation."[9]

In the House itself, Rep. Hays kept pushing back the date of his promised bill; his committee did not begin markup sessions until March 26. In April, the Senate, by a 53-32 vote, passed a reform bill that combined parts of the original bill with a call for public funding of presidential and congressional primary and general election campaigns. Among the amendments offered was one by Sen. James Buckley, New York Conservative-Republican, requiring an immediate certification by the federal court of appeals of any court test of the constitutionality of the bill's provisions—an opportunity of which he and other opponents availed themselves when the bill became law and which led to the Supreme Court's *Buckley v. Valeo* ruling.

On Aug. 8, 1974, a few hours before Nixon announced his resignation as President, the House version of a campaign reform bill was approved 355-48. The House version differed sharply from the Senate bill. While it was much more limited in scope, it did call for public funding for presidential elections and added public financing of presidential nominating conventions.

After further delaying tactics by Hays, the conference committee began meeting in September. The impasse on the public finance issue was not settled until early October. As finally passed by large margins in both houses, the bill included public funding only for presidential elections. It did not change significantly the flat grant provisions for the general election, but it extended government financing to include both matching funds for the presidential prenomination period and flat grants to the political parties for their national nominating conventions.

President Ford signed the bill Oct. 15, 1974, in a White House ceremony to which all members of Congress were invited. A long-time opponent of public funding, the President expressed doubts about some sections of the law but said, "the times demand this legislation."[10]

Federal Election Commission

Established by the 1974 Amendments, the Federal Election Commission was formally organized in April 1975. It was designed to draw together the administrative and enforcement functions that previously were divided among the three supervisory officers—the Comptroller General, the Secretary of the Senate and the Clerk of the House of Representatives—as mandated by the FECA of 1971[11]

When the law took effect Jan. 1, 1975, only two of the commission's six members had been nominated, and the name of one of these was to be later withdrawn. In the absence of a commission, the Clerk of the House and the Secretary of the Senate continued to carry out their roles in administering the 1971 law, particularly as to disclosure requirements which continued in force during the transition period. However, the enforcement provisions of the law could not become operative until the FEC became operative. By that time, a number of 1976 presidential candidates had announced and were going about the matter of raising money in accordance with the new law.

The law specified that four members of the commission would be nominated by Congress and two by the President.[12] The original nominee of Senate Majority Leader Mike Mansfield was Joseph E. Meglen of Billings, Mont. He was Mansfield's treasurer in his two previous Senate campaigns. When objections were raised as to Meglen's qualifications for the $38,000-a-year post, and he had reconsidered the need to move to Washington for what appeared to be essentially a full-time job, Meglen had his name withdrawn. The Senate then nominated Thomas E. Harris of Arkansas, former associate general counsel of the AFL-CIO. Senate Minority Leader Scott named Joan D. Aikens of Swarthmore, Pa., the head of the Pennsylvania Council of Republican Women. The two nominees from the House were both former representatives—Robert O. Tiernan of Rhode Island, named by Democratic Majority Leader Thomas P. O'Neill, and Vernon Thomson of Wisconsin, nominated by House Minority Leader John J. Rhodes. President Ford's two nominees were also former representatives: Thomas B. Curtis, Republican of Missouri; and Neil O. Staebler, Democrat of Michigan. The members of the commission were finally sworn in by the President on April 14, 1975. Curtis was elected chairman and Staebler, vice chairman. The Secretary of the Senate and the Clerk of the House of Representatives were made ex officio members without voting power.

While recognizing the need for an evenhanded approach at a time of widespread cynicism about the electoral process, the commission nevertheless had a stormy first year.[13] Its very existence was under court challenge from the beginning. As a result of the *Buckley v. Valeo* ruling of January 1976, the manner of appointment of members of the commission was changed substantially. The FEC was in existence only nine months when the Supreme Court declared the method of selection (some by the legislative branch) unconstitutional because it violated the separation of powers doctrine. That meant that the FEC could not carry out the executive functions of enforcing the law or certifying matching fund payments to presidential candidates.

Moreover, the FEC soon drew fire from certain members of Congress who were not pleased with the commission's early operations or its early decisions. The first two regulations the FEC wrote were rejected by Congress. (Regulations are rulings written by an agency such as the FEC to interpret, implement and "flesh out" the skeleton of a law as enacted by Congress.)

The congressional attack on the proposed regulations was evidence of the particular problems built into the structure and functioning of the federal government's newest regulatory agency. Historically, regulatory agencies tend over a period of time to be captured by the industries they are established to regulate. In the case of the FEC, the original method of appointment of its members, with four appointed by the legislative branch, led to early trouble. Of the six original appointees, four were former members of the House of Representatives. This eased their confirmation by a majority of both houses, in itself an unusual procedure. The procedure was changed by the Congress in the 1976 Amendments to conform to the usual practice of presidential nomination and senatorial confirmation.

But because the FEC has the power to regulate congressional campaigns, the potential conflict between the new commissioners' experience and their friendships on Capitol Hill and their need for impartial handling of congressional elections was apparent. In order to achieve credibility as an independent agency, there was a clear need to establish the FEC's independence from the Congress it was in part established to regulate. Some members of Congress, it turned out, did not want the FEC to be very independent where congressional elections were concerned. The proposed regulations, advisory opinions and procedures touched the daily lives of members, whether campaigning or not, in ways some found objectionable and others considered outside the commission's province.

Another problem for the FEC was that the regulations it wrote had to be submitted to Congress along with an explanation and justification. If neither the Senate nor the House disapproved by a formal vote within 30 "legislative" days (days each house is in session), the commission could prescribe such regulation, and it would have the force of law.

Both the method of partial congressional appointment and the review of its regulations were unusual and tended to threaten the independence of the FEC. Of course, FEC funds were appropriated by Congress, another potential pressure point. Members of the FEC claimed that the commission sought a balanced relationship with Congress, but discord soon developed.

Early FEC Regulations Rejected

Congressional Expense Accounts. In its initial proposed regulation, on congressional expense funds, the FEC, whether intentionally or not, served to alert Congress to the power which the new agency could claim and to how that power might be perceived by some members to be directed at times against them or against traditional practices they did not want discontinued. This regulation was submitted to Congress in July 1975 and dealt with the so-called "office slush funds" maintained by some members. It required that they be disclosed at regular intervals and made them subject to the then-new limitations on political contributions and expenditures.

The funds in question, formally known as "constituent service funds," usually come from contributions made outside the campaign framework. They are used to supplement funds provided by the government to pay for day-to-day operations of congressional offices. These "office funds" are used for such items as newsletters, travel back home and office expenses beyond those authorized by Congress. Not enough money is provided by the government to meet the perceived needs of some members of Congress, so they pay for them out of their own pockets, if personally able, or by raising special funds. There is a legitimate question as to whether so-called representational expenses are sufficient in some cases; for example, a member from a distant state, who wants to return home frequently, may need to spend additional money to do so. Of course, some trips are for election purposes but many combine both representational and political functions.

In its proposed regulation, the FEC held that funds raised independently of those authorized "should be viewed as political and not legislative funds,"[14] requiring disclosure in quarterly campaign finance reports. Even more controversial was the requirement that contributions and spending from the accounts be treated as campaign funds under the limitations set by law for the next election of the member maintaining the fund.

Congressional reaction was immediate and included threats to veto the ruling. The Senate subsequently did veto

145

the ruling. It did so by a one-vote margin (48-47), with many senators reluctant to appear to be voting in favor of "slush funds." Apparently, some senators voted with the FEC only because they knew their votes were not needed to defeat the measure. None of the 1976 presidential contenders then in the Senate voted against the FEC regulation.

A compromise proposal, which would treat the funds as political only in election years and would also include comparable funds used by congressional challengers as well as by the President and Vice President, was then worked out with Senate leaders. It ran into sharp opposition, however, in the House Administration Committee headed by Wayne Hays of Ohio.

The Supreme Court ruling that expenditure limits were unconstitutional effectively removed that problem from the proposed regulation and caused its consideration to be suspended until the Federal Election Commission was reconstituted.

Even after the FEC was reconstituted, the fourth draft of the regulation was changed under pressure from some members of Congress. The FEC deleted from the proposed regulation a $100 limit on cash contributions. Since the election law set that limit on cash campaign contributions, the change put congressional office funding on a different basis. Similarly, the FEC retreated on its position that office account reports should be filed as attachments to campaign fund reports. Legislators objected that to do so would give the appearance that these funds represented campaign money, and they insisted on maintaining a distinction. The expense account reports were required once each year—on January 31—but in election years, quarterly reports were required.

The proposed regulation was prepared in response to a large number of requests from members of Congress asking whether their office accounts were subject to the limitations in the law. It proved to be an unfortunate tactic for the FEC to seek to regulate a congressional custom before writing basic regulations dealing with the substance of the law, that is, disclosure, limitations and government funding. The FEC was responding to many requests for advisory opinions on many subjects, some of them marginal, but some from members of Congress who were persistent in seeking quick answers. Basic regulations were given lesser priority.

Point of Entry. Members of Congress attacked the second proposed FEC regulation, which was more basic to the law than the office fund regulation. The proposed point of entry regulation required that originals of all candidate and political committee fund reports be filed first with the FEC; then the FEC would provide microfilm copies of the reports to the Secretary of the Senate and the Clerk of the House within two working days. Such a system would have provided more effective disclosure under efficient procedures, but it was rejected by the House. Under the 1971 law, there were three supervisory officers, each independent of the other. The 1974 Amendments failed to specify clearly the role of the secretary and the clerk in relation to the FEC, but the law seemed to require an arrangement whereby candidates for the Senate and their committees would continue to file with the secretary, candidates for the House and their committees would continue to file with the clerk, and candidates for President and Vice President and their committees as well as multi-candidate (party or special interest or issue) committees would file with the FEC. Clearly, the secretary and the clerk had to provide copies of filed reports to the FEC, which was responsible for administering and enforcing the law. The proposed regulation interpreted the law broadly, but it was considered desirable to make it possible for candidates or committees to file all reports at a single address and to reduce costs of photocopying and postage for committees supporting candidates for more than one federal office.

The initial point of entry regulation met with the approval of the Senate but not the House. Rep. Hays, through whose committee the proposal had to move, argued that the law as it then stood sufficed and that the Clerk of the House "ought not to have a whole bunch of people handling these papers before they get to him."[15] The presumed prerogative of the House to receive the reports first was argued for two reasons: (1) The U.S. Constitution states that each house is the judge of its own membership, and hence custody of the original reports was essential in case any questions of contested elections or of unethical behavior in fund raising or spending arose; and (2) some members checked their disclosure filings with personnel in the Office of the Clerk of the House before filing verified reports, and they were concerned that the FEC would not provide the same service to help them to avoid possible violations of law. The second reason was more important in the rejection vote because assurances had been made when the House was debating the 1974 Amendments that the leadership would guarantee that the original filings would continue to be with the House clerk.

Reluctantly, the FEC bowed before the opposition and revised its proposal on filing reports—reversing the procedure so that candidates filed first with the clerk and the secretary, who then passed on copies to the FEC. However, this proposed regulation also was deferred until after the FEC was reconstituted. The FEC chairman, Thomas B. Curtis, said the change would produce "added cost and confusion."[16]

Clearly, some of the early criticism of the FEC by Congress was unjustified. Some FEC decisions were inevitable and merely implemented a law that was complex and in part badly drafted. The problem for the FEC was to treat Congress at arm's length to ensure its own independence while being responsive to Congress' oversight authority.

The regulations that had been rejected by Congress were rewritten, and along with one on disclosure, had been cleared by Congress but not issued when the Supreme Court released its landmark decision, *Buckley v. Valeo.* While Congress rewrote the law to reconstitute the commission, three other proposed regulations that had been prepared were not submitted, and hearings on one other were canceled. Thus, the FEC was in operation for more than a year without a single regulation in force. A few days after the commission was reconstituted in May 1976, 10 sets of draft regulations were published for public comment. These incorporated provisions based on the 1976 Amendments.

Constitutional Challenge

In addition to its early liaison and communications problems with Congress, the new FEC's future was clouded almost immediately by a legal suit challenging not only the constitutionality of most of the major provisions of the 1974 Amendments but also the commission's very existence.[17]

The 1974 Amendments invited legal challenge because Congress failed to take seriously the warnings of experts and others that important constitutional issues were involved. Reformers were so enthusiastic that they pushed to the outer bounds of strict regulation. They urged and Congress agreed to a tight system of limitations, arguing that as long as private independent expenditures were permitted, limitations could be placed on them as well as on contributions. Overall candidate expenditure limits were thought to be constitutional because they were considered necessary for an effective system of regulation that would restrain excessive spending. Traditionally, excessive spending had been unfair to candidates without personal wealth or access to large contributions. A system of regulation with low and effective limitations was the goal also of some reformers and others who sought to "starve" electioneering by reducing the money available to a point where Congress would enact public funding of senatorial and House as well as of presidential campaigns.

In *Buckley v. Valeo,* the courts confronted a difficult judicial task. There were dilemmas to be resolved that made the issue one of appropriate debate for the decade in which the United States marked its bicentennial. The problem, in its simplest form, was for the courts to balance the First Amendment rights of free speech and free association against the clear power of the legislature to enact laws designed to protect the integrity of the election system. Involved were questions of public discussion and political dialogue. Basically, the plaintiffs sought to ensure that the reforms, however well-meant, did not have a chilling effect on free speech or on citizen participation.

An unusual provision of the law had authorized any eligible voter to start federal court proceedings to contest the constitutionality of any provision of the law. The amendment had been designed to speed along any case by permitting questions of constitutionality to be certified directly to the federal court of appeals, which was obliged to expedite the case. A case was brought a few days after the law became effective on Jan. 1, 1975. Plaintiffs covered a broad spectrum of liberals and conservatives, individuals and organizations and included Sen. James L. Buckley, New York Conservative-Republican, Eugene J. McCarthy, former Democratic senator from Minnesota, Stewart R. Mott (a large contributor), the Conservative Party of the State of New York, the New York Civil Liberties Union, the Mississippi Republican Party, the Libertarian Party and the Conservative Victory Fund, among others. Defendants included, along with the Attorney General, the FEC, the Secretary of the Senate and the Clerk of the House, and three reform groups, Common Cause, the Center for Public Financing of Elections and the League of Women Voters.

The case was argued before the U.S. Court of Appeals for the District of Columbia, which in an Aug. 15, 1975, opinion sustained most of the law's provisions. Appeal was then made to the U.S. Supreme Court, the arguments were heard, and on Jan. 30, 1976, a little over a year after the case was initiated, the Supreme Court ruled in a *per curiam* opinion that was joined in all aspects by three justices and joined in part by others. (There was one major dissent.) The Supreme Court decision reversed many major points that had been considered and upheld by the court of appeals. The impact of the decision has been great not only on the regulation of federal elections but also on state and local law.

The central question was posed by Justice Potter Stewart during oral arguments: Is money speech and speech money? Or stated differently, is an expenditure for speech substantially the same thing as speech itself because the expenditure is necessary to reach large audiences by the purchase of air time or space in the print media. The decision resolved the conflict by asserting the broadest protection to First Amendment rights to assure the unrestrained interchange of ideas for bringing about popular political and social change. Accordingly, the court majority concluded that individual expenditure limitations imposed direct and substantial restraints on the quantity of political speech. This applied to limits on both individuals and on candidates in their personal expenditures on their own behalf as well as on spending by or on behalf of a candidate. However, an exception was made with reference to overall candidate expenditure limits, with the court holding that candidates who accepted public funding when provided by the government could also be obliged to accept campaign expenditure limits as a condition of the granting of the public money. The court made clear that independent spending by individuals and groups could be considered as a protected form of free speech only if the spending were truly independent. Independent spending could not, then, be coordinated with the candidate or his campaign organization nor consented to by the candidate or his agent.

On the other hand, the court upheld the limits on individual and group contributions to campaigns, asserting that these constitute only a marginal restriction on the contributor's ability to engage in free communication. Saying that free expression rests on contributing as a symbolic act to help give a candidate the means to speak out with views congenial to those of the contributor, the court also asserted that the quantity of speech does not increase perceptibly with the size of the contribution. Hence limits on contributions were constitutional. The Supreme Court found that there was a real or imagined coercive influence of large contributors on candidates' positions and on their actions if elected, leading to corruption or the appearance of corruption, and it said that contribution limits were acceptable because they serve to mute the voices of affluent persons and groups while also restraining the skyrocketing costs of political campaigns.

The Supreme Court sustained all the disclosure requirements of the law, sanctioned the forms of public funding provided by the federal law, and upheld the concept of a bipartisan regulatory commission to administer and enforce the law so long as the agency was within the executive branch of the government and its members were appointed by the

President. These are the three main directions in which regulation of political finance will proceed, perhaps modified to some extent by efforts to retain contribution limits (though the limits may be increased to help provide more seed money to mount campaigns and to offset unlimited spending by wealthy candidates on their own behalf) and by expenditure limits when candidates accept government funding (though their effectiveness is offset by unlimited independent spending by individuals and groups).

1976 AMENDMENTS

When the Supreme Court required appointment of all members of the commission by the President within 30 days, the Congress began the process of revising the law. The reconstitution of the FEC took 111 days.

The proposed revision was complicated by the suggestion of controversial changes in the law. Among the proposals was one to extend public funding to senatorial and House campaigns. When the Congress failed to act within the 30-day period, an additional stay of 20 days was granted by the Supreme Court. When Congress again failed to act promptly, the FEC on March 22, 1976, lost its executive functions, without which it could not certify payments of matching funds to candidates then seeking their party's presidential nomination. Until the law was revised, government funds could not be paid out, causing the candidates to economize while relying solely on private funds. The commission also officially lost its powers to render advisory opinions, promulgate regulations, process complaints, initiate civil enforcement actions and refer criminal cases to the Attorney General.

Much of the delay occurred because Congress was unable or unwilling to act promptly. President Ford requested a simple reconstitution of the FEC in order to permit the FEC to continue to operate through the 1976 election. He argued against becoming bogged down in other controversial changes. Instead, Congress undertook significant revisions dealing with compliance and enforcement procedures, the issuing of advisory opinions and the róle of corporate and labor political action committees.

Some observers thought the delay was purposeful, designed by Democratic congressional leaders to help the nomination prospects of Sen. Hubert H. Humphrey (who was not an active candidate but was thought by many to be a potential one if other candidates failed) and to hurt the candidates actively contesting in the primaries, and by Republican congressional leaders to assist President Ford's prospects against Ronald Reagan. The suspension of matching funds came at a critical time, forcing candidates to rely wholly on private funds and loans during the Pennsylvania, Texas and other crucial primaries.

The Senate and the House initially passed substantially different bills. A conference committee finally reached agreement on a substitute bill,[18] but Congress by then was in spring recess, and with the presidential primary season in full sway, seven remaining contenders for their parties' nominations—six Democrats and one Republican, Ronald Reagan—asked the Supreme Court to permit the matching funds to be paid out immediately, before the court-ordered reconstitution took place. The court denied the plea but left the way open for the appeals court to modify its ruling. The court of appeals turned down the request, as did the Supreme Court twice upon further appeals.[19] The appeals were made on grounds of violation of First Amendments rights to speak effectively, compelling candidates to raise money under tight contribution limits while running crucial campaigns without expected funds. In effect, the rules had been changed in mid-campaign, but the courts failed to find grounds to intercede.

Key Senate Republicans delayed final approval of the conference committee report until early May. Then the focus shifted to the White House, where President Ford took a week to sign the bill, while the Nebraska primary went by. Ford refused to say that he would sign the bill, while the other candidates sought his assurances he would sign it in order to make it easier for them to borrow money against the promise of matching funds.

153

After signing the law May 11, Ford took another six days to reappoint five commissioners and name former Rep. William L. Springer to replace Chairman Curtis, who had resigned. This held up matching money for the Michigan and Maryland primaries. The Senate promptly reconfirmed the reappointed commissioners. Within hours of being sworn in, the renewed FEC certified $3.2-million due for various candidates and $1-million to the major party national conventions. The FEC had continued to process submissions for matching funds while certifications were suspended.

The Ford campaign was relatively healthy financially throughout the hiatus. Reagan charged that President Ford benefited from "interest-free credit" from the government, which billed the President Ford Committee while other candidates needed advance money before their chartered planes would fly. Ultimately the delays did not especially help Ford, nor did Humphrey become an active candidate. The effect on Ford's campaign was not clear, because Reagan went into debt in this period of time yet won primaries in Texas, Indiana, Georgia and Alabama, while Ford's cash advantage was slowly dissipated. The delays did not hurt Carter seriously, though he lost nine of the last 14 primaries in a winning campaign for the nomination; given his momentum, prompt matching funds could have helped him in the later primaries.

President Ford considered vetoing the 1976 Amendments.[20] One reservation he said he had about the bill was whether or not the provision for a congressional veto of FEC regulations was constitutional. Accordingly, he instructed the Attorney General to test the provision in the courts. A short time later, Ramsey Clark, a former Attorney General, and a Ralph Nader organization, Public Citizen Litigation Group, filed a suit to test the same question.

AN EVOLVING FEDERAL ELECTION COMMISSION

Curtis' Resignation

Several times during his year as the first chairman of the FEC, Thomas B. Curtis had threatened to resign.[21] He threatened to resign when Rep. Wayne Hays sought to curb the power of the FEC by attaching an amendment to an unrelated bill that was reported favorably by the House Administration Committee. The proposed Hays amendment would have reversed the provision in the 1974 Amendments whereby a proposed regulation went into effect automatically 30 legislative days after submission to the Congress unless either the Senate or the House disapproved it during that time period. The Hays version stipulated that proposed regulations would go into effect only if both houses approved them within the 30-day working period. This would have had the effect of radically altering congressional control over the FEC by empowering either house to kill any regulation simply by bottling it up in committee for the necessary period. By failing to call a committee meeting, the chairman of the committee in either chamber could, in effect, exercise a personal veto. The FEC opposed this amendment, and Curtis said he would resign if it became law. Hays eventually backed down, but the Curtis threat to resign became reality on April 30, 1976, when he wrote a 23-page letter to President Ford asking that he not be renominated to the commission when it was reconstituted.

Curtis raised two issues at the time of his resignation. First, he contended that a truly independent FEC, which he considered essential, would be possible only if the commissioners were part-time and paid on a per diem basis. They would thus be able to maintain complete independence of action because of private income derived from their principal occupation. Congress seems headed in the opposite direction, however; the 1976 Amendments required the commissioners to relinquish their private business activities within a year of becoming members.

Second, Curtis raised questions about congressional controls on the FEC stating that multiyear authorizations were desirable to avoid congressional pressure on the FEC's independence—a crucial point that Congress will need to deal with. The 1976 Amendments provided an authorization of $6-million per year.

Upon its reconstitution, the FEC could not agree on a Democrat as chairman to succeed Curtis. The members were divided over who could best deal with the Congress. So in a compromise action, Vernon W. Thomson, a Republican member, was elected chairman and Thomas E. Harris, a Democrat, was elected vice chairman. The chairmanship is limited by law to one year, presumably to avoid accretion of power by either party. The plan was to have bipartisan rotation of the chairmanship.

Advisory Opinions

By December 1975, the FEC *Annual Report*[22] noted that 76 advisory opinions (AO) and 48 informal opinions of counsel (OC) had been issued. The FEC ceased submitting regulations and issuing AOs following the Supreme Court decision. Instead of advisory opinions, the commission issued only opinions of counsel in areas previously covered by AOs. No new ground was broken and OCs also were stopped after March 22, when the Supreme Court stays were terminated. The FEC undertook evaluation of all regulations and AOs following the Supreme Court decision and began to eliminate those dealing with limitations declared unconstitutional by the court. It also began to revise others dealing with disclosure or public funding and related to limits no longer effective. Many of the AOs were criticized by practitioners and scholars for being narrow and legalistic, for inflexibly following the rigidities in the law and for failing to consider traditional political practices. They were also criticized for failing to relax some possibly unconstitutional provisions of the law.

When Congress rewrote the law in 1976 to reconstitute the commission, it also set new standards for the FEC in writing advisory opinions, stipulating that the FEC cannot issue rules of general applicability but must apply AOs only to specific facts presented in a request. Any rules of general applicability were required to be incorporated into regulations, which then were subject to congressional disapproval. But the commission itself was to determine how broadly or narrowly to interpret the law.

The enactment of the 1976 Amendments brought about a number of procedural changes put into effect by the FEC. Advisory opinions may be requested by holders of federal office, candidates for federal office, political committees, the national committee of a political party or authorized agents of any of the foregoing persons if the agent discloses the identity of his or her principal. This is a rather narrow list since it seems to exclude state election commissions from seeking AOs concerning the relationships of federal to state law.

Advisory opinions may only be issued concerning the application of a general rule of law to a specific factual situation involving the requestor. A "general rule of law" must be stated in regulations. Opinions cannot be issued for hypothetical questions.

Advisory opinions issued by the commission may be relied upon by any person involved in the specific transaction dealt with in the request or any person involved in a transaction indistinguishable from the transaction in the request provided in either case that such persons act in good faith and in accordance with the provisions and findings of the AO.

An early advisory opinion related to President Ford's travel when engaged in Republican Party activities.[23] This issue touched on the role of the President as a party leader and on nonelection party building and fund-raising activities. In 1975, the Republican National Committee allocated $500,-000 to support the President, Vice President and their aides when engaged in a party role. When the FEC ruled that President Ford's 1975 costs for travel need not be charged against his 1976 campaign spending limit, the Democrats took a partisan view that the expenditures should be included within Ford's spending limits. When Ronald Reagan challenged Ford for the Republican nomination by announcing his candidacy in November 1975, the Republican National Committee promised equitable treatment for all candidates but continued to finance Ford's travel for party building.

Political Action Committees

Perhaps the most controversial and widely publicized advisory opinion dealt with corporate political action committees.[24] It was entitled "Establishment of Political Action Committee and Employee Political Giving Program by Corporation." However, it was widely called the Sunpac AO because it was written in response to a request submitted by the Sun Oil Company. The opinion was responsible for some of the delay in reconstituting the FEC, because the legislation incorporated provisions written in response to this AO.

In a 4-2 decision, the FEC voted to permit corporations to support the election campaigns of candidates for President, Vice President, the Senate and the House so long as the money came from voluntary employee contributions. However, it cautioned corporations that there is a potential for coercion in soliciting employees and set guidelines for solicitation.

The commission's guidelines on solicitation of political contributions by employees to such funds were: first, that no superior should solicit a subordinate; second, that the solicitor should inform the solicited employee of the political purpose of the fund for which the contribution is solicited; and third, that the solicitor should inform the employee of the employee's right to refuse to contribute without reprisal of any kind.

The 1976 Amendments, as finally enacted after much contention over the provisions dealing with political action committees, permit corporations through their political action committees to solicit, without any limit, their stockholders, executive or administrative personnel, and their families for contributions. "Executive or administrative personnel" is defined as those employed by a corporation who are paid by salary, rather than on an hourly basis, and who have policymaking, managerial, professional, or supervisory responsibilities. Corporate committees can solicit employees who are not stockholders or administrative or executive personnel twice a year but only through mail addressed to their homes. Solicitation of any other sources is forbidden.

Unions, through their political action committees, can solicit, without limit, their members and their families for contributions. Union committees, however, can solicit corporate stockholders, executive or administrative personnel or employees twice a year but only through mail addressed to their homes. Any method used by a corporation to solicit contributions must be made available upon written request to a union representing any of its members working for that corporation, its subsidiaries, branches, divisions and affiliates. The union must reimburse the corporation for the expense.

A trade association or its political action committee can solicit contributions from the stockholders and executive or administrative personnel of the association's member corporations if separately and specifically approved by the corporation. The corporation, however, cannot approve any such solicitation by more than one trade association in any calendar year.

Corporations, unions, and membership organizations must report expenditures that are directly attributable to a communication expressly advocating the election or defeat of a clearly identified candidate if in excess of $2,000 per election. This provision does not apply when a communication is primarily devoted to subjects other than the express advocacy of the election or defeat of a clearly identified candidate. Whoever solicits employees must inform them of the political purpose of the separate segregated fund as well as of their right to refuse to contribute without fear of reprisal.

The law also imposes a $5,000 ceiling on individual contributions to a political committee in a calendar year. (A $20,000 limit applies to a committee of a national political party.) It also imposes a $5,000 ceiling on multicandidate committee contributions to any other political committee in any calendar year, and it places political committees established, financed, maintained, or controlled by any corporation, union, or any other person under one joint contribution limit. Thus, contributions made by a political action committee established by a subsidiary, department, division or local unit of a corporation or union are counted toward the contribution limit of a political action committee established by a parent or sister organization. This is designed to prohibit proliferation of such committees by each office or facility of a company or each local of a union. This anti-proliferation provision may violate the *Buckley v. Valeo* ruling.

Voluntary Compliance

A major goal of the commission has been to induce voluntary compliance. Expertise began to develop in the private sector following the FECA of 1971, as candidates and political committees turned to lawyers, accountants and computer specialists for advice on how to comply with the law. Once the FEC began functioning, it became the major source of information and education on compliance. No agency, however, can command full compliance without a large staff. Thus, it fell to the private sector, to candidates and their advisers, to set standards which have brought a high degree of voluntary compliance. Once it is realized that the FEC is serious about evenhanded administration and enforcement of the law, self-regulation can be expected to bring substantial compliance with the law.

During 1975, the FEC opened 57 compliance actions, of which 31 were closed. Only one was referred to the Attorney General. Five cases were settled by conciliation or voluntary compliance, and the remainder, 81 per cent, were decided to have had no basis in fact or to be outside the scope of the act or the jurisdiction of the commission. In the first year, civil enforcement powers were not exercised, and conciliation was the main method used to resolve complaints. Nevertheless, several compliance actions were criticized by some members of Congress, one because an investigation was undertaken on the basis of an anonymous complaint. In the 1976 Amendments, the Congress reduced FEC powers by constricting the standards the FEC must follow in compliance actions and specifically forbade the commission to undertake any investigation or action on the basis of an anonymous complaint. Complaints must be in writing, signed, sworn and notarized.

After investigation of a formal complaint, the commission must determine whether there is "reasonable cause to believe" that a violation has been committed and make public any determination. The commission must seek to correct the matter through "informal methods of conference, conciliation, and persuasion." All attempts at conciliation, and all conciliation agreements must be made public.

The commission has exclusive primary jurisdiction with respect to civil enforcement. If a conciliation agreement is not reached, and if the commission determines there is "probable cause" to believe a violation has occurred, it may institute civil actions for relief, including temporary or permanent injunctions, restraining orders or other appropriate orders. The commission also has the power to seek civil court enforcement of court orders and of conciliation agreements. In addition to civil enforcement, the commission has the authority to refer certain serious offenses to the Department of Justice for criminal prosecution. These are "knowing and willful" violations involving the making, receiving or reporting of any contribution or expenditure having a value in the aggregate of $1,000 or more, or having a lesser value in certain cases.

Audits

In its first year of operation, the FEC audit staff worked to educate presidential candidates, undertaking management review audits for those seeking to qualify for public funds, and it processed candidate submissions for matching fund certifications.

The FEC is required to conduct audits of candidates receiving matching funds after the matching period, which follows the national nominating conventions, or after withdrawal. When candidates withdraw, funds can only be used for qualified campaign expenses, and so audits are necessary to make such determinations.

Open Meetings

The FEC decided at the outset to be a "sunshine" agency, held regular open meetings except when dealing with personnel actions or enforcement, adopted a code of ethics for its members and employees and provided easy public access to its records and discussions, including the opening of a store-front public room for inspection of political fund reports. During 1975, the FEC processed 25,000 pages of filed reports and received from the three previous supervisory officers almost a million pages of filed reports for the years 1972-1974. Emphasizing educating the public and seeking voluntary compliance, the commission mailed some 66,000 items during 1975 explaining the law. It also began a public seminar program across the country and supplied speakers to numerous conferences and meetings.

Clearinghouse on Election Administration

The FEC assumed responsibility for the Clearinghouse on Election Administration, which carries on activities and publishes studies relating to registration of voters, voting and election administration.[25] The clearinghouse serves as a communication link among federal, state and local election agencies. It contracted with the Congressional Research Service of the Library of Congress to publish periodically a federal-state election law survey analyzing federal and state legislation and judicial decisions[26] and also to issue an occasional survey of state election laws.[27] The clearinghouse has been a useful national center in the neglected field of election administration and has served as a catalyst in election law research.

The 1974 Amendments relieved the supervisory officers under the 1971 law of responsibility for compiling fund data for 1973 and 1974 (after they had published compilations for 1972).[28] The FEC has undertaken a comprehensive, detailed and costly computer program designed to assist in data collection and analysis related to its responsibilities. Reports will be issued periodically.

Some notion of the volume of work involved is indicated by the FEC's estimate that during 1976, some 100,000 campaign fund disclosure statements will be filed by 2,500 federal candidates and 7,500 political committees.

FEC printouts of contributors will include only 1975-76 data. Data from the 1973-74 period will have to be collated by private researchers if a full picture of 1976 financing is to be available.

SUMMARY

Official apathy toward reform has been a Washington tradition—John F. Kennedy was the first modern President to consider campaign finance a critical problem. His appointment of a bipartisan Commission on Campaign Costs started a chain of events which, after faltering in the 1960s and early 1970s, came to a sudden climax in a period of two months with passage of the Federal Election Campaign Act of 1971 and the Revenue Act of 1971.

The first federal prohibition of corporate contributions was enacted in 1907, the first disclosure law in 1910 and an amendment governing prenomination spending the following year. Disclosure in primaries was challenged in 1921 in the famous *Newberry* case, in which the Supreme Court held that congressional authority did not extend to prenomination activities. This narrow interpretation was rejected in 1941 by the Supreme Court, but Congress did not reassert its power to require prenomination disclosure until 1972.

The basic law covering disclosure until 1972 was the Federal Corrupt Practices Act of 1925. The Hatch Act of 1940 limited amounts an individual could give, but it was easily circumvented, as were the federal gift tax regulations. Individuals simply made many smaller gifts to multiple committees working for the same candidate.

The post-World War II Presidents, Truman, Eisenhower, Kennedy and Johnson, all were concerned about methods used to raise money to pay for political campaigns. Truman and Eisenhower endorsed the recommendations of Kennedy's Commission on Campaign Costs in 1962. The recommendations met with coolness from Congress, however, and the new Johnson administration had other priorities.

The Baker and the Dodd cases in 1966 refocused attention on reform, as did the Long Act which provided for the first federal subsidy for presidential elections. That act and the debate in 1967 over its repeal proved to be the forerunners of the two pieces of legislation passed by Congress in 1971 that were major turning points in the history of campaign finance: the Federal Election Campaign Act and the Revenue Act. The latter provided tax credits or deductions for political contributions and also a tax checkoff to subsidize presidential campaigns during general elections. The FECA required fuller disclosure than ever before—a provision that was to play a key role in the Watergate affair. The FECA also set limits on expenditures in the communications media.

Watergate brought new pressures for reform, leading to passage of the 1974 Amendments to the FECA, which created the Federal Election Commission, extended public funding to presidential nomination campaigns and set overall limits on spending.

Controversial issues involving campaign financing focused on the new Federal Election Commission soon after its establishment; the FEC had a stormy first year with its very existence under court challenge from the beginning.

The FEC drew fire from congressional critics, and its first two regulations were rejected by the Congress.

The legal challenge to the FEC came in the Supreme Court's *Buckley v. Valeo* ruling in January 1976. The court upheld the limits on campaign contributions, but it struck down the provisions limiting campaign spending except when candidates have received government funds for their campaigns. It also sustained the disclosure requirements of the law, and while it upheld the concept of the FEC, it ruled that such an agency must be within the executive branch and its members appointed by the President. The required reconstitution of the commission's membership took 111 days—much of the delay coming in the midst of the 1976 primary elections.

During 1975 and 1976 the FEC issued numerous advisory opinions and informal opinions of counsel, some of which have come under criticism on grounds that they were too narrow and legalistic.

A major goal of the FEC has been to induce voluntary compliance. The commission also is required to conduct audits of candidates receiving matching aid. From the outset, the FEC has been a "sunshine agency," holding regular open meetings and providing easy public access to its records and discussions.

This chapter has covered only portions of the work of the FEC. A major program of the FEC is the distribution of government funds to candidates for President. This government funding program, which operated for the first time in

1976, will be examined in Chapter 10. In the next chapter we take a brief look at the experience of the states with regulation of campaign finance.

NOTES

1. This chapter is derived in part from: Herbert E. Alexander, *Money in Politics* (Washington, D.C.: Public Affairs Press, 1972), chaps. 11-13, pp. 183-251. Also see Louise Overacker, *Money in Elections* (New York: The Macmillan Company, 1932), p. 107; Alexander Heard, *The Costs of Democracy* (Chapel Hill: The University of North Carolina Press, 1960), pp. 334-335; and David W. Adamany and George E. Agree, *Political Money: A Strategy for Campaign Financing in America* (Baltimore: The Johns Hopkins University Press, 1975).
2. Robert L. Peabody, Jeffrey M. Berry, William G. Frasure, and Jerry Goldman, *To Enact a Law: Congress and Campaign Financing* (New York: Praeger Publishers, 1972).
3. *Newberry v. United States,* 256 U.S. 232 (1921).
4. *United States v. Classic,* 313 U.S. 299 (1941).
5. *Financing Presidential Campaigns,* Report of the President's Commission on Campaign Costs (Washington, D.C.: Government Printing Office), April 1962.
6. P.L. 92-225.
7. P.L. 93-443.
8. P.L. 94-283.
9. Christopher Lydon, "President Urges Campaign Reform with Gift Limits," *The New York Times,* March 9, 1974.
10. John Herbers, "Bill to Reform Campaign Funds Signed by Ford Despite Doubts," *The New York Times,* October 16, 1974.
11. Paul T. David, "The Federal Election Commission: Origins and Early Activities," *National Civic Review,* vol. 65, no. 6 (June 1976), pp. 278-283.
12. A discussion of the history and impact of the 1974 Amendments can be found in David Adamany and George Agree, "Election Campaign Financing: The 1974 Reform," *Political Science Quarterly,* vol. 90, no. 2 (Summer 1975), pp. 201-220.
13. For a continuing commentary on the FEC and election law generally, see *Campaign Practices Reports,* a newsletter published biweekly by Publications Plus, Inc., Washington, D.C., Karen Fling, ed. Also see the Federal Election Commission *Record* and various guides, compilations and reports of the FEC.
14. Richard D. Lyons, "Congress Leaders Fight Curbs on 'Slush Funds.' " *The New York Times,* September 15, 1975.

15. Warren Weaver Jr., "Wayne Hays Today Will Again Tackle Election Board on Rule," *The New York Times,* October 20, 1975.

16. Warren Weaver Jr., "Election Panel Revises Campaign Reporting Rule," *The New York Times,* November 26, 1975.

17. For many of the briefs and documents, including the Supreme Court decision in *Buckley v. Valeo,* see *Special Report of the Joint Committee on Congressional Operations, Identifying Court Proceedings and Actions of Vital Interest to the Congress,* Committee Print, 94th Cong., 2d sess. (Washington: U.S. Government Printing Office, 1976). For a critique of the decision see Albert J. Rosenthal, "The Constitution and Campaign Finance Regulation after *Buckley v. Valeo,*" in "Political Finance: Reform and Reality," *The Annals,* vol. 425 (May 1976), pp. 124-133. For various opinions, see Federal Election Campaign Act Amendments, 1976, *Hearings before the Subcommittee on Privileges and Elections of the Committee on Rules and Administration,* February 18, 1976, 94th Cong., 2d sess.

18. *Federal Election Campaign Act Amendments of 1976,* Conference Report, Report No. 94-1057, U.S. House of Representatives, 94th Cong., 2d sess.

19. "Campaigning Funding Plea Turned Down," Associated Press, *The Washington Post,* May 1, 1976.

20. See statement by the President, White House press release, May 11, 1976.

21. See letter to the President, April 30, 1976, FEC release.

22. *Annual Report 1975,* Federal Election Commission, Washington, D.C., March 1976, pp. 30-32.

23. James N. Naughton, "Suddenly the Questions are Far-Reaching as Ford's Travels," *The New York Times,* September 19, 1975.

24. See Edwin M. Epstein, "Corporations and Labor Unions in Electoral Politics," in "Political Finance: Reform and Reality," *The Annals,* vol. 425 (May 1976), pp. 33-58; Michael J. Malbin, "Corporate PAC-backers Chart a Trail Through Congress," *National Journal,* April 10, 1976; Michael C. Jensen, "The New Corporate Presence in Politics," *The New York Times,* December 14, 1975; David Ignatius, "Firms Get a Slow Start in Inducing Employees to Give to Politicians," *The Wall Street Journal,* May 20, 1976.

25. See, for example, *A Study of Election Difficulties in Representative American Jurisdictions: Final Report* (Washington, D.C.: U.S. General Accounting Office, January 1973); *A Study of State and Local Voter Registration Systems: Final Report* (Washington, D.C.: U.S. General Accounting Office, August 1974); *Election Administration Bulletin* (Washington, D.C.: U.S. General Accounting Office, May 1974); *Federal-State Elec-*

tion Law Survey: An Analysis of State Legislation, Federal Legislation and Judicial Decisions (Washington, D.C.: U.S. General Accounting Office, July 1973); *Survey of Election Boards Data Base* (Washington, D.C.: U.S. General Accounting Office, May 1974); *Survey of Election Boards: Final Report* (Washington, D.C.: U.S. General Accounting Office, May 1974); *Survey of Election Boards: Summary of Written Comments* (Washington, D.C.: U.S. General Accounting Office, July 1974); *Describe, Analyze, and Compare the Currently Available Methods of Vote Counting Equipment and Make Appropriate Recommendation: Final Report,* Prepared for: U.S. General Accounting Office, Office of Federal Elections, Clearinghouse on Elections (Vienna, Va.: Analytic Systems, Inc., December October 1974); *Experimental Voting System Supplement,* Prepared for: U.S. General Accounting Office, Office of Federal Elections (Vienna, Virginia: Analytic Systems, Inc., December 1974); *Election Laws Examination with Respect to Voting Equipment,* Prepared for: U.S. General Accounting Office, Office of Federal Elections (Vienna, Va.: Analytic Systems, Inc., January 1975); Roy G. Saltman, *Effective Use of Computing Technology in Vote Tallying,* Prepared for: Clearinghouse on Election Administration, Office of Federal Elections, General Accounting Office (Washington, D.C.: Information Technology Division, Institute for Computer Sciences and Technology, National Bureau of Standards, March 1975).

26. For a continuing survey of federal and state election laws, and relevant litigation, see *Federal-State Election Law Survey: An Analysis of State Legislation, Federal Legislation and Judicial Decisions,* Prepared for the Federal Election Commission by the American Law Division of the Congressional Research Service, Library of Congress, Washington, D.C.

27. *Analysis of Federal and State Campaign Finance Law: Quick-Reference Charts,* Prepared for the Federal Election Commission by the American Law Division of the Congressional Research Service, Library of Congress, Washington, D.C. (June 1975).

28. Printouts were: *Alphabetical Listing of 1972 Presidential Campaign Receipts,* vols. I and II, Office of Federal Elections, General Accounting Office (Washington, D.C.: U.S. Government Printing Office, November 1973); *The Annual Statistical Report of Contributions and Expenditures Made During the 1972 Election Campaigns for the U.S. House of Representatives,* pts. I and II, by W. Pat Jennings, as Clerk of the House of Representatives and supervisory officer (Washington, D.C.: U.S. Government Printing Office, April/June 1974); *The Annual Statistical Report of Receipts and Expenditures Made in*

Connection with Elections for the U.S. Senate in 1972, prepared under the direction of Francis R. Valeo, Secretary of the Senate, supervisory officer for Senate elections (Washington, D.C.: U.S. Government Printing Office, October 1974).

7

Regulation of Political Finance: The States' Experience

During the period that new federal laws governing campaign financing were conceived and enacted, some noteworthy experimentation in election reform was taking place in many of the states. In the past four years, almost every state has changed its election law in a significant way. Each of these states must now make its law conform to the 1976 Supreme Court ruling. As will be seen, the pattern of reform followed by the states has contrasted in important ways with provisions of recent federal legislation.

BIPARTISAN ELECTION COMMISSIONS

Some 25 states have bipartisan, independent commissions that oversee elections. Members of the commissions, in most cases, are appointed by the governor; in a few of the states they are appointed by the governor and legislature jointly.

The commissions represent an attempt to isolate as much as possible from political pressures the functions of receiving, auditing, tabulating, publicizing and preserving the reports of political and campaign receipts and expenditures required by law. The commissions generally have replaced partisan election officials, such as secretaries of state, who traditionally were repositories of campaign fund reports but whose partisanship as elected or appointed officials did not make them ideal administrators or enforcers of election law. Some commissions have strong powers, including the right to issue subpoenas and to assess penalties—powers which also are available for the administration and enforcement of contribution limits and of public funding in states providing it.

While bipartisan election commissions theoretically are insulated from political pressures by virtue of their independent status and the equal representation of the two major parties, they face many constitutional and enforcement problems. The method of choosing the Federal Election Commission was challenged successfully in *Buckley v. Valeo* on the ground that congressional appointments violated the constitutional separation of powers; an Alaska court rejected a challenge to that state's law which claimed that appointment to the election commission from lists submitted by the Democratic and Republican Parties represented unwarranted statutory protection of those parties.[1] However, an Illinois court ruled that the manner of selection of the bipartisan State Board of Elections contravened the state constitutional prohibition against the legislative appointment of officers of the executive branch.[2] Members of the Illinois board were nominated by the majority and minority leaders of each house of the legislature; each leader nominated two persons, and the governor selected one of the two.

Commissions having civil prosecutorial power must refer apparent criminal violations to appropriate enforcement officers—normally an attorney general or district attorney, who is a partisan official with discretion on whether to pursue the referrals. While these officials are often less well equipped than the commissions to deal with election violations, there is no alternative to referring criminal violations to them.

DISCLOSURE

Although as recently as 1972 nine states did not require disclosure of political funds, now only North Dakota does not require it. Forty-three states require some disclosure both before and after elections. Pre-election disclosure is essential if voters are to be able to assess information before they enter the voting booth.

Full disclosure of political income and disbursement is widely recognized as a basic requirement in eliminating campaign abuses. Full and frequent disclosure is a keystone of regulation. It is now fully sanctioned by the Supreme Court and is the most common form of regulation of money in politics.

A quotation from Justice Louis D. Brandeis is often used to preface discussions of the central importance of disclosure laws:

> Publicity is justly commended as a remedy for social and industrial diseases. Sunlight is said to be the best disinfectant; electric light the most efficient policeman.[3]

Although these words of Brandeis were directed at the secret manipulations of the money trusts when he wrote them in 1913, they can be considered to apply equally to secrecy surrounding the use of money in politics. Since shortly after the turn of the century, when the National Campaign Publicity Law Organization began working for a public reporting system for campaign contributions and expenditures at the federal level, there has grown a strong belief that public disclosure of political campaign finance is a desirable end.

Requirements that political costs be reported and made public rest on the recognition of the principle that a contribution to or expenditure for a political activity is a public act committed for a public purpose. That purpose is the official function of electing citizens to office—and it invariably costs money. If the voters are given full and accurate information on the financing of candidates, political parties and committees, it is argued, they will be better able to act in their best interests when casting votes. Publicity has a unique cleansing power which tends to reduce the potential influence of financial pressure on elected officials by inhibiting the contributor's expectation of favors and the official's willingness to grant them. Moreover, publicity provides information concerning the distribution, unequal or otherwise, of financial resources among rival candidates and parties and may serve to keep expenditures at reasonable levels through the fear that excessive spending will cause the electorate to react adversely.

Thus, the argument goes, an effective public disclosure system will provide financial accountability, increase public confidence in the electoral process and curb excesses and abuses by increasing the political risk for anyone engaged in unfair or illegal campaign practices.[4]

At the same time, advocates claim that legislation promoting publicity is not intended to restrict the individual nor to hold up the actions of anyone to criticism. No stigma is attached to contributions when made public; on the contrary, financial support of candidates and parties is considered a legitimate and desirable form of political participation.

An objection to disclosure of campaign contributors is that it constitutes an invasion of privacy.[5] In this view, the act of contributing is comparable to the act of voting, and the secrecy of the one is considered as important as the secrecy of the other. Each, in this view, expresses a private right of the citizen. Accordingly, to compel disclosure of political contributors is to cast doubt upon their motives, as well as to hold them up to possible scorn and potential criticism. If the stated purposes of publicity are not always achieved, however, as its critics say, then perhaps the logical approach simply would be to improve the law.

Challenges to disclosure laws have come in the form of a series of suits by the Socialist Workers Party (SWP), supported by the American Civil Liberties Union at the federal level[6] and in several states. The SWP has charged that disclosure laws reveal the names of its supporters, making them targets of police and FBI surveillance and harassment. Although several states have reduced minor party reporting requirements, the U.S. Supreme Court has declared disclosure acceptable for minor parties. The court left open the question of damages allegedly suffered by a minor party because of disclosure.

CONTRIBUTION LIMITS

Although contribution limits have been sanctioned by the Supreme Court, how widely they will be imposed is still to be determined. Eventually, they will be assessed in the light of the court's ruling permitting unlimited spending by candidates on their own behalf and unlimited direct spending by individuals and groups who are independent of the candidates. These elements of the decision threaten to disadvantage candidates running against millionaires willing to spend their own funds.

Twenty-two states limit individual contributions. Other forms of prohibition, such as of corporate or labor contributions, are also part of the state pattern of regulation. Twenty-four states prohibit contributions by corporations, while several others prohibit contributions only if the corporation is heavily regulated (for example, public utilities, banks and insurance companies). Four states—Delaware, Florida, Maryland and New York—and the District of Columbia permit corporations to contribute but set limits on the amounts they can give. Only eight states prohibit labor union contributions to political activity—a wide disparity considering that the federal law treats corporations and unions alike by prohibiting contributions from either.

Restrictions on Business and Labor

The unequal treatment of business and labor at the state level needs to be corrected but corrected in realistic terms that recognize that economic interests have a persuasive claim—and perhaps constitutional rights—to be allowed to participate in the political process. Even under federal law or in states prohibiting corporate or union activity, political action committees can be established to seek voluntary contributions from employees or members. The federal law, in fact, permits corporate or union resources to be used for the establishment and administration of a separate segregated fund to be used for political purposes by a corporation or labor organization, provided that no coercion or condition of employment or membership is involved in the solicitation of

Table 7-1 Regulation of Political Finance by the States

State	Election Commission	Disclosure Before & After[a]	Individual Contribution Limits	Expenditure Limits[b]	Public Subsidy	Tax Provisions Credit	Tax Provisions Deduction	Tax Provisions Checkoff
Ala.				✓				
Alaska	✓	✓				✓		
Ariz.		✓	✓	✓				
Ark.		✓					✓	
Calif.	✓	✓		✓			✓	
Colo.		✓						
Conn.	✓	✓	✓	✓				
Del.		✓	✓	✓				
Fla.		✓	✓	✓				
Ga.	✓	✓		✓				
Hawaii	✓	✓					✓	✓
Idaho		✓			✓			
Ill.	✓	✓						
Ind.				✓				
Iowa	✓	✓		✓	✓		✓	✓
Kan.	✓	✓	✓	✓				
Ky.	✓	✓	✓				✓	
La.		✓						
Maine	✓	✓	✓	✓	✓			✓[c]
Md.	✓	✓		✓	✓			✓[c]

Mass.		✓	✓	✓	✓			✓c
Mich.	✓	✓	✓	✓	✓		✓	✓
Minn.	✓	✓				✓	✓	
Miss.	✓	✓	✓	✓				
Mo.	✓	✓	✓					
Mont.		✓	✓		✓		✓	✓
Neb.		✓					✓	
Nev.		✓						
N.H.	✓	✓	✓	✓	✓			✓d
N.J.		✓	✓	✓				
N.M.		✓	✓	✓	✓			✓
N.Y.		✓	✓	✓				
N.C.	✓	✓		✓				
N.D.		✓		✓				
Ohio	✓	✓	✓	✓				
Okla.	✓	✓		✓				
Ore.		✓					✓	
Pa.			✓			✓	✓	
R.I.	✓	✓		✓	✓			✓
S.C.	✓	✓		✓				
S.D.	✓	✓						
Tenn.		✓						
Texas		✓						
Utah		✓		✓	✓		✓	
Vt.		✓		✓				✓
Va.		✓	✓	✓				
Wash.	✓	✓						

Table 7-1 Cont.

State	Election Commission	Disclosure Before & After [a]	Individual Contribution Limits	Expenditure Limits [b]	Public Subsidy	Tax Provisions Credit	Tax Provisions Deduction	Tax Provisions Checkoff
W.Va.		✓	✓	✓				
Wis.	✓	✓	✓	✓				
Wyo.			✓	✓				
D.C.	✓	✓	✓	✓		✓		

a Only one state, North Dakota, requires no disclosure. Six states (Alabama, Indiana, Nevada, New Mexico, Pennsylvania and Wyoming) require disclosure only after an election. In some states, disclosure requirements are not identical for primary and general elections.

b Expenditure limits were declared unconstitutional by the Supreme Court Jan. 30, 1976, in *Buckley v. Valeo*. The states checked above had expenditure limits. Their laws will have to be modified to conform to the court's ruling.

c Maine, Maryland and Massachusetts have surcharge provisions. Maryland's law is due to go into effect in 1978.

d New Jersey enacted a state income tax after the subsidy program became law to be applicable in the 1977 gubernatorial elections; the new income tax system included a checkoff for the future.

SOURCES: Based on data as of July 1, 1976, combined from: *Analysis of Federal and State Campaign Finance Law: Summaries* and *Analysis of Federal and State Campaign Finance Law: Charts*, prepared for the Federal Election Commission by the American Law Division of the Congressional Research Service, Library of Congress, Washington, D.C. (December 1975); *The Book of the States, 1976-77* (Lexington, Kentucky: The Council of State Governments, 1976), XXI, pp. 223-226; Fling, Karen, ed. "A Summary of Campaign Practices Laws of the 50 States," *Campaign Practices Reports*, Report 2, Washington, D.C.: Plus Publications Inc., January 1976; *State Statutes Regulating Political Finance*, prepared by the Citizens' Research Foundation, Princeton, New Jersey, July 1974.

contributions to the fund. In addition, corporate and union funds can be used to communicate with stockholders, employees or members and their families and to carry on non-partisan registration and get-out-the-vote campaigns aimed at stockholders, employees or members and their families.

Some fairly common activities of corporations and unions can readily be curbed. For example, they often make contributions-in-kind. Such a contribution may take the form of a fee paid a political figure for making a speech; it may involve the loan of an airplane or the gift of a free ride. Corporation or union personnel may be permitted to devote salaried time to a political activity; officers or directors may make personal contributions which are reimbursed through expense accounts, bonuses, "flower funds" or other dodges. These are activities that enforceable state prohibitions can curb. Most definitions of "contribution" in law now include loans and in-kind gifts.

Some state laws prohibit campaign contributions and other spending relating to politics or campaigns for state and local offices by persons doing an annual business of more than, say, $5,000 with units of government represented by those offices, or who are directors or shareholders owning or controlling, say, 10 per cent or more of a corporation or business or association engaged in such transactions. Further, persons who own or operate any corporation or business or association regulated by the state or are directors or shareholders owning, say, 10 per cent or more of stock in such a corporation or business similarly can be prohibited from making political contributions. Labor unions and their officers having contracts with the unit of government in question are similarly prohibited. Such laws carry criminal penalties and usually provide procedures for the initiation of citizen complaints.

Spiro Agnew Case

An example of the malignant links that can develop between money and politics is the case of former Vice President Spiro Agnew. Although untainted by Watergate, Agnew was forced to leave office by a scandal of his own making.

While the Agnew case was dramatic, in that it reached to the highest levels of the federal government, it had all the dimensions of classic political corruption. It was ironic that Agnew, the Nixon administration's champion of morality and a politician admired for his candor, stood accused of tax evasion and related white-collar crimes.[7]

What began as a routine investigation of corruption in Baltimore County in 1972, where a Democrat, N. Dale Anderson, had succeeded Agnew as county executive, led ultimately to the Vice President's doorstep. On Aug. 14, 1973, four days after Agnew's Maryland campaign finance reports were subpoenaed, members of the Salute to Ted Agnew Night Committee (which had supported President Nixon and other federal candidates in 1972) were indicted for violating the Maryland Fair Election Practices law. This case was discovered to fit a larger pattern of contributions to Agnew from persons already under investigation for alleged kickbacks and bribes, and it led to the grand jury investigation of Agnew for alleged bribery, extortion and tax fraud. Agnew's resignation from office was one of the conditions of a plea bargaining agreement under which he would plead no contest to the single count of tax evasion while the federal government would publish a 40-page account of how he allegedly extorted bribes for 10 years while serving as Baltimore County executive, governor of Maryland and Vice President. According to witnesses, Agnew had used political office to hand out county and state contracts in exchange for personal payoffs from seven engineering firms and one financial institution, pocketing well over $100,000.[8]

Contributions and Improper Influence

There is no lack of illustrations of the abuses of political contributions. The seamy side of campaign financing achieves only occasional headlines, but it does obtain sufficient prominence to create the impression that political money is more often tainted than not. This not only contributes to public cynicism about political money but also affects basic citizen attitudes toward politicians and the entire political process. To the degree that negative attitudes persist, parties and candidates have difficulty raising sufficient funds from legitimate sources and may be forced to turn to funds from questionable sources.

The extent to which campaign contributions are received with expressed or tacit obligations cannot be measured, but it is undoubtedly greater at the state and local levels than at the federal level. Not only criminal elements, but respected business executives and professionals use campaign contributions to obtain favor and preference on contracts, jobs, tax rulings and zoning. Some relationships are openly acknowledged. In many places, systematic solicitation of those who benefit from the system occurs.

In Indiana, for example, the Two Percent Club, composed of certain government employees who are assessed at the rate of 2 per cent of their salaries, is a formal basis of financing the party in power.[9] In other cases, contributions are made to both parties as a hedge, in an attempt to purchase goodwill and access, if not actual contracts, regardless of who is elected.

On the other hand, instances exist which are clear cases of extortion or conspiracy to receive campaign money in return for favors or preferment. In New Jersey, a former Democratic secretary of state was convicted in May 1972 on federal charges of bribery and extortion in seeking $10,000 in political contributions from a company that sought a contract to build a bridge. His successor, a Republican, was similarly indicted and convicted in October 1972 on grounds of extorting $10,000 in political contributions for the state Republican Party in return for attempting to fix the awarding of a state highway construction contract. Clearly, corruption crosses party lines.[10]

But even where there is no clear-cut official malfeasance, it may be customary for the beneficiary of government favor to show his gratitude by contributing. An official choosing between two persons for an appointment or a contract is usually more inclined toward the contributor than toward the stranger, toward the applicant or bidder who is likely to supply campaign funds than the one who does not. Much of politics is built on a system of rewards, but the American system of private financing often leads to favoritism. Even where laws governing Civil Service employment and state contracts make favoritism illegal, specifications can be rigged or inside information made available to the chosen.

Criminal Funds. The amount of money supplied by criminal elements is a subject on which there are few facts. Part of the problem is the difficulty in distinguishing campaign gifts from other exchanges of money. Organized crime has ample cash available with which members can and do seek to influence the political or campaign decision-making processes and even monopolize the political processes in some areas.

More than two decades ago, the Second Interim Report of the Special Senate Committee to Investigate Organized Crime in Interstate Commerce (the so-called Kefauver committee) concluded that one form of "corruption and connivance with organized crime in State and local government" consisted of: "Contributions to the campaign funds to candidates for political office at various levels by organized criminals...." Such criminal influence is bipartisan; "not infrequently, contributions are made to both major political parties, gangsters operate on both sides of the street."[11] Little has changed to revise this description.

Unfortunately, the extent of such activity is still unknown. Some scholars have estimated that perhaps 15 per cent of the money for state and local campaigns is derived from the underworld.[12] Excluding the federal level where the incidence of such behavior is presumed to be low, this would mean that almost $30-million might have come from criminal elements in 1976. If such money is concentrated in nonfederal campaigns, there is special reason to study legislation at the state and local levels designed to regulate such behavior.

If political money is relatively scarce and alternative unfettered sources of financing such as government funds are not readily available, prohibitions and limitations may be skirted. Too few laws at the federal or state levels have been designed to assist candidates and parties in obtaining alternative sources of funds so that they need not rely on large contributions from special interests.

Enforcement

The line between outright bribery and campaign contributions may often be a thin one, but where there is no accounting whatever of campaign funds or of sources of income it is easy to rationalize that one was meant to be the other. Statutory disclosure brings at least some discipline to transactions involving money and elected public officials, and if laws are enforced, even more discipline will result.

Political finance is an area of self-regulation by those affected, by those who have arrived successfully under the old rules of the game. Incumbent legislators vote on proposals to improve the law or, more often, find ways to block the legislation before it gets to a vote. Prosecutors, attorneys general or district attorneys, whether elected or appointed, are most often party regulars who may be reluctant, under pressure of loyalty or gratitude, to enforce laws that have traditionally been underenforced.

Government sets an unfortunate climate if enforcement agents fail to do their job. That climate can readily lead to public cynicism. The impact on society cannot be calculated but must be presumed to be an important link in the chain of hypocrisy that is perceived by society in general and the less favored in particular. Levels of confidence in government are thereby lowered, creating alienation from the entire political process.

Vigorous prosecution is salutary in educating political actors that the law cannot be ignored. If the risk of violating the law is made greater by knowledge that government agencies are alert, serious, evenhanded and persevering, then practitioners will learn to comply.

Government prosecutors have shown they can be successful. It is often the case that those who are found to be in violation are punished for tax fraud, extortion, conspiracy, larceny or bribery but rarely for stretching an already flexible code of campaign finance. It is probably safe to assume that until some candidates, campaign managers, treasurers and contributors are severely punished for "white collar" violations of election laws, the old habits of laxity will persist.

STATE PUBLIC FUNDING

The future of American elections will be greatly affected by developments in the 50 states. Some of the states have moved more steadily and experimentally than the federal government in efforts to deal with political money. An understanding of what is happening at the state level is therefore useful.

Tax Checkoff. Eight states have income tax checkoff provisions similar to the federal tax checkoff. In four of the eight—Idaho, Iowa, Rhode Island and Utah—the money raised is distributed without restrictions to political parties, rather than to candidates as at the federal level. In the other four, the money goes to the parties but with restrictions: in Montana, the money must be used for gubernatorial campaigns only; in Minnesota, the money must be distributed by the parties to selected categories of candidates according to formula; in North Carolina, the money goes from the parties to specified general election candidates only; in New Jersey, the money has to be used to support gubernatorial general election campaigns.

Surcharge Provisions. Three additional states have enacted surcharge provisions. In Maine, any taxpayer who is due a tax refund may stipulate that $1 of the refund be paid to a specified political party; if no refund is due, the taxpayer may add $1 to his tax liability. Maryland's law, which will be in effect for the 1978 election, provides that the taxpayer can agree to a $2 surcharge to be paid into a Fair Campaign Financing Fund. As might be expected, the rate of taxpayer participation is considerably lower under a surcharge program—near 1 per cent in Maine, 3.4 per cent in Maryland—than it is in checkoff programs—up to 25 per cent in Minnesota—in which tax dollars that would have been paid in any case are diverted to political uses. A Massachusetts surcharge took effect July 1, 1976.

In four states where voters may name the party to receive the tax money—Iowa, Minnesota and Rhode Island by checkoff, Maine by surcharge—the Democrats are being designated more often than the Republicans, ranging from about 3 to 1 in Rhode Island to about 3 to 2 in Iowa. The Democratic edge has led some observers to be concerned about the implications for Republican state parties. These observers worry that the system could lead to a "strong-get-stronger-weak-get-weaker" situation. Since the difficulties of forming a new party are great, such a situation could lead to one party dominating a state, with a fractionalized multiparty minority. In Rhode Island, Minnesota and Idaho, suits have been filed against the checkoffs, claiming the distributions to be discriminatory and unconstitutional.

Distribution of Funds. Ways in which the parties may spend public funds vary from state to state. In Minnesota, though taxpayers can check off a party designation if they wish, the distribution requirements are such that the money

Table 7-2 Distribution of Checkoff Funds to Political Parties, 1974 and 1975

	1974	*1975* [a]
Iowa		
Democratic	$92,376	$ 96,333
Republican	60,870	55,257
Minnesota [b]		
Democratic Farmer Labor (DFL)	Not in	253,000
Republican	Effect	125,500
Rhode Island [c]		
Democratic	58,000	89,000 estimate
Republican	30,000	25,000 estimate
Maine (surcharge)		
Democratic	4,859	3,617
Republican	2,668	1,919

[a] 1975 figures are preliminary.
[b] Totals include allocations from general funds which are split evenly between DFL and Republicans. Voter designations were as follows: DFL-50 per cent, Republican-17 per cent, general fund-31 per cent, minor parties-2 per cent.
[c] Totals include allocations from general funds plus a $25,000 "bonus" to Democrats by virtue of holding all five elected statewide offices.

goes directly to candidates—whether from the party designations or the general fund—with no flexibility provided the party and no funds available for general party use. Forty per cent of the money must be used in the five statewide campaigns, with a fixed percentage designated for each of the five races. The remaining funds are apportioned 30 per cent for state senate races and 30 per cent for state representatives. Within those quotas it is divided equally among candidates. With such restrictions, there is little the party can do with the money to try to bring a candidate into line with party policy or to urge a program upon him; he would receive the money no matter what.

Iowa, by contrast, allows a great deal of flexibility in the way the funds are distributed. Other than requiring that candidates at the same level receive the same amount of money from their party—all six congressional candidates of one party, for example, must get the same amount—the state party may allocate the money as it wishes so long as it is spent for legitimate campaign purposes. In Iowa (particularly among the Democrats), the money in some instances has been used for strengthening the party effort; in others, the money has aided candidates.

In 1974, Iowa Democrats had some $93,000 to spend. They allocated $7,000 each to the two statewide races—for governor and the U.S. Senate—and $1,000 each to the six U.S. House races. The remainder was spent on more of a general party effort: $4,000 for a brochure, $14,000 on a voter identification program, $13,000 on a project known as TEAM (To Elect A Majority) aimed at the legislative races and $5,000 on telephone lines to aid the TEAM project. Iowa Republicans spent $16,354 of public funds on the senatorial race, $5,000 each on the races for governor and lieutenant governor and $3,000 each on the six U.S. House campaigns. Both parties in Iowa have supported the checkoff system. The Republicans spent $3,200 on radio tapes urging its use, and both state chairmen have made joint appearances on public service stations supporting the checkoff.

In Rhode Island, the Democrats had $58,000 in public funds to spend on the 1974 contests. They distributed about

$16,000 of this to local candidates or committees, including a mayoral election campaign which got $5,000. Money was also used on a get-out-the-vote drive. The Republicans in Rhode Island in 1974, with $30,000 in public funds, sent no money down to the county or state level. The Republican funds went toward the party's general operating expenses in the state as well as to the campaigns at the statewide level.

With or without a tax checkoff system, states which offer government support to state campaigns usually do so on a matching incentive basis. For example, New Jersey law provides for a matching program under which a gubernatorial candidate in the general election, after reaching a threshold of $40,000 in private contributions not exceeding $600 each, can be eligible for matching funds of two dollars for each dollar raised. New Jersey enacted a state income tax after the subsidy program became law, so funds must be appropriated for the first test of the program scheduled to go into operation in the 1977 gubernatorial elections; the new income tax system included a checkoff.

Public Funding and Political Parties

Although public subsidies in campaigns provoke many arguments, scant attention has been paid to the implications of the various plans for the political system in general and the two-party system in particular. Questions of fairness, cost, administration and enforcement need to be asked, assumptions challenged and an understanding developed of the conditions that ought to be met if subsidies are to be provided. Public financing is not a panacea, and it will bring fundamental changes in the political structure and electoral processes.

The main questions raised about public funding are who should receive the subsidy and how and when it should be made. The goal of government subsidization is to help serious candidates. A subsidy system should be flexible enough to permit those in power to be challenged. However, it should not support candidates who are merely seeking free publicity, and it should not attract so many candidates that the electoral process is degraded. Accordingly, the most difficult

policy problems in working out fair subsidies are definitional:
How does one define major and minor parties and distinguish
between serious and frivolous candidates without doing
violence to equality of opportunity or to "equal protection"
under the federal or state constitution? Any standard must be
arbitrary, and certain screening devices must be used, based
upon past vote, numbers of petitions, numbers of smaller
contributions to achieve qualifying levels or other means.

While it is desirable to increase competition in the electoral arena, there are certain related considerations. One is
whether the provisions of government funding can induce
two-party competition in predominantly one-party areas by
means of providing funding to candidates of the minority party; competition may be extremely hard to stimulate. Another
is whether government domination of the electoral process
will follow government funding.

As the states establish systems of public financing, the
large number of elected officials—a hallmark of this country's
political system—will become obvious. In the United States,
more than 500,000 public officials are elected over a four-year
cycle. Long ballots require candidates to spend money in the
mere quest for visibility, and the long ballot and frequent
elections combined bring both voter fatigue and low turnout.
In New Jersey, there are statewide elections at least every six
months because the gubernatorial and state legislative campaigns are held in odd-numbered years. New Jersey, however,
elects only one statewide public official—the governor—and
then lets him appoint the rest. As financial pressures mount,
states probably will give increasing consideration to reducing
the number of elective offices, thus diminishing the amounts
of money (whether public or private) needed to sustain the
electoral system.

Public funding of political campaigns, when the money
is given directly to candidates, could accelerate the trend
toward candidate independence and further diminish the role
of the two major parties. With government funding available
and made doubly attractive by limits on private contributions, the candidate's need to rely on party indentifica-
tion is greatly lessened. Supported even partially with

government funds, the candidate is even less beholden to his party. While traditionally the parties have not provided much money to candidates, they have eased fund raising for candidates by opening access to party workers for volunteer help and to contributors for money. To the extent that such obligations are reduced, the trend may be toward candidates even more independent of the parties than in the past. The trend could produce two results: (1) greater difficulty in providing coherent majorities in legislatures; and (2) the spread of California-style personalized politics.

All of this would seem less of a problem in presidential campaigns because the party identification of the candidate is widely known. The Nixon re-election example is instructive. Massive funds independent of the party facilitated the distinct separation of Nixon's campaign from that of the Republican Party, to the detriment of both.

If public financing made directly to candidates is extended to U.S. Senate and U.S. House campaigns, reduced party loyalty might result, fragmenting both majorities and minorities. It also could lead to factionalism and splinter parties. At the least, one can speculate that subsidies to candidates without reference to parties will lead to more independence in legislatures and an erosion of party loyalty. At a time when there is concern over executive-legislative relationships and over executive encroachment and weak legislatures, further splintering of Congress or of state legislatures could accelerate the diminishing role of the legislative branch. The operation of checks and balances would be less constant if legislatures were further weakened. An elected office holder who ignored the demands of the leadership would not be fearful of being frozen out of a re-election bid or denied adequate funds because government would provide at least partial funding. The parties can be an important part of the balancing act. To maintain strength, the parties would require public funding independent of any government money given to candidates. If policy makers decide that strengthening political parties is desirable, candidate-funding—at least in the general election period—could be channeled through the parties.[13]

STATE TAX INCENTIVES

To the extent that campaigns are funded with public funds, the role of large contributors and special interests is reduced. Where there is less emphasis on private money, there is theoretically less chance for corruption or favoritism. In addition to direct public financing, the federal government and 12 states provide some form of indirect public support. The states offer a tax deduction on state income tax for political donations similar to the federal deduction (42 states impose an income tax). Three states, Alaska, Oregon and Minnesota, and the District of Columbia have tax credits similar to the federal one. The District of Columbia abandoned a highly controversial requirement in its new election code that taxpayers identify the candidate to whom they gave funds when claiming a tax credit for the contribution. The tax credit is a powerful incentive because it visibly reduces the amount of taxes paid.

Alternatives to Subsidies

Other forms of direct or indirect government assistance can be suggested. Rather than provide money, governments can supply services that relieve parties and candidates of the need for certain expenditures. For example, some state governments provide campaign help through the assumption of greater responsibilities for registration of voters, distribution of voter information pamphlets and election day activities. Moreover, public funding can help meet the transition costs between election day and inauguration day.[14]

Among the most important of such services would be government-sponsored universal voter registration. This would vastly reduce the costs to political parties and candidates of performing an essentially public function and would also reduce dependence on special interests for their registration activities. Such assistance would, furthermore, be likely to increase participation in elections in a nation with complex registration requirements and a highly mobile population.

SUMMARY

As new federal laws have developed, noteworthy experimentation in campaign financing has occurred in many states; almost every state has changed its election laws significantly in the past five years:

1. Twenty-five states now have bipartisan election commissions, representing an attempt to isolate from political pressures the collection and reporting of information required by law that bears on campaign finance. The commissions also serve as civil enforcement agencies.

2. All but one state (North Dakota) require disclosure of political funds, 43 mandating it both before and after elections. Full disclosure is widely recognized as a basic step in eliminating campaign abuses.

3. Twenty-two states limit the size of individual contributions.

4. Some states have been more experimental than the federal government in dealing with public funding. Eight states now have checkoff provisions on state income tax forms; in half of these the money goes to the political parties for distribution, not directly to candidates as federal law provides. In the other four it also goes to the parties but with restrictions as to use, for example, only to gubernatorial or other specified candidates. Fourteen states have tax incentive programs similar to those at the federal level, 12 through tax deductions, three with tax credits. (Oregon allows both deductions and credits.)

NOTES

1. *Abramczyk v. State of Alaska,* Superior Court, 3rd Judicial Circuit, No. 72-6426 (1975).
2. *Walker v. State Board of Elections,* Illinois Circuit Court, 7th Judicial Circuit, No. 364-75 (1975).
3. Louis D. Brandeis, "What Publicity Can Do," *Harper's Weekly,* December 20, 1913, p. 10.
4. Arguments for disclosure of lobbying expenses and personal disclosure by public officials and candidates are based on similar principles.

5. Compare the widespread American belief in publicity with the conclusion of a Swedish government investigating committee that to compel the disclosure of political contributors would place free government in jeopardy by conflicting with the principle of secrecy of the ballot. *The Commercial and Financial Chronicle*, January 24, 1952, p. 7. For a more detailed account of a similar investigation in Norway, see Jasper B. Shannon, *Money and Politics* (New York: Random House, 1959), pp. 75-77.

6. *Socialist Workers Party v. Jennings*, Civ. No. 74-1338 (D.D.C.).

7. See *United States v. Spiro T. Agnew*, Crim. A. No. 73-0535, U.S. District Court, District of Maryland, October 10, 1973.

8. On October 2, 1973, Maryland Gov. Marvin Mandel named an 11-member task force to study the awarding of state contracts without competitive bidding. Under the chairmanship of Professor Abel Wolman of Johns Hopkins, the results were published on December 15, 1973, in "Report of the State of Maryland Task Force on Non-Competitive Contracts."

9. Robert J. McNeill, *Democratic Campaign Financing in Indiana, 1964* (Bloomington, Ind., and Princeton, N.J.: Institute of Public Administration at Indiana University and Citizens' Research Foundation, 1966), pp. 15-19, 35-40.

10. For a discussion of these New Jersey and other state cases, see George Amick, *The American Way of Graft* (Princeton, N.J.: The Center for Analysis of Public Issues, 1976).

11. *Second Interim Report of the Special Senate Committee to Investigate Organized Crime in Interstate Commerce*, 82nd Cong., 1st sess., Report No. 141, p. 1

12. According to Alexander Heard, this estimate "embraces funds given in small towns and rural areas by individuals operating on the borders of the law who want a sympathetic sheriff and prosecutor, but who are not linked to crime syndicates. The estimate applies chiefly to persons engaged in illegal gambling and racketeering. It does not extend, for example, to otherwise reputable businessmen who hope for understanding treatment from building inspectors and tax assessors." Alexander Heard, *The Costs of Democracy* (Chapel Hill, N.C.: University of North Carolina Press, 1960), p. 164, fn 73, also pp. 154-168; also see Harold D. Lasswell and Arnold A. Rogow, *Power, Corruption and Rectitude* (Englewood Cliffs, N.J.: Prentice-Hall, Inc., 1963), pp. 79-80; and Donald R. Cressey, *Theft of the Nation: The Structure and Operations of Organized Crime in America* (New York: Harper & Row, Publishers, 1969), p. 253.

13. There is an extensive literature on party responsibility. Among the more recent books and articles see, for example: Austin

Ranney, *Curing the Mischiefs of Faction: Party Reform in America* (Berkeley: University of California Press, 1975); and Herbert E. Alexander, "The Impact of Election Reform Legislation on the Political Party System," an unpublished paper prepared for the 1975 Annual Meeting of the American Political Science Association, San Francisco, Calif., September 5, 1975. For earlier literature, see Herbert E. Alexander, *Responsibility in Party Finance* (Princeton, N.J.: Citizens' Research Foundation, 1963).

14. For a complete discussion of proposals, see Herbert E. Alexander, *Regulation of Political Finance* (Berkeley and Princeton: Institute of Governmental Studies, University of California and Citizens' Research Foundation, 1966), pp. 16-36.

8

The 1972 Election: Watershed in U.S. Politics

The 1972 election was a watershed in the history of American political campaigns—not only because of the series of events we now know as Watergate but also because the first major revision in federal law regulating political finance in nearly 50 years took effect in mid-campaign. Although caution must be taken in comparing spending in 1968 and 1972 because of the new disclosure provisions that applied in the latter year, some observations are warranted.

Including some $1.2-million in expenditures by the minor parties, the total spending, prenomination and post-nomination, to elect a President in 1972 came to $137.8-million. Republican and Democratic totals were fairly close, $69.2-million and $67.3-million, respectively. Four years earlier, about $100-million had been spent by Republicans, Democrats and minor parties on the presidential contest.

The Republicans in 1968, in both the prenomination and general election campaigns, spent some $45-million, $20-million of it in the primaries. Four years later, their presidential primary spending was negligible (two rivals spent about $1.2-million challenging the incumbent, President Nixon), but the Republicans' total bill was even higher than the Democrats' because so much was spent on Nixon's behalf in the general election campaign.

The Democrats spent $37-million in 1968; they spent $25-million in the primaries and $12-million in the general election. In 1972, the comparable figures were $32.6-million for the nomination, $30-million in the general election.

In both years, then, the Republicans outspent the Democrats in the general election by about 2 to 1. But in 1972 the amounts the parties were splitting by that ratio were about twice as large as they had been four years earlier.

MONEY AND POLITICS IN 1972

Both the secret stashes of money that bought "dirty tricks" and new regulations with respect to the handling of campaign funds attracted a spotlight to political finance as an issue in 1972.

The issue raised many questions: How could the rules be changed to prevent new Watergates? Was it time to consider again the role of government in financing and regulating campaigns? Should there be direct government funding of election campaigns? And perhaps above all, how might the changes that the events of 1972 were bound to bring impact on the political system?

The root of the problem—whether the eavesdropping plans of the operatives of the Committee to Re-Elect the President (CRP), the resignation of Vice President Spiro Agnew or the parade of executives of some of America's leading industries pleading guilty to campaign infractions—was money. The Republicans had an excessive amount of money available and, as a consequence, had the flexibility to indulge themselves in the ventures that led to Watergate. Unrealistic laws, badly administered and rarely enforced, invited noncompliance. Referring to the illegal corporate contributions to the Nixon campaign from some Texas firms, including the laundered Mexican checks which first tied the Watergate burglars to the Committee to Re-Elect the President, attorney Richard Haynes said, "That's how you give your tithe."[1]

In politics, too much money can be as damaging as too little money. A campaign with a lean budget does not indulge in elaborate espionage and sabotage schemes. The Nixon fund-raising team had the benefit of its successful 1968 effort together with the added advantages of incumbency and a divided opposition. In those circumstances, it was relatively easy—too easy—to raise more than $60-million, twice as much as had ever before been raised on behalf of a presidential candidate.

Indeed, the Nixon campaign had much more money than was necessary to defeat Sen. McGovern. The excess funds could well have been used to assist the Republican Party in other contests.

Actually, the Democrats, with a large debt from their 1968 campaigns in addition to a chronic shortage of funds, would have seemed more vulnerable to the demands of special interests in return for contributions.

The fund-raising techniques of the Nixon campaign were well honed. Testifying before the Senate "Watergate" committee, Robert Melcher, counsel to American Ship Building Co. (which was subsequently fined for an illegal 1972 contribution), described the impression that George Steinbrenner III, chief executive officer of the company, had received from Herbert Kalmbach about the desirability of a $100,000 gift:

> ...they would be happy to receive any contribution, but that if you were in the $25,000 class or if you were in the $50,000 class, you would be amongst many, many thousands, and that you probably would be lost in the shuffle or wouldn't be remembered.[2]

It is ironic that the Republicans, the traditional advocates of the private financing of politics, did more through the excesses and abuses of the Nixon campaign in 1972 to create an atmosphere conducive to the adoption of public financing than the Democrats and committed lobbying groups could have achieved.

The Committee to Re-Elect the President

The Committee to Re-Elect the President represented in some ways the culmination of a number of trends in

American politics over many decades—all of which served to weaken the role of the political party. Historically, the parties suffered when civil service and professionalization replaced patronage in the late 19th century. So too were parties weakened when the establishment of primaries took candidate selection out of the hands of party leaders; when government, in the New Deal era, began to provide social services similar to those the urban party organizations had offered to attract the allegiance of voters; when television focused dramatically on the candidate separate from his party; and when broader education led to increased ballot splitting. American politics now has become so candidate-oriented the parties often seem irrelevant.

The Committee to Re-Elect the President was the prime example of a candidate's committee, responsible and responsive perhaps to the candidate, but to no one else—not to the voters, not to the contributors and certainly not to the candidate's party. The CRP was only concerned about electing one man to office and not about the future of the party. A few days after the Watergate break-in, in June 1972, an official at the Republican National Committee commented: "All they care about at CRP is Richard M. Nixon. They couldn't care less about the Republican Party. Given the chance, they would wreck it."[3]

A principal architect of the CRP was H. R. Haldeman, Nixon's chief of staff. Early in 1971, his staff assistant, Jeb Stuart Magruder, was released from his White House position and given the job of creating the new committee; Magruder set up an office across Pennsylvania Avenue from the White House.

The organization evolved into two entities: the Committee to Re-Elect the President, responsible for the political activity, and the Finance Committee to Re-Elect the President (FCRP), responsible for fund raising and campaign spending. The two divisions were headed by two Cabinet members in Nixon's first administration—former Attorney General John Mitchell at CRP and former Secretary of Commerce Maurice Stans at FCRP. In time, some 35 individuals left the White House staff to join the CRP or FCRP.

While it has been condemned for many of its financial practices, the organization was a model of central control which many campaign organizers, familiar with the normal chaos of national campaigns, could envy. The organization was planned, in part, to help the campaign comply with the new law. Most of the money raised for Nixon went through the central campaign and was spent according to central authority. Spun out from the central Finance Committee to Re-Elect the President, and much more tightly controlled than the state and local McGovern committees, were FCRPs in all 50 states and special committees associated with the CRP for radio, television and the print media. There was also a Democrats for Nixon organization at the national level, plus 14 state or regional affiliated committees. Beyond this there was a miscellany of state and local Nixon committees (particularly in California) which were not part of the CRP network. There were also committees supporting Vice President Agnew and a small number of ethnic or heritage committees.

The Nixon-Agnew committees raised $62.7-million ($60.2-million through the FCRP and its satellites, $2.4-million by Democrats for Nixon and 14 affiliates). In addition, the Republican Party at the national level, including Senate and House campaign committees, raised $9.3-million, making the Republican national total $72-million. Spending was in proportion, as Table 8-1 shows. These figures give some notion of the magnitude of the Republican apparatus in 1972, the financial equivalent of a middle-sized corporation.

Expenditures by the Nixon campaign (combining prenomination and post-nomination spending by expense category) are shown in Table 8-1. These amounts represent spending from 1971 through mid-1975, all related to Nixon's 1972 nomination and election. For example, legal fees of $2-million were paid by the CRP to defend some campaign officers who were indicted. An unusual expenditure was a payment of $775,000 made by the CRP to the Democratic National Committee in settlement of its civil damage suit against the CRP for activities directed against the DNC and its officials. Some Nixon contributors were irate that their

Table 8-1 Pre- and Post-Nomination Expenditures of the Committee to Re-Elect the President and Related Organizations in 1971 and 1972

Expense Category	$ Millions
Advertising (broadcast, including production costs and fees)	$ 7.0
Direct mail to voters (not including fund raising)	5.8
Mass telephoning to voters	1.3
State organizations (primary elections, personnel, storefronts, locations, travel, voter contact, etc.)	15.9
Campaign materials	2.7
Press relations, publications, and literature	2.6
Headquarters (campaign, personnel, rent, telephone, travel, legal, etc.)	4.7
Travel and other expenses of President, Vice President, surrogates, and advance men	3.9
Citizen group activities	1.9
Youth activities	1.0
Polling (including White House-directed surveys)	1.6
Convention expenses	.6
Election night	.2
Fund raising (direct mail—$4-million, and major events—$1-million)	5.0
Fund raising (national administration and gifts for contributors)	1.9
Legal fees	2.1
Democratic settlement	.8
Democrats for Nixon	2.4
TOTAL[a]	$61.4

[a] Does not include $1.4-million in miscellaneous cash, some used for "dirty tricks" or "hush" money in 1972-73, and some used for political or other purposes in 1969-70-71, not directly related to the 1972 presidential election.

gifts to the Republican cause eventually found their way into Democratic coffers. Surplus CRP funds amounting to $1.2-million remained in mid-1975 to pay off additional legal fees.

The Democrats

Sen. George McGovern spent nearly $12-million in winning the 1972 Democratic presidential nomination. His rivals for the nomination spent close to $21-million on primaries, convention expenditures and other prenomination costs. There were also four avowed Democratic vice presidential candidates in 1972 who spent another $328,000—bringing the total Democratic prenomination costs in 1971-72 to $33.1-million.

Spending varied widely primary by primary, depending on the individual candidate's strategies, on geography and on the size of the electorate. The McGovern forces spent more than $4-million in California alone—one-third of his total prenomination costs. The California primary was seen from the beginning as the linchpin of his strategy. By contrast, in Wisconsin where his clear victory in a crowded field established him as a major contender, McGovern spent only $440,000. The Massachusetts primary, which the South Dakota senator also won, cost him $316,000, Ohio cost $231,000, Florida, where the McGovern plans called for only minimal campaigning in a state conceded to Wallace, cost only $28,000.

Sen. Edmund S. Muskie, another prenomination contender, made his biggest investments in the Wisconsin and Florida primaries—over half-a-million dollars in each state—but lost both badly. The candidate who probably spent the most to get the least in the 1972 primary season was Rep. Wilbur D. Mills. His last-place finish in the Massachusetts primary, with 3 per cent of the vote, came at a "cost" of about $10 a vote ($150,000 spent for 15,000 votes). In New Hampshire, Mills got even less for his money—3,500 votes at an estimated expenditure of $200,000, or an approximate cost of $57 a vote.

Once McGovern was nominated, some $30-million was spent on his behalf in the general election: by the central McGovern committee (McGovern Inc.) and its satellite committees; by state and local affiliates and autonomous committees; and by committees organized to finance two vice presidential campaigns, the early campaign by Sen. Thomas F. Eagleton and the latter one by R. Sargent Shriver.

In addition to the spending by the various candidate committees, about $4.5-million was spent by the Democratic

National Committee and its satellite committees. That sum included costs of the telethon staged by the Democrats on the eve of the nominating convention and of a variety of other political activities.

Table 8-2 gives an accounting by expense category of general election costs for five McGovern central committees and accounts. Additional spending occurred through other accounts and by numerous state and local committees. This table accounts for $18.5-million of the total of about $30-million, plus loan repayments of $2.6-million (not counted as expenditures because to do so would duplicate amounts and distort the total).

Costs of the Conventions

Both political parties met their 1972 convention costs in large part with a fund-raising device developed in 1936—selling corporations space for advertising in the convention program books. The Republicans raised $1.6-million and the Democrats $1-million through this means. Beyond this, the Republicans received $100,000 from the City of Miami Beach Tourist Development Authority and $52,450 from the Governor's Committee of Florida. Democrats, who also met in Miami Beach, received equivalent money, goods and services from the host city. To support the convention, local contributors presented the Democrats with $297,139, and a discounted Miami Beach Tourist Development Authority note provided another $69,388.

That was the traditional way the parties have met their convention costs. In the selection process, various cities make financial bids in cash and kind as they vie for designation as the convention site, a prize which brings millions of dollars of extra business, publicity and tax revenue to a city.

The dispute over whether the International Telephone and Telegraph Corporation (I.T.T.) won favorable settlement of antitrust cases in return for pledging to help finance the 1972 Republican convention in San Diego, the site originally chosen, focused particular attention on another long-term practice in convention financing. That practice was support from the business communities in cities vying for the conven-

Table 8-2 Presidential Expenditures by Five Central McGovern Committees in the 1972 General Election

Expense Category	Amount
1. Media—broadcasting	
A. TV and radio time	$ 5,035,000 [a]
B. TV and radio production	793,000
2. Media—nonbroadcasting	
A. Newspapers and magazines	962,273
B. Telephone canvassing	96,160
3. Direct mail	3,135,334
4. Campaign materials	176,049
5. Crowd events	25,200
6. Personal services	
A. Staff payroll	914,401
B. Outside professional services and consultant fees	269,763
7. Office expenses	822,339
8. Air charter	
Net cost	755,473
(Gross cost—$1,898,795; press and Secret Service reimbursement—$1,143,322)	
9. Field campaign	
A. Transportation	286,485
B. Other expenses	431,378
10. Transfers	
A. To state McGovern committees	3,074,541
B. To other organizations (e.g., for voter registration)	1,498,610
C. Payment of preconvention debts	267,410
Total expenditures	18,543,416
Loan repayments	2,634,969 [b]
Total disbursements	$21,178,385

Note: These figures cover the expenditures from national campaign headquarters in Washington, D.C. Additional expenditures were made by numerous state and local committees not closely controlled by McGovern headquarters during 1972.

[a] Total network and non-network broadcast spending by McGovern is reported at $6,210,788 for the general election period (in Federal Election Campaign Act of 1973, appendix A, *Hearings* before the Subcommittee on Commerce, U.S. Senate, 93rd Cong., 1st sess. [1973]. Hereafter referred to as FCC *Survey, 1972.)*

[b] Loan repayments are not counted as expenditures in order to avoid double counting.

tions. Traditionally, business firms kept convention costs down by furnishing many free services to conventioneers. Cars provided by the automobile companies were put at the disposal of convention leaders, special buses were provided for delegates and the press and hospitality suites and message centers were set up in the convention hotels, all at corporate expense. Many practices such as these were illegal for the 1976 and future national conventions under the 1974 Amendments and guidelines established by the Federal Election Commission.

The I.T.T. Case. The I.T.T. affair dealt with questions basic to government relationships with business and with corporate influence on government. What was at issue was not that I.T.T. had offered from $100,000 to $400,000 (the amount varied, depending upon the source of information) to help San Diego finance the Republican convention—to have done so would have been traditional corporate practice. Rather, at issue was whether I.T.T.'s pledge had subsequently won I.T.T. privileged treatment from the Justice Department in an anti-merger ruling.

Although later testimony revealed that President Nixon had directed then Deputy Attorney General Richard Kleindienst to delay the appeal of an antitrust ruling to the Supreme Court, it was never conclusively established that the Nixon administration's settlement of the suit was in return for I.T.T.'s 1971 pledge to the convention.

The out-of-court settlement between the Justice Department and I.T.T. in July 1971 came just eight days after the selection of San Diego as the GOP convention site for 1972. Later testimony revealed that top I.T.T. executives and Nixon administration officials had met repeatedly in secret to discuss the suit and that while the negotiations were going on I.T.T. offered the money to underwrite the convention.

The Republicans decided to move the 1972 convention from San Diego to Miami Beach, giving delays and rising costs as the official reasons for the switch. Without doubt, however, the I.T.T. affair was a major reason for the shift.

Increased Convention Costs. The costs of national conventions have soared in recent decades. As recently as 1952, conventions cost the major parties only about $340,000 each; 20 years later the Democrats spent $1.7-million, the Republicans $1.9-million. Perhaps the most significant factor in the increased costs has been the need to accommodate the increasing number of news media representatives covering the conventions. There are probably more than twice the number of news people at conventions than delegates and alternates. Television represents the fastest growing component of the press at conventions because of the special equipment required and the growing size of crews.

Security measures have also become a major cost in recent years. Miami Beach in 1972 received federal grants to help train and equip police to handle demonstrations. The total cost to Miami Beach of both conventions in 1972 was at least $3-million.

Federal grants were made again for security precautions taken in 1976 for the Democrats' meeting in New York and the Republicans' in Kansas City. But, as we have seen, federal funding has replaced to a considerable extent the private, corporate and host city financial support to the parties to pay for the national nominating conventions. As much as $2.2-million was provided for this purpose in 1976 to each of the major parties. No minor party qualified for proportionate funding in 1976.

Secret Funds

Cash "under the table" has been a fact in politics for many years, but in 1972 the use of secret funds reached an unprecedented level. This was especially true in the Nixon re-election campaign and events growing out of the Watergate break-in. The total amount of secret money involved ran into millions of dollars—in contrast to the $18,235 secret fund that Sen. Nixon, as a vice presidential candidate, sought to explain in his 1952 "Checkers" speech.[4]

At least three secret funds were exposed by the Nixon transcripts and Watergate testimony. The funds overlapped and accounts of their sources and uses conflict.

One fund was Herbert Kalmbach's, the earliest to be created and the largest of the three; part of it helped pay for "dirty tricks." The fund was created originally from nearly $1.7-million left over from the 1968 campaign. Between 1969 and the end of 1971, Kalmbach collected another $300,000, bringing the fund to about $2-million.

A second secret fund was created when the Kalmbach account was closed out in early 1972 and the $234,000 which remained was transferred to the treasurer's fund in the Finance Committee to Re-Elect the President. The money later was moved on to become part of a $350,000 fund requested by the White House for H. R. Haldeman to use for nonelection issue polling. While amounts in the treasurer's fund fluctuated, a later disclosure showed an aggregated cash fund of $919,000. Into this fund went many of the illegal corporate contributions to the Nixon campaign, as well as the $89,000 in cashier's checks on a Mexico City bank which eventually wound up in the bank account of one of the Watergate burglars.

The third secret fund was controlled by H. R. Haldeman. As noted, it was created largely from money left over from Kalmbach's fund. During the election campaign, the fund was largely untouched, except for $22,000 that John Dean, the President's counsel, withdrew to pay for a pro-administration Vietnam advertisement and as a "loan" for his honeymoon. The money was used primarily to pay "hush money" to Watergate defendants; a total of $155,000 was passed on for this purpose in the spring of 1973.

Another fund was held by Charles (Bebe) Rebozo, Nixon's close friend. Rebozo has asserted that $100,000 came to him, in two payments of $50,000 each, from representatives of the billionaire recluse, Howard Hughes. He says he kept the money and returned it untouched in 1973. Many allegations have been made as to the size and use of the fund. But none of the allegations has been proved.

Contributions Returned

The Finance Committee to Re-Elect the President returned large sums of money to corporations and individuals after knowledge of illegal or improper contributions became public. However, the FCRP had use of most of the money—which totaled $1.6-million—through portions of the campaign period. The FCRP returned a total of $465,000 to corporations that had made illegal campaign contributions and more than $1-million to seven individuals (Table 8-3).

Officials of the Finance Committee to Re-Elect the President also claimed that contributions totaling more than $2.5-million, including $1-million from Italian financier Michele Sindona, were rejected because of proposed conditions or possible embarrassment about the source of the contributions.

Some contributions, mainly illegal corporate gifts, also were returned by Democratic presidential hopefuls Hubert H. Humphrey, Henry M. Jackson and Wilbur D. Mills.

Table 8-3 Contributions Returned by the Finance Committee to Re-Elect the President, 1971-1973

Corporation or Individual	Amount of Contribution	Date Returned
American Airlines	$ 55,000	7/11/73
Ashland Oil Inc.	100,000	7/17/73
Braniff Airways Inc.	40,000	NA
Goodyear Tire & Rubber	40,000	8/10/73
Gulf Oil	100,000	7/26/73
Minnesota Mining & Mfg.	30,000	9/11/73
Phillips Petroleum Co.	100,000	8/17/73
Total Corporate Repayments	$465,000	
Robert H. Allen	$100,000	1/24/73
Walter T. Duncan	305,000	5/73
Ernesto Lagdameo	30,000	7/72
C. Arnholt Smith	200,000	3/28/72
Eric Ho Tung	15,000	9/7/72
Robert L. Vesco	250,000	1/31/73
Cornelius Vanderbilt Whitney	250,000	12/2/71
Total Individual Repayments	$1,150,000[a]	

[a] Does not include $100,000 returned to Howard Hughes by Rebozo.
NA Not Available

PARTY SPENDING

American politics—particularly at the presidential level—centers around candidates, not parties. Campaigns often work to project a candidate's personality, and they do not always stress party identification. Money is often contributed to the candidate or his campaign committee rather than to the party. Thus, party solicitation, even when undertaken, may find serious competition for the available dollar.

Emphasis on the candidate, not his party, was particularly marked in 1972, and it extended to both major party candidates. The Committee to Re-Elect the President focused wholly on Nixon.[5] And on the Democratic side, the battle between the party regulars and the insurgent McGovern forces had some of the same impact in divorcing the candidate from the party.

However, despite the competition they faced from the candidates' appeals for funds, the Democratic and Republican national party organizations in 1972 managed to raise in the vicinity of $14-million—adding up the receipts from the various sustaining funds or associate programs that each maintains, as well as the money raised by the Democratic National Committee through its July 1972 telethon (discussed in Chapter 4).

Republican Party Financing

While its efforts were somewhat overshadowed by the large amounts of money pouring into the committees directly involved in Nixon's re-election, the Republican National Finance Committee (RNFC) raised $8.6-million in 1972. A large part of that was spent in direct or indirect support of the Nixon administration and the presidential campaign.

The Republican practice has been to form separate finance committees to conduct fund drives for the regular operating organizations. At the national level, the party is made up of a number of committees. A brief description of each follows:

The *Republican National Finance Committee* (RNFC) is the fund-raising arm of the Republican National Committee

(RNC). It raises money for the overall budget of the RNC. The finance committee also serves as a budgeting agent for all national party fund-raising committees. Moreover, the RNFC assists state and local party organizations in developing their financial programs. The *Republican National Committee* itself is the administrative arm of the party. It provides counsel and management advice to candidates and party committees at every level. The RNC emphasizes voter identification, registration and get-out-the-vote activities, candidate recruitment and research. It manages the national nominating conventions every four years.

The *National Republican Congressional Committee* (NRCC) provides direct campaign and financial support for Republican members of the U.S. House of Representatives. In addition, it has art, photography, research and public relations departments to provide professional campaign guidance to Republican candidates for election or re-election to the House. Part of its income is derived from its joint sponsorship, with the Republican Senatorial Committee, of the annual dinner, in Washington, D.C., honoring Abraham Lincoln.

Established in 1948, the *Republican Senatorial Committee* (RSC) is the campaign support organization for incumbent and non-incumbent candidates for the U.S. Senate. It makes direct campaign contributions and provides radio, television, photography and campaign management counsel. Its financial support comes almost entirely from the annual Washington dinner.

The *Republican Boosters Club* was launched in the fall of 1964 to provide direct campaign aid to non-incumbent candidates for the House and Senate in selected districts. Funds are raised through annual memberships. All expenses of the Boosters Club are paid by the congressional and senatorial committees.

Each year, the proposed budgets of each of the operating committees of the party are presented to the RNFC for approval. After approval of all budgets, each state is allocated a target for money raising within that state during the year in support of the national GOP committees. This quota is determined by the RNFC, using a performance factor based on the individual state's demonstrated ability to raise funds for the national organizations over several years. All contributions from individuals are credited against the quota of the state in which they reside.

In most states, Republican finance committees are set up independently to supply funds to the state committees. Quota and allocation agreements may be made under which the political organizations retain some funds—normally those derived from fund-raising dinners—but the rest may be raised and allocated through the state or metropolitan finance committees.

Where it operates, the system is businesslike, and it helps to avoid multiple solicitation, a source of irritation in political fund raising. The system relieves politicians of onerous fund-raising tasks by using volunteers. Ideally, money is raised where it is available and spent where it is needed through finance committee allocations to operating committees. Political fund raising is considered a year-round, election and nonelection year activity, requiring full-time staff to produce steady and reliable income.

In 1962, the *Republican National Sustaining Fund* was organized. An annual sustaining membership costs $15 per contributor, but contributions of up to $100 are accepted. Other categories include: RN Associates for annual contributions of $1,000 and above; the Republican Campaigner Program for annual contributors of $100 to $499; and the Republican Victory Associates for those contributing $500 to $999. The proportionate amounts the RNC raised from these sources is shown in the following summary of 1972 income:

RN Associates	$1,448,960.00
Sustaining Fund	5,282,262.00
Campaigners Programs	944,507.00
1971 "Salute" Dinner	236,845.00
Gala Dinner	490,996.00
Speaker Commission	3,214.00
State Payments	53,480.00
Special Projects and Miscellaneous	103,340.00
TOTAL	$8,563,604.00

These figures illustrate the importance of small contributions to the RNC. Prior to Nixon's renomination in the summer of 1972, the appeals to the small contributors were conducted solely by the RNC; $5.3-million was raised by the sustaining membership program during this period, with an average gift of $20 coming from about 250,000 contributors. After Nixon's nomination, the direct mail program was combined with CRP mailings in direct support of Nixon's re-election.

Although contributions to the Republican National Committee dipped sharply in 1973, as the Watergate disclosures emerged, the amounts gathered annually by this program began to climb again in 1974, and by 1975, President Ford's first full year in office, the amount raised via this route rose to a new annual record. The amounts raised since 1962 are presented as follows:

Republican National Sustaining Fund, 1962-1975

1962	$ 700,000	1969	$2,125,000
1963	1,100,000	1970	3,040,000
1964	2,369,000	1971	4,369,000
1965	1,700,000	1972	5,282,000
1966	3,300,000	1973	3,964,000
1967	3,500,000	1974	4,759,482
1968	2,400,000	1975	5,971,877

Democratic Party Financing

The *Democratic National Committee* (DNC) confronted a particularly challenging set of problems in 1972. Although the staff at the rival Republican headquarters may have often felt eclipsed by the Committee to Re-Elect the President, it at least had the satisfaction of both beginning and ending 1972 in the black. The DNC, however, began the year with a $9.3-million debt left over, for the most part, from the 1968 Humphrey campaign.

The first Democratic telethon, held in 1972, launched the effort to reduce the DNC debt. By means of annual telethons, as well as settlement of some loans and debts for a few cents on the dollar, the DNC debt had been whittled down to $2.6-million by mid-1976.

Democrats solicit contributions systematically in appropriate geographic areas and in industries, such as textiles in New York and entertainment in New York and California, which tend to be Democratic. Moreover, intense solicitation occurs in liberal and labor circles. Finally, they appeal to such traditional sources as contractors.

The tumultuous events at the Democrats' national convention in Chicago in 1968 brought a number of problems: the Democrats had been expecting to renominate President Johnson when the convention was planned. The convention was accordingly scheduled as late in the summer as possible, leaving little time to heal the wounds. Nor were there any plans to raise the funds which would be needed. The nominee, Vice President Hubert H. Humphrey, was forced to borrow large sums in order to campaign, and a substantial portion of those debts were still unpaid four years later.

The Democratic Party neglected to court small contributors while it was in power in the 1960s, relying instead on large contributions. When large contributions were no longer forthcoming, the search for money at times became frantic. Since that time, the DNC has pursued a small gifts, direct mail program which is augmented by the annual telethon.

Throughout the 1960s, various attempts were made to bring more structure and discipline to the Democratic fund-raising efforts. After the 1960 presidential campaign, it was decided to merge the financial operations of the DNC with the congressional campaign committees. However, while the DNC agreed to provide the funds to the Senate and House committees, the organizations remained autonomous in other respects, spending and allocating funds to candidates independently.

During the Johnson administration, disbursements to congressional candidates were made increasingly with an eye to the interests of the White House, a break with the past when funds had been given chiefly to bolster the Democratic leadership in each house. Tensions developed as the White House sought control over the distribution of the funds to candidates, and in 1966 it was announced that each committee would raise its own funds.

The Democratic finance structure was supplemented by the establishment of a *Democratic National Finance Committee* (DNFC) early in 1960. Its purpose was to assist party financial operations by building a network of members in each state and territory to aid the efforts of the party chairman, treasurer and national committee members.

In 1972, the Democratic national convention passed a resolution to set aside 8 per cent of all DNC income to defray the expenses of delegates who needed financial help to attend the 1976 convention. The money was never allocated, on grounds that the DNC was still in debt and could not pay it off and meet operating expenses as well. The convention funding provided by the federal government cannot be used to defray delegate expenses.

The Democrats also held two "miniconventions" after their regular national convention in July 1972—one planned, the other thrust upon them—which together cost the party about $510,000. The first was the convention hastily convened in Washington, D.C., in August 1972, after Sen. Eagleton had left the ticket; it met for the purpose of ratifying Sargent Shriver as the replacement choice as Democratic vice presidential nominee. The total cost to the DNC was about $10,000.

A far more extensive meeting—costing an estimated $500,000—was a three-day Democratic meeting in Kansas City, Mo., in December 1974. The meeting, on party organization and policy, was attended by 1,700 grassroots delegates and 338 ex officio delegates consisting of Democratic elected officials. The convention had been called by the 1972 national convention, but it was the culmination of the reform movement that reached back to 1968. At the Kansas City meeting a new party charter was ratified—the first comprehensive charter written by any political party in the nation's history.

Congressional Spending

The intense interest in presidential spending in 1972 generated by the accounts of the misdeeds in the Nixon re-election campaign overshadowed the $90-million also being spent that year on campaigns for the other elected branch of the federal government—the Congress.

Of the total of $35.5-million spent on the 33 senatorial races in 1972 (the Democrats made a net gain of two seats), the Republicans spent $19.8-million and the Democrats $14.3-million. A total of $8.1-million was spent in Senate primary campaigns, $26.4-million in the general elections.

The Democratic Senatorial Campaign Committee disbursed $726,000 to Democratic Senate candidates in 1972, while its counterpart, the National Republican Senatorial Committee, spent $1.4-million on aid to Republican Senate candidates. Contributing to these committees, but earmarking donations for favorite candidates, has long been popular. It creates good will with the members of the campaign committee and with the Senate leadership, and, of course, the candidate learns the source of the money.

On the House side, a total of $54.3-million was spent, $11.2-million of it on the primaries. Here, the Democrats outspent the Republicans by nearly $5-million, much of the difference coming in primary expenditures. In the general election campaigns for the House of Representatives, the expenditures by the two parties were much closer—$20.2-million spent by Democratic candidates, $18.8-million spent by Republicans.

In the disbursements of the House committees, the National Republican Congressional Committee gave $625,000 to Republican candidates for the House. Additional funds were spent directly on their behalf, as noted previously. The Democratic Congressional Campaign Committee and the Democratic National Congressional Committee together gave over $1-million to Democratic House candidates in the general election.

Both the Democrats and Republicans had additional party-affiliated committees operating in 1972. The Republican Congressional Boosters Club gave a total of $1.3-million, spread among Republican Senate and House candidates in the general election. The Democrats had a National Committee for the Re-election of a Democratic Congress, which raised money independently but gave its proceeds to the Democratic Senatorial Campaign Committee ($261,000) and the Democratic Congressional Campaign Committee ($377,000) rather than to candidates directly. Each of these party committees was a separate fund-raising vehicle designed to gather funds from among the party faithful. Some of the funds collected were contributed by corporate or professional political action committees; some were given by individuals. Frequently, funds were earmarked for specific candidates, but most were for use at the discretion of the committee officials.

A considerable part of the funds went to incumbents. Challengers usually got a token amount, depending on the availability of funds and upon their ability to persuade officials that they could be successful if adequately funded.

There were also a number of committees in 1972 that were not tied to a party structure but were identified as supporting only Democratic or only Republican candidates for Congress. These committees were designed to support certain kinds of candidates or to promote certain general goals within a party. One example is the Committee for Twelve which supported 12 liberal Democratic House candidates, spending $190,000. Another example is the DSG Campaign Fund, which spent $252,000 in support of Democratic candidates for the House (DSG stands for the Democratic Study Group, an organization of more than 150 House Democrats who work together on legislative goals). Six Democratic-oriented groups not affiliated with the party spent $1.5-million in 1972.

Although Republicans had nine groups in a similar category, they only spent $310,000 on behalf of Republican candidates for the House and Senate. Examples were: Congressional Victory Committee, supporting Republican candidates for both Senate and House, spending $63,000; and Negroes for a Republican Victory, spending $58,000.

SPECIAL INTEREST AND IDEOLOGICAL GROUPS

Spending by labor in 1972 was greater than the expenditures by business, professional, health and dairy com-

Table 8-4 Spending by Labor and Other Special Interest Groups in 1972

	Adjusted Gross	Direct Expenditures	Transfers
Labor Spending			
Reported under Corrupt Practices Act	$ 320,000	$ 170,000	$ 150,000
Reported under FECA	7,350,000	1,280,000	6,070,000
COPE-related spending by AFL-CIO[a]	810,000	810,000	———
Total	$8,480,000	$2,260,000	$6,220,000
Other Special Interest Spending			
Reported under CPA	$ 260,000	$ 170,000	$ 90,000
Reported under FECA			
Business/Professional	3,450,000	350,000[b]	3,100,000
Dairy	1,600,000	100,000	1,500,000
Education[c]	1,020,000	120,000	900,000
Health-related	1,310,000	110,000	1,200,000
Rural-related[d]	400,000	50,000	350,000
Total	$8,040,000	$ 900,000	$7,140,000

[a] Disclosed in 1972 for the first time, in compliance with Government Accounting Office directive.

[b] Corporate committees had minimal direct spending; this is largely attributable to associations with ongoing operations.

[c] All education committees are included in this category, regardless of affiliation.

[d] Includes rural electric co-ops, agriculture committees, etc., other than dairy.

mittees combined—$8.5-million by the unions compared with just over $8-million by the other groups. These figures are shown in Table 8-4; the direct expenditures column reflects spending for rent, salaries and related expenses incurred in operating the committee, while the transfers column reflects the amounts these committees transferred to candidates or other committees for them to spend on campaigning. Most of the money was transferred to committees supporting candidates for the Senate and House of Representatives.

Table 8-5 Spending by Ideological Groups in 1972

	Adjusted Gross	Direct Expenditures	Transfers
American Conservative Union	$ 209,000[a]	$ 209,000	$ ——
Americans for Constitutional Action	126,000	119,000	7,000
Americans for Democratic Action	75,000	75,000	——
Campaign Fund for the Environment	14,000	9,000	5,000
Committee for Responsible Youth Politics	20,000	8,000	12,000
Concerned Seniors for Better Government	39,000	——	39,000
Congressional Action Fund	102,000	65,000	37,000
Congressional Alliance '72	21,000	21,000	——
Conservative Victory Fund	379,000[a]	259,000	120,000
Council for a Livable World	166,000	135,000	31,000
League of Conservation Voters and LCV-CF	92,000[a]	30,000	62,000
National Committee for an Effective Congress	670,000[a]	266,000	404,000
One Percent Fund	9,000[a]	9,000	——
Set the Date	6,000	6,000	——
United Congressional Appeal	52,000	20,000	32,000
Universities National Anti-War Fund	8,000	3,000	5,000
Vote for Peace	110,000	37,000	73,000
Women for Peace	71,000	71,000	——
Young America's Campaign Committee	71,000[a]	71,000	——
Totals	$2,240,000	$1,413,000	$ 827,000
Reported under FECA	$2,240,000	$1,413,000	$ 827,000
Reported under CPA	408,000	287,000	121,000
Total	$2,648,000	$1,700,000	$ 948,000

[a]The gross figures used here are taken from the House compilation, the transfers from Common Cause. The Senate publication gives somewhat different figures, where noted, but the final totals are almost identical.

Although labor was split over McGovern's candidacy, greatly eroding the usual solid Democratic support by union political action committees, labor's reported gross disbursements rose above those in other years. However, the increase was almost entirely due to more comprehensive reporting requirements affecting two sources of union funds: the previously unreported AFL-CIO spending from union dues for COPE (Committee on Political Education) staff and operational costs, and the first-time filings of scores of state and local union political committees.

Business and professional groups were also active. The figure of just over $8-million for their reported gross disbursements does not include the illegal corporate and dairy contributions.

In addition to these two major groups, a number of other special interests reported their spending as required by law. These were groups of an ideological nature, such as the Americans for Democratic Action on the left and the Americans for Constitutional Action on the right. Or they were groups with an interest in a particular issue, such as the Campaign Fund for the Environment. Altogether, such groups spent a total of $2.6-million in 1972. Their diversity and their ranges of funding are shown in Table 8-5.

The total raised and spent by all these special interests—$19-million—is impressive. Of this amount, almost $14.5-million was given to candidates, party or campaign committees to spend as they saw fit. The rest was spent directly in operating the committees.

POLITICAL BROADCASTING IN 1972[6]

The Federal Election Campaign Act of 1971 affected broadcasting in several significant ways in 1972. First, the law limited the amounts candidates for federal offices could spend on radio, television, cable television, newspapers, magazines, billboards and automated telephone systems in any primary, runoff, special or general election to 10 cents times the voting-age population of the geographical unit covered by the election, or $50,000, whichever was greater. Second, it restricted spending by candidates to no more than 60 per cent of their media expenditures on broadcast advertising. And third, it provided that the broadcast media could not charge candidates (at any level) more than the lowest unit rate charged any other advertiser for the same class and amount of time, for a period extending 45 days preceding a primary election or 60 days preceding a general or special election. At other times, rates could not exceed the charges made for comparable use.

The provisions limiting broadcast expenditures varied in significance for campaigns for different offices. In the presidential general election, the limits on spending did not directly determine in 1972 the level of broadcast spending—both Nixon and McGovern spent well under the $8.5-million limit set for presidential and vice presidential candidates in the post-nomination period. For the Democrats, the limit was much higher than they had ever spent on broadcasting in a presidential general election campaign, and the $6.2-million actually spent by McGovern on broadcasting was the highest Democratic total up until that time. While the Republican spending in 1968 had been well over this amount ($12.6-million), in 1972 their much lower broadcast expenditure ($4.3-million) was more a result of campaign strategy than of legal constraints.

The most striking increase in Nixon's nonbroadcast spending was in the use of direct mail as a medium of communication. In some cases, direct mail was viewed as a means superior to broadcasting in reaching specially targeted groups.

Senate and House Spending. The new spending limits may have had more direct impact in nonpresidential contests. The 1972 broadcasting costs for senatorial races ($6.4-million) were much lower than in 1970 when $16-million was spent, and even lower than in 1968 when $10.4-million was spent. In most Senate and House campaigns, the actual spending was much less than the allowed limit. In the 34 senatorial races, four candidates appear to have overspent the general election limit; two of them were running against one another, while of the remaining two who overspent, one won and one lost. Nine House candidates appear to have exceeded the spending limit in the primary and general election each; three of these were winners. No prosecutions of any of these apparent violations occurred.[7]

While the broadcasting costs of House campaigns did increase from $6.1-million in 1970 to $7.5-million, the increase is slight compared to the rise in spending in gubernatorial races, where a 50 per cent jump (from $6.2-million to $9.7-million) was recorded between 1968 and 1972. In 1968, broadcast expenditures for all other state and local offices made up 23 per cent of the total spent on broadcasting that year; in 1972, that proportion increased to 40 per cent.

Lowest Unit Cost Regulation. Of more general importance in limiting expenditures was the FECA requirement that broadcasters charge political candidates the lowest unit cost for the same advertising time available to commercial advertisers. Thus, broadcasters could not charge premium rates for candidates who wanted prime time for a few weeks before the election but had to charge the same unit rate as, say, for a local department store which advertises 52 weeks in the year, qualifying for quantity discounts. An unanticipated consequence was that as the profitability of political broadcasting declined, somewhat less time was made available by broadcasters for political use. Total broadcast spending, therefore, was kept down by a combination of a reduction in actual cost and a limited supply of available time.

The FECA provisions were seen by some, chiefly broadcasters themselves, as creating difficulties and hardships. Increased amounts of paperwork, for example, were inevitable in the certification process. The lowest unit rate provision was of particular concern to broadcasters. Some saw it as discriminatory because the print media were not similarly regulated; others worried about the economic consequences. Broadcasters tried and were unsuccessful in having the lowest unit rate provision thrown out. They were successful (along with newspaper publishers) in the *ACLU v. Valeo* decision,[8] which declared unconstitutional the enforcement procedures for the media limitations. Those procedures had placed responsibility for certification on media vendors. This meant that broadcasters and publishers had to obtain from a candidate a certification that each expenditure would not cause him to exceed the limit. The courts relieved vendors of this responsibility without actually declaring the limit itself unconstitutional. However, this media limit was repealed in the 1974 Amendments. Thus, of the three provisions of the 1971 law mentioned at the beginning of this section, only the third item, or the lowest charge provision, survived in the 1974 Amendments.

'Actualities'. One widely used means of gaining free time, in effect, was the feeding of tapes by the campaign organizations to local stations for use as news clips. Both presidential campaigns in 1972 spent several hundred thousand dollars to produce and distribute taped recordings of candidates and spokesmen to hundreds of radio stations across the country for free rebroadcast during news programs. Audio feeds, or "actualities" as they are sometimes called, are essentially analogous to the printed press release.

Two staff "radio reporters" accompanied McGovern in all his travels, taping everything he said, and then selecting several segments for transmission to Washington, D.C., headquarters. From there, the feeds were telephoned to 16 regional centers and then telephoned to individual stations. Stations were also able to phone McGovern and Nixon headquarters at special numbers in Washington to receive the "actualities." In what may become more common practice in future campaigns, the McGovern California primary effort even employed a video tape crew to travel mornings with the candidate and then reproduce video tape feeds for transport to California television stations in time for the evening news broadcasts.

Influence of Broadcasting

Certainly in terms of cost and the attention it received, political broadcasting was of prime importance in the 1972 campaign—yet measured in terms of total political expenditure, its importance declined. The decline in relative importance was due to (1) new FECA regulations regarding broadcast charges and spending limits and (2) recognition that the ability of broadcasting to influence voters was also limited. Both parties found that direct mail and telephone contacts may well be more effective in addressing various groups directly.

In spite of the $10.8-million spent by the presidential candidates for political broadcasts in the general election, the public support indicated for them in public opinion polls changed only slightly from the conventions until election day. In winning one of the largest pluralities in presidential campaign history, Nixon spent significantly less on political broadcasting than his opponent, McGovern, and less than he had spent in the much closer 1968 election. McGovern's broadcast strategy was one of maximum exposure; Nixon's was one of minimal exposure. Also striking, in terms of the role of broadcasting, was the failure of such "media candidates" as John Lindsay, former New York City mayor, who invested heavily in broadcasting.

None of this should suggest that television and radio broadcasting are of no real importance in determining the success or failure of a campaign or that candidates will in the future so regard them. Rather, it appears that the power of broadcast media as a tool of political communication is limited and that the effectiveness and the extent of media usefulness will vary from one election and candidate to another. The large-scale use of the media in a campaign is not necessarily the most effective strategy, although its absence may be harmful. The onset of regulation of broadcast spending, therefore, has coincided with (and may have contributed to) the beginning of a critical re-evaluation of the role of broadcasting in political campaigning. Together, they have at least temporarily brought to a halt a spiral of rising political broadcast spending.

SUMMARY

Total spending to elect a President in 1972 amounted to $137.8-million; that sum compared with $100-million reported spent to elect a President in 1968 (when disclosure provisions were less strict). In both years, Republicans outspent the Democrats in the general election by about 2 to 1.

Ironically, it was the Republican campaign abuses and excesses that created an atmosphere conducive to the passage of legislation providing public funding of presidential campaigns—a step historically opposed by many Republicans.

The Committee to Re-Elect the President was in many ways the logical culmination of a number of trends observable for decades. All of these trends tended to weaken political parties. The CRP was a prime example of a committee responsible only to the candidate, not to the party. For all its abuses, the CRP was a model of central control. In the Democratic campaign, by contrast, there was less centralization, even after McGovern had been nominated.

Both parties for many years had met their convention costs largely with a fund-raising device dating back to 1936—corporate advertising in the convention program books. In 1976, federal funding for conventions replaced to a considerable extent the corporate and host city financial support. Consequently, the possibility of an I.T.T. case is unlikely in the future.

The use of secret funds, a long-time political fact, reached an unprecedented level in 1972, with the total of such funds running into millions of dollars. Watergate testimony and transcripts exposed at least three secret funds—one funded "dirty tricks," the second funded the actual Watergate break-in and the third provided "hush money" for some Watergate defendants.

The Finance Committee to Re-Elect the President returned $1.6-million in illegal or improper contributions but only after these corporate or individuals gifts had been exposed.

Emphasis on candidate, not party, was particularly marked in 1972, yet the national party organizations raised $14-million in that year.

Spending for Senate and House campaigns in 1972 totaled $90-million. A large component was funds contributed by organized labor and the business community.

221

Such funds amounted to more than $16-million ($8.5-million by unions, over $8-million by business, professional, health and dairy groups); most went to help support congressional campaigns.

The use of broadcasting by campaigners was affected in significant ways by the 1971 campaign reform act: the total amount that could be spent was limited, and broadcasters were told their rates for politics could not exceed those charged their most-favored commercial advertiser. This probably impacted most heavily on congressional spending, since both parties were well within the presidential limits. Increasingly it is understood that the influence of broadcasting in elections is limited and that its usefulness varies from campaign to campaign. That new understanding and the new laws have at least temporarily stopped the rising spiral of spending for political broadcasting.

Chapter 9 reviews campaign finance in the 1974 midterm election year, a transitional year under new reforms.

NOTES

1. Carl Bernstein and Bob Woodward, *All the President's Men* (New York: Simon and Schuster, 1974), p. 55.
2. Senate Select Committee on Presidential Campaign Activities, *Final Report,* pt. 2, No. 93-981, 93rd Cong., 2d sess. (Washington, D.C.: Government Printing Office, June 1974), p. 452.
3. Bernstein and Woodward, *op. cit.,* p. 29.
4. See Richard M. Nixon, *Six Crises* (Garden City, New York: Doubleday and Co., 1962), p. 129.
5. Bruce F. Freed, "This Time Everbody's Got a CREEP," *The Washington Monthly,* November 1975, p. 35.
6. See *Surveys of Political Broadcasting, Primary and General Election Campaigns,* Federal Communications Commission, for the years 1960, 1962, 1964, 1966 and 1970; and *Federal Election Campaign Act of 1973,* appendix A, *Hearings Before the Subcommittee on Communications of the Committee on Commerce,* U.S. Senate, 93rd Cong., 1st sess. (1973), hereafter referred to as FCC, *Survey 1972.*
7. "Broadcast Spending: Presidential, Senate Costs Drop," *Congressional Quarterly Weekly Report,* May 12, 1973, pp. 1134-1136.
8. 366 F. Supp. 1041 (D.D.C., 1973).

9

The 1974 Election:
A Transitional Election Year

Although the new limits on large contributions did not take effect until after the 1974 congressional elections, there were abundant signs in 1974 that many big donors had been made exceedingly gun shy by the Watergate atmosphere. Republican fund raisers, in particular, found money hard to raise. The combination of disclosures, indictments, convictions and new laws slowed the flow of money. The 1974 campaigns were in a sense a transition between the methods of raising and spending political money under the "old politics" and the methods that would be mandated in 1976.

A number of candidates found it politically popular to impose a voluntary limit on the amount they would accept from an individual contributor. Former Attorney General Ramsey Clark, seeking the Democratic senatorial nomination in New York, adopted a limit of $100 ($200 from a husband and wife). He was still able to raise $858,000. Sen. Charles McC. Mathias Jr. (R Md.) adopted similar limits and actually returned over $14,000 to contributors who had made contributions in excess of $100. Some candidates imposed voluntary limits of $1,000, the individual contribution limit adopted in the 1974 Amendments (which were signed by the President during the course of the campaign), or of $3,000, the limit proposed in Senate bills in 1974.

Throughout 1974, pressures for change were many. The Watergate, Spiro Agnew and other scandals had exposed practically every corrupt election practice. The media continued to cover closely the development of election legislation and generally editorialized in favor of reform, including the concept of public funding. Common Cause continued its role, lobbying and monitoring congressional political fund reports.

The impending demise of the big contributor, ironically, seemed to have the unforeseen effect of spotlighting and increasing the impact of the political action committees of special interest groups. Because of the decrease in large individual contributions, the proportion of total receipts received by congressional candidates from special interest groups appeared to be larger than ever.

The rush to fill the vacuum created by limitations on individual contributors had been building before Watergate. Spending by interest groups was increasing, election by election, during the decade 1964-74. A survey by the Common Cause Campaign Finance Monitoring Project midway through 1974 found that registered special interest groups then had almost twice as much money available for the 1974 congressional races as the same groups had reported spending in the entire 1972 congressional campaigns—some $17.4-million compared with $9.7-million.[1]

A subsequent Common Cause survey on the state of congressional campaign fund raising as of Dec. 31, 1974,[2] found that the candidates running in the 1974 elections reported raising a total of $91-million, $14-million of which was raised by 873 candidates who lost in the primaries. Of the $77-million raised by candidates who ran in the general election, incumbents had received $36.9-million, their challengers $19.8-million, another $16.7-million went to candidates in races where there were no incumbents; $2.5-million was raised by unopposed candidates. (These figures are somewhat distorted because amounts raised and spent in the prenomination period are combined with general election funding, thus appearing to enlarge the differential although some of the money was spent on an entirely different campaign, namely the primary. Common Cause claims it is impossible to differentiate primary from general election spending because of the nature of the reporting process.) In any case, a 2 to 1 ratio in favor of the incumbents was found by the Common Cause Campaign Finance Monitoring Project in both the 1972 and 1974 congressional elections.[3]

CONGRESSIONAL SPENDING AND RECEIPTS

Almost $74-million was spent by the congressional candidates who ran in the 1974 general elections, according to reports filed with the Secretary of the Senate and Clerk of the House during the period Sept. 1, 1973 to Dec. 31, 1974. That amount compares with $66.4-million reported spent in 1972 from the beginning of the disclosure period on April 7 through Dec. 31, 1972. There were 468 Democratic candidates, 407 Republicans and 288 minor party and independent candidates. The major party candidates spent $72,705,369, or 98.3 per cent of the total; the minor party and independent candidates spent $1,206,274.

The 1,163 candidates in 1974 reported contributions of about $73.4-million for the period Sept. 1, 1973 to Dec. 31, 1974, with another $3.7-million held as cash on hand at the outset of the reporting period, for a total of just over $77-million available for the 1974 elections. Comparison with the earlier September 1974 report shows that about $37-million of the total—nearly half—came in during the final two months of the campaign or following the election.

Spending on House Races

Some $45-million was reported as spent by those candidates for the House of Representatives in the 1974 general elections. There were 1,058 such candidates (434 Democrats, 376 Republicans and 248 minor party or independent candidates).

The Democrats spent $23.7-million, the Republicans $20.6-million and the other candidates a little over $739,000 in the elections. The Republican Party suffered large losses, apparently as a result, in part, at least, of voter reaction to Watergate and related scandals. Analyses showed a wide shift away from the Republicans, a switch marked in every region, ethnic group and economic classification, and it was a shift that observers termed negative—against the Republicans rather than for the Democrats.[4]

There were 323 House incumbents who ran in the 1974 general election against major party challengers; they reported expenditures of $20.5-million (expenditures of $12.9-million were reported by their challengers). There were 52 races in which no incumbent competed in the general election. The expenditures in those races divided $5.7-million for the Democrats and about $4.1-million for the Republicans. In 60 House races (59 Democratic, one Republican), the incumbents had no major party opposition; they reported expenditures of just over $1-million.

The overall spending limits then being proposed in the 1974 Amendments for House races ($70,000 in a primary or general election plus a 20 per cent overage for fund-raising costs, or $84,000 in each election) would have affected only 23 (less than 3 per cent) of the 810 major party House candidates. Those 23 candidates reported spending beyond the $168,000 combined limit under consideration; 17 of them won; six lost.

There were 40 races in 1974 in which a House incumbent was defeated by a challenger. Only one of those successful challengers spent more than the $168,000 limit established in the 1974 Amendments; however, 21 of the 40 challengers outspent the incumbents they defeated, tending to substantiate the claim that challengers often need to spend more than incumbents in order to contest effectively. Overall, the challengers were "outspent" by the incumbents in 78 per cent or 253 of the 323 House races involving incumbents and major party challengers.[5]

Spending on Senate Races

In the 34 Senate elections in 1974 a total of $28.9-million was spent—$16.6-million by 34 Democratic candidates, $11.8-million by 31 Republican candidates and just under $500,000 by 40 minor party and independent candidates. Twenty-two senators with major party challengers sought re-election in

1974; they spent a total of $13.1-million. Their challengers spent some $7.3-million.

There were nine Senate races in which no incumbent competed in the general election. In two of those, the incumbents, both Democrats, were defeated in the primary. Democratic spending by candidates who ran in those contests totaled $4.8-million; similar Republican spending amounted to $2.4-million. Three Democratic senators ran unopposed, they reported spending $741,367.

Of the 65 major party candidates for the Senate, 17 exceeded what would have been their limit if the 1974 Amendments had been in effect (10 cents per voter in a primary, 15 cents in a general election). Nine of the 17 were incumbents, four were challenging an incumbent and four were in races without an incumbent. Eleven of the 17 "overspenders" won. None of the minor party candidates for the Senate exceeded what would have been the spending limits had the law then been in effect.

Two of the 22 major party challengers to incumbents were elected in 1974. Gov. Wendell Ford of Kentucky defeated Republican Sen. Marlow Cook, outspending Cook by $1,006,670 to $524,569 (the spending limit under the new law would become $551,040). In Colorado, Gary Hart, McGovern's campaign manager in 1972, defeated Republican Sen. Peter Dominick, though he was outspent by $502,343 to $352,557 (the Colorado spending limit would become $412,560).

In nine Senate races involving incumbents, the winner received less than 55 per cent of the vote in the general election (the 55 per cent figure is used as a rough rule of thumb to identify marginal or "swing" states or districts). One was the Kentucky race in which Gov. Ford won with 53.5 per cent of the vote. The other eight were contests in which the incumbent won.

Special Interest Groups

By mid-1974, registered special interest groups were reporting that they had already accumulated $17.4-million in their campaign war chests.⁶ Some of this went to pay various administrative costs of operating the committees, for educational programs, voter registration drives and the like, but a summing-up of special interest group activity during the year shows that some $12.5-million of the funds was contributed directly to congressional candidates.

The biggest spenders were labor groups which donated $6.3-million to congressional candidates in 1974. The largest single contributor within labor ranks was the AFL-CIO's Committee on Political Education (COPE) and its state affiliates; COPE handed out nearly $1.2-million to candidates. Other major union contributions were from the United Auto Workers ($843,938) and the maritime unions ($738,314).

Competing with labor were the special interest groups from business, professional, agricultural and dairy interests—together, their contributions to 1974 congressional candidates totaled $4.8-million. Business groups contributed the largest share of that amount—$2.5-million. Interest groups in the field of health contributed more than $1.9-million of the total, while the agriculture and dairy interests donated $361,040. Various ideological interest groups such as the Americans for Constitutional Action and the National Committee for An Effective Congress contributed $723,410 to congressional candidates; miscellaneous groups gave another $682,215. The largest spenders in all special interest categories are shown in Table 9-1.

Big Individual Contributors

If the post-Watergate atmosphere and the pending legislation made some large contributors wary, it by no means eliminated them from the 1974 political scene. Some $22.5-million was contributed to House and Senate candidates by donors who gave $500 or more. Had the 1974 Amendments been in effect and contributors held to a $1,000 per candidate limit, $3.8-million in individual contributions (not counting loans) to the candidates in the congressional general elections—about 5 per cent of the total raised in contributions during the period Sept. 1, 1973 to Dec. 31, 1974—would have been eliminated.

Table 9-1 Individual Interest Groups: Largest Contributors to 1974 Congressional Candidates

1. American Medical Assns.*	$1,462,972
2. AFL-CIO COPEs	1,178,638
3. United Auto Workers	843,938
4. Maritime Unions	738,314
5. Machinists	470,353
6. Financial Institutions	438,428
7. National Education Assns.	398,991
8. Steelworkers	361,225
9. Retail Clerks	291,065
10. BIPAC (National Assn. of Mfrs.)	272,000
11. National Assn. of Realtors	260,870

* The American Medical Political Action Committee (AMPAC) asserts that it has no branches or subsidiary groups, and accordingly, claims the designation by Common Cause of "American Medical Associations" is incorrect. AMPAC contributed $969,405 to congressional candidates in 1974.

SOURCE: Common Cause

During this period, 24 individuals gave contributions aggregating more than $25,000 to the congressional races—a total of $1.6-million. Under the 1974 Amendments, individuals can give no more than $25,000 to candidates for federal offices in any calendar year. Had the law been in effect, it would have eliminated $1-million of those contributions.

One of the largest single contributors in 1974 was H. Ross Perot, chairman of the board of Electronic Data Systems, Inc., of Dallas, Texas, a major supplier to the government of data processing for the Medicare and Medicaid programs. The House Ways and Means Committee has jurisdiction over the Medicare and Medicaid programs.

Perot made contributions of at least $31,900 to members of the Ways and Means Committee. Two of his contributions were made after the election to members of the committee who ran unopposed in the primary or general election, Omar Burleson (D Texas), and Joe D. Waggonner (D La.), both of whom received $5,000. Perot also gave $5,000 to Joel T.

Broyhill (R Va.) and $2,500 to Donald G. Brotzman (R Colo.); both were defeated in the general election. They received the contributions after they had lost. In addition, Perot contributed $2,500 to James R. Jones (D Okla.) and $500 to James G. Martin (R N.C.); they both received their money on Dec. 30, 1974, about two weeks after they were named to serve on the Ways and Means Committee in the new Congress.

Perot also contributed to Rep. Daniel J. Flood (D Pa.), chairman of the Appropriations Subcommittee on Labor, Health, Education and Welfare. He gave at least $26,000 to members of the Senate Finance Committee, which has jurisdiction in the Senate over the Medicare and Medicaid programs. In all, at least $57,900 of Perot's contribution went to members of Congress who were associated with either the Ways and Means Committee or the Senate Finance Committee.

THE 1974 ELECTION IN THE STATES

As one moved across the country in 1974, one could see political financing reform at work in various ways. California voters approved Proposition 9, an initiative proclaimed by its sponsors to be the toughest and most far-reaching piece of campaign finance legislation ever enacted in this country. As will be seen, it was something less than that. Massachusetts, in earlier decades of the century widely known for political corruption, saw a winning gubernatorial candidate run his campaign in conformance with the letter and the spirit of a strict new disclosure law. In Pennsylvania, on the other hand, reform legislation could make little headway against entrenched political interests, and in Ohio the gubernatorial candidate who championed reform lost to one who ducked the issue.

The brief accounts that follow document some of the experiences that marked the transition in election law application and observance in the states in 1974.[7]

California: Proposition 9[8]

Campaign finance was a major issue in California in 1974. The state's voters clearly indicated how they felt about the issue with their overwhelming (70 per cent) approval of Proposition 9, which strengthened already strict disclosure and enforcement requirements and introduced new provisions limiting total spending. The key provisions dealing with disclosure were not unusual, but the spending limitations were. In an effort to overcome the advantage of incumbency, candidates who were in office were limited to spending 10 per cent less than their challengers. Other limits for party state central committees and ballot-measure campaigns were carefully spelled out. The spending limits became unenforceable following the U.S. Supreme Court's *Buckley v. Valeo* ruling. Other provisions of Proposition 9 include:

Conflict of Interest. Public officials must disclose financial holdings that present a potential conflict of interest, and they are disqualified from making public decisions in areas of conflict.

Lobbyist Regulation. Lobbyists must register with the secretary of state, rather than with a legislative committee as previously required. They cannot give gifts to, or spend more than $10 a month on behalf of, a public official. They cannot make or arrange political contributions. Those who hire lobbyists or who spend at least $250 a month to influence legislative or administrative decisions must report expenses over $25, their gifts to officials, candidates or members of their families, and business transactions exceeding $1,000 with firms in which an official or candidate is an owner.

Enforcement and Penalties. A five-member, bipartisan Fair Political Practices Commission enforces the provisions of the law. The secretary of state receives and files and the Franchise Tax Board audits the reports. Knowing and willful violation of the law is a misdemeanor, and anyone convicted of violating the law is prohibited from holding elective office or acting as a lobbyist for four years. Fines of up to $10,000, or three times the amount of an illegal contribution, are provided for.

Despite the claim of proponents that Proposition 9 was the strictest of state laws, it placed no limits on individual or group contributions, and it neither prohibited nor limited corporate or labor union contributions. In choosing expenditure rather than contribution limits, Proposition 9 went in a direction opposite to that the U.S. Supreme Court was to take later in *Buckley v. Valeo.*

In an unusual move, business and labor formed a coalition that opposed Proposition 9. However, the major groups in opposition were not able to spend enough money to oppose it effectively—the committees favoring Proposition 9 outspent foes of the measure by more than 3 to 1 ($600,000 to less than $170,000). A coalition of reformist groups, led by the People's Lobby and Common Cause, worked successfully for its approval.

One of Proposition 9's major champions was Edmund G. Brown Jr., then California secretary of state. His backing of the measure, designed to reduce the role of big money in California politics, was a helpful factor in his November gubernatorial victory. Yet in his campaign, Brown spent $1.6-million to defeat, among others, San Francisco Mayor Joseph Alioto (who spent $1.7-million) in the Democratic primary, and then Brown spent nearly $2-million in the general election campaign.

Florida: Askew's $100 Limit[9]

Gov. Reubin Askew launched his re-election bid with the promise that he would not accept any contributions exceeding $100. It proved to be a successful campaign strategy in a state where not only Watergate but also some of the worst scandals in Florida's history were focusing voters' attention on the need to reduce the impact of big money on politics.

Under a new campaign finance law passed by the Florida legislature in 1973, candidates for statewide offices could accept no more than $3,000 from an individual. The highly popular Askew, however, decided to take advantage of what he sensed to be a mood for reform by pledging to stick to the $100 limit. "It gave our people a chance to go out and do a lot of groundwork," Askew said later. "When they are working, they are not spending—and, generally, much of the money spent on campaigns is wasted." Although his opponents charged that the governor at times circumvented his pledge, by asking corporations, for example, to produce a series of $100 givers, his strategy worked with voters. Askew got contributions from 8,876 donors, a Florida record, raised $594,510 in all, and defeated his Republican opponent, Jerry Thomas, by a vote of 1,118,954 to 709,438.

Massachusetts: Spirit of Reform[10]

Few states in the union have had such familiarity with corruption and graft as Massachusetts; "a little something on the side" for campaign workers was at one time second nature to the politics of Boston. In 1974, however, both the Republican and Democratic candidates for governor, the incumbent Francis W. Sargent and the challenger Michael S. Dukakis, ran as champions of a new campaign-finance disclosure law; both men had been involved in the drive for the new law for several years.

As the campaign opened, the Massachusetts legislature was considering a bill to make public funds available for financing the gubernatorial election. Governor Sargent offered to return all the money he had raised before the beginning of the year if the public funds were available for the race. However, the bill did not pass.

Sargent spent more than Dukakis, but he lost. The Democratic candidate reported that he had received $846,509 in contributions and spent $817,497; Sargent, the Republican, spent just over $1.1-million.

Dukakis worked to raise money from small contributors. He returned all contributions from state employees or contractors who did business with the state.

New York: Carey's Loophole[11]

The attention of reformers in New York State in 1974 was focused initially on the senatorial primary campaign of former U.S. Attorney General Ramsey Clark who, like Gov. Reubin Askew of Florida, pledged to take no contributions over $100. Clark raised some $858,000 in this fashion and won the

Democratic nomination for the U.S. Senate. However, in the general election he was defeated by Sen. Jacob K. Javits who raised and spent more than $1-million. A tenth of that sum came from 26 persons who contributed $3,000 or more each.

In the gubernatorial race, U.S. Rep. Hugh Carey first defeated his long-time rival Howard J. Samuels for the Democratic nomination and then went on to defeat Gov. Malcolm Wilson in the general election.

New York had a new election law, signed by Gov. Wilson in May 1974, which stipulated that a statewide candidate could spend no more than $105,000 of his family's money in the primary and no more than $250,000 in the general election. Persons not related to the candidate could contribute no more than $21,000 to a single campaign. Loans were to be counted as contributions if unpaid by the primary or general election day.

Despite the ceilings in the new Election Procedures Reform Act, Carey's spending in the primary, totaling $2.5-million, included over $1-million in contributions, loans and guaranteed loans from his brother Edward, a wealthy oil producer. The degree of his brother's wealth was largely unknown before the campaign. It has been estimated that the annual sales of the Carey Energy Group, which he leads, ran to about $1-billion.

The effective date of the New York law was June 1, 1974. Carey launched his campaign in January with a $750,000 guaranteed loan (by his brother) from the Bank of Commerce. The campaign treasurer and the legal finance expert were vice presidents of New England Petroleum Corporation (NEPCO), the major supplier of fuel to utilities in New York and New England. Edward Carey is the sole NEPCO stockholder. With the money, Carey launched a TV-radio spot campaign that was to cost $1.5-million by the end of the campaign.

The Carey campaign had to repay enough of his brother's loan by the Sept. 10 primary to bring the candidate below the $105,000 limit or be subject to prosecution under the new election law. By early August, Edward Carey had lent or guaranteed loans totaling nearly $1.2-million, but only $225,000 of this amount had been lent since June 1, the effective date of the new law. Additional money totaling some $142,500 from the brother was loaned in August, and it appeared to the Carey opponents in the Samuels camp that Carey would be unable to go below the limit by the primary. But then about $300,000 was contributed from other sources, permitting loan repayments to the candidate's brother and bringing the loan amount within the limit. Some $80,000 of the new contributions came in on one day, in the form of $20,000 loans each from a NEPCO vice president, a law partner of Gov. Carey, the candidate's personal physician, and the candidate's daughter. Between Aug. 31 and Sept. 3, more than $200,000 in new loans were made to the campaign from diverse sources—another NEPCO vice president, the president of a NEPCO Canadian subsidiary, three partners in Lehman Brothers (a Wall Street investment house), an oil attorney and a real estate attorney. By Sept. 9, the day before the primary, Edward Carey's loans had been brought below the limit—thanks to new loans from two other Carey brothers; $20,000 from Joseph Savoca of Commonwealth Oil of Puerto Rico; $20,000 from John Gorman of Eller Terminals, a NEPCO subsidiary; $5,000 flown in from NEPCO's Washington, D.C., representative, Robert Trevisani, and $5,000 from three companies, one in Italy and two in Panama, that were controlled by the man whose agency had built NEPCO's Bahamian refinery.

Carey's spending in the primary, in which he defeated Samuels by 600,000 to 387,000 votes, totaled $2.5-million to his rival's $1.6-million. Media expenditures accounted for about $750,000 of Carey's costs, only $120,000 of Samuels'. In the general election, to which Edward Carey donated very little, Hugh Carey spent some $2.5-million to his opponent's $2.7-million. Carey received 2.9 million votes, and Wilson received 2.1 million. The Democrat spent about 80 cents a vote in the general election (compared with $4 a vote in the primary), the Republican about $1.20 a vote.

Ohio: Victory for the 'Old Politics'[12]

Former Gov. James A. Rhodes, a spokesman for the "old politics," won a comeback bid for a third term in 1974, defeating Gov. John J. Gilligan, who ran as a champion of campaign reform. Gilligan said he had "disclosed every dime" given to his campaign. The Republican victor, on the other hand, had been under attack throughout the campaign for questionable fund-raising practices.

Rhodes, for example, had failed to report in his June 1974 disclosure statement the names of any contributors to a November 1973 $25-a-plate chicken luncheon in Columbus; the names were not given on grounds that gifts of $25 or less were exempt from reporting requirements. Rhodes argued that there had been 6,355 single tickets sold for the lunch, that is, no one individual gave more than $25; reporters, however, discovered letters that had been sent to businessmen urging them to purchase and resell as many tickets as they could afford. Rhodes' response to all charges was to "stick with the issues," and to attack Gilligan's alleged mismanagement of the state government.

Ohio voters clearly seemed to decide the election on issues other than campaign reform. Gilligan and another statewide candidate came out strongly for reform, and they both lost. Rhodes virtually ignored the question, and he won.

In a memo on campaign strategy that he wrote in July 1974, Gov. Gilligan suggested that perhaps some of Rhodes' contributors would be telling their stories before a grand jury. Actually, it was Gilligan's campaign people who had to make grand jury appearances after the election. Charges were filed against 14 campaign workers who were placed on the state payroll for a number of weeks after the election. Although they received state pay, they did not report for work; they worked instead as part of the Recount Planning Group, a successor to a Gilligan campaign group. Thirteen of the 14 were eventually found guilty, and three were sentenced to six months in jail.

Kansas: Reaction Against Reform[13]

In January 1973, two judges of the county district court in Topeka declared key sections of the existing election laws unconstitutional. The Watergate affair plus scandals in Kansas involving state architectural contracts at the University of Kansas Medical Center led the state legislature to give top priority to the twin issues of campaign finance and government ethics in its 1974 session. The legislation that emerged from that session drew strong criticism from many candidates following the 1974 campaign.

In the race for the U.S. Senate, Robert Dole, a first-term incumbent and the Republican National Chairman at the time of the Watergate break-in, was opposed by Rep. William R. Roy, a two-term Democratic member of the U.S. House. Because of Dole's previous position, the Republicans had given the race top priority, hoping to demonstrate that Watergate had not "rubbed off" on the former chairman.

The race was closely fought, and before Dole was returned to the Senate by Kansas voters he had spent $1,073,423, and Roy had spent $737,669. A statewide race in the state had never before cost more than $1-million. The campaigns cost so much that they tended to siphon off money from other candidates, causing fund-raising problems elsewhere in Kansas.

Four Republican contenders vied in the primary campaign for nomination for governor, from which Robert Bennett, president of the state senate, emerged the victor. Bennett won the primary by 530 votes, spending $98,816 on his nomination campaign.

The Democratic gubernatorial primary was uncontested; the nominee was state Attorney General Vern Miller, who entered the race after the incumbent Democratic governor, Robert Docking, decided not to seek re-election. (Docking's brother had been implicated in the state architecture scandals, but the governor denied that this played any role in his decision not to run again.)

In the general election campaign, a substantial part (about 12 per cent of contributions) of Miller's financial support came from organized labor. Bennett enjoyed much more support from his state party organization than Miller did from the Democratic organization. Miller was the heavy favorite to win at the start of the race, but as the campaign progressed, Bennett pulled ahead in state polls; as his stock improved, so did his fund-raising ability. When it was all over, Bennett had recaptured the state house for the Republicans, and his campaign treasury had a surplus.

During this first campaign under the new finance law, candidates had to contend with much extra paperwork as a result of the detailed reporting requirement. The 11-member Governmental Ethics Commission, which had been created to oversee the new law, was besieged with requests for interpretations of the law; by the end of the year, 69 opinions had been issued. Both losers and winners criticized the law; Bennett spoke to the major criticism when he said that he felt the new commission seemed to want "almost to bend over backwards to enforce the letter rather than the spirit of the law."

In the 1975 legislative session, modifications in the law were enacted. Some of the changes weakened provisions of the law; others attempted to shore up weak points that had been discovered. The chief justice of the state supreme court expressed his reluctance to appoint two members of the Ethics Commission (citing a new judicial code directing judges to refrain from political activity), and that authority passed to the governor, who already had authority to appoint three of the 11 members.

When the Ethics Commission made its final report for 1975, it made numerous substantive recommendations. The 1976 legislature, however, ignored the recommendations, and unsuccessful attempts were made in both houses to cut the commission's budget by more than half. Meanwhile, a bill to provide a tax checkoff system of political funding died in the 1975 legislature.

SUMMARY

The 1974 campaigns were transitional between the methods of raising and spending political money under the "old politics" as they existed in 1972 prior to the Federal Election Campaign Act effective date of April 7, and those that were mandated by the 1974 and 1976 Amendments.

In 1974, a number of candidates imposed a voluntary limit on the amount they would accept from an individual contributor. Throughout the year, pressures for change were many, with campaign contributions and costs placed under a spotlight by the media.

The impending demise of the big contributor, ironically, had the unforeseen effect of increasing the impact of the political action committees of special interest groups. Special interest money figured larger than ever in the coffers of congressional candidates.

More than $74-million was spent by congressional candidates running in the 1974 general elections. Some $45-million was spent by House candidates, and $28.9-million was spent on Senate races. House incumbents who ran outspent their challengers by nearly 2 to 1, $20.5-million to $12.9-million. The 22 senators who sought re-election spent $13.1-million; their challengers spent $7.3-million.

Registered special interest groups had built a war chest of $17.4-million by midway in the year, nearly twice as much as they spent throughout the whole 1972 congressional election period. Some $12.5-million in funds were contributed directly to candidates for the Senate and House. Labor groups were the biggest spenders, donating $6.3-million. Business, professionals, agricultural and dairy interests contributed $4.8-million to candidates.

The big contributors were still in evidence in 1974—some $22.5-million was contributed to congressional campaigns by donors who gave $500 or more. Twenty-four individuals gave contributions aggregating in excess of $25,000.

Political activity in the individual states in 1974 reflected the variety of reactions to Watergate and other political campaign abuses. Californians passed Proposition 9, one of the toughest campaign finance laws in the country. In Massachusetts, a state with a long history of corrupt politics, the two gubernatorial candidates ran as champions of a new comprehensive campaign-finance reform act.

In Florida, the incumbent governor ran successfully for re-election by limiting individual contributions to $100. Kansas had its own scandal involving awards of architectural contracts; this heightened the impact of Watergate in a state where the Republicans spent much of their money in re-electing Sen. Dole, who had been the Republican national chairman at the time of the Watergate break-in. Sen. Dole received the Republican nomination for Vice President in August 1976.

But both Ohio and New York witnessed something of the "old politics." In Ohio, the incumbent governor, a backer of campaign-finance reform, was defeated by a candidate who was attacked for questionable fund-raising activities. In New York, the winning candidate for governor took advantage of a three-day "loophole" before the primary, enabling his wealthy brother to support his candidacy with $1.2-million in gifts and loans.

In Chapter 10, we examine the unique aspect of campaign finance in 1976—public funding of presidential campaigns.

NOTES

1. "Common Cause Releases Analysis of June 10 Reports of Interest Groups," Common Cause news release, July 10, 1974.
2. All of the data on 1974 congressional spending are available directly from the Common Cause Campaign Finance Monitoring Project; some summary data are from "Summary of Key Findings by the Common Cause Campaign Finance Monitoring Project for 1972 and 1974 Federal Elections," Common Cause, April 24, 1975, and a later analysis of the 1974 data, "The Political Money Tree," *In Common*, Spring 1976, vol. 7, no. 2, pp. 7-14.
3. *1974 Congressional Campaign Finances*, vols. 1-5, prepared by Common Cause Campaign Finance Monitoring Project, 1976.
4. David E. Rosenbaum, "Wide Voter Shift from G.O.P. Shown," *The New York Times*, November 7, 1974.
5. For a series of case studies of congressional campaigns in 1974, see Alan L. Clem, *et al., The Making of Congressmen: Seven Campaigns of 1974* (North Scituate, Mass.: Duxbury Press, 1976).
6. Common Cause news release, July 10, 1974, *op. cit.*
7. The accounts are derived from Herbert E. Alexander, ed., *Campaign Money: Reform and Reality in the States* (New York: The Free Press, 1976).
8. *Ibid.,* chap. 5, "California: A New Law," by William Endicott, pp. 110-141.

9. *Ibid.,* chap. 3, "Florida: The Power of Incumbency," by William Mansfield, pp. 39-77.
10. *Ibid.,* chap. 6, "Massachusetts: Corruption and Cleanup," by Robert Healy, pp. 142-161.
11. *Ibid.,* chap. 11, "New York: Loopholes and Limits," by Sam Roberts, pp. 276-305.
12. *Ibid.,* chap. 10, "Ohio: A Tale of Two Parties," by Brian T. Usher, pp. 252-275.
13. *Ibid.,* chap. 7, "Kansas: Reform and Reaction," by Al Polczinski, pp. 162-186.

10

The 1976 Election: Public Funding for President

The 1976 presidential election campaigns were the first in which government funding was available. Three kinds of funding were available for different phases of the campaigns:[1]

1. A flat grant of $21.8-million (the amount is adjusted to movements of the Consumer Price Index) was provided for each of the candidates of the major parties in the general election period. Smaller amounts were available for qualifying minor party candidates, though none qualified in advance of the 1976 election.

2. Grants of about $2.2-million (also adjusted) to each of the major parties to arrange for and run the national nominating conventions were provided. Again, lesser amounts would have been provided for qualifying minor party conventions, but none was eligible in 1976.

3. Matching funds were provided for qualifying candidates seeking the nominations for President. (The complex formula will be explained below.)

GENERAL ELECTION

In the general election period, a presidential candidate nominated by a major party who decides to take the funds available to him will be eligible for $21.8-million. That may seem a large and inviting sum to the casual observer of the political scene. But if a candidate accepts the funds, that is all he may spend of money within his control. As the Democratic nominee in 1972, George McGovern spent $30-million, and the Nixon campaign spent almost twice that amount, although over a longer period of time. The 1976 funding level seems even more modest when the 33 per cent inflation factor between 1972 and 1976 is taken into consideration. A presidential candidate who does not accept government funds may spend as much as he can raise, thus making the private funding route attractive for candidates who are wealthy and willing to spend their own money for their own campaigns or who are confident of their ability to raise more money than that provided by the federal government.

A candidate in the general election who accepts the government funds is limited to spending the grant he receives from the government. He cannot raise private funds in addition. His party, however, can spend up to two cents per voting age citizen, or about $3.2-million more, on his behalf. Spending by the party will depend, of course, upon the party's ability to raise sufficient money to cover its operating expenses and its costs on behalf of other candidates, apart from the presidential and vice presidential candidates. In addition, the *Buckley v. Valeo* decision allows independent spending in unlimited amounts by individuals and groups, so long as it is not controlled by the candidate or coordinated with him or his campaign. There is no way to estimate how much money will be spent this way and, since it is outside the candidate's control, whether it will be wasted, helpful or harmful. Since the candidate who accepts government funds cannot raise money privately, he will not need to mount a fund-raising campaign. This will result in some saving to his campaign. In 1972, for example, the McGovern campaign spent about $3.5-million in mail costs for fund-raising purposes, $1-million in newspaper ads and additional funds in appeals tagged on at the end of paid broadcasts. Hence, with party help up to the limit and no fund-raising costs, the available money is adequate—but certainly not generous.

If one assumes both major presidential candidates spend the full grant ($21.8-million) and party allotment ($3.2-million), totaling $25-million, then their combined total of $50-million contrasts with the $90-million spent by Nixon and McGovern in 1972. Consequently, the cost of electing a President will be reduced in 1976 from the $133-million spent in 1972, even though there were no significant Republican prenomination costs in 1972 but high ones in 1976.

The legislation which did the most to stimulate early thinking about government subsidies to election campaigns was the Long Act of 1966, which would have allotted to each major party's national committee about $30-million (in 1968 dollars) for the general election period. As noted earlier, the law never became operative, but public financing was revived in the Revenue Act of 1971. The major difference was that the subsidies from the tax checkoff fund created by the Revenue Act of 1971 go directly to the presidential candidates, while the 1966 law would have provided the money to each political party for its use on behalf of its nominee.

Provisions for distribution of federal funds were changed again in the 1974 Amendments to the FECA. They authorized two additional uses for money raised through the checkoff system.

NATIONAL CONVENTIONS

Both major party national committees may receive up to $2.2-million to help pay the costs of the national nominating conventions. This raised issues early in the work of the Federal Election Commission (FEC), which help to illustrate the difficult questions the commission faced. An expenditure limit of the same amount as the subsidy was imposed for the two major parties. The parties requested advisory opinions on supplemental contributions and services traditionally provided by the host state and city governments and by corporations. The commission ruled that state and local governments could provide services and facilities but that corporations could not directly or indirectly assist except in special circumstances. Only if a corporation provided certain services to the public, could it similarly assist at the convention. For example, lowered hotel rates would be considered a corporate contribution unless such rates were available to other conventions.

The commission took special care to ensure that corporations could not "launder" funds by contributing them to a government agency which then would provide the convention service. At first, the commission held that only retail corporations based in the convention city which could expect to receive some reasonable rate of return in terms of sales of goods or services during the convention could contribute or make in-kind contributions. In the face of criticism that not enough money could be raised in these circumstances, the commission broadened the opinion to include national corporations if they had local operations. Given the financial straits in which New York City, the site of the Democratic convention, found itself, and the curtailing of certain corporate activity, the commission did seek to ease the problem by broad interpretation.

PRENOMINATION CAMPAIGNS

The 1974 Amendments also provided that candidates for the presidential nomination could receive up to about $5.5-million each in tax-generated funds for preconvention campaign expenses. To qualify for the money, a candidate must show to the satisfaction of the FEC that he has raised $5,000 in private contributions of $250 or less in each of 20 states. During the prenomination campaigns in 1976, through August 26, 15 presidential candidates qualified for a total of more than $24.1-million. In the prenomination period (unlike the post-nomination period when a flat grant of government funds is provided and no private fund raising by the candidate is allowed), the government provides limited matching funds based on the fund-raising ability of qualifying candidates. Thus candidates for the presidential nomination need to raise private funds which then are matched on a limited basis. Accordingly, a 20 per cent overage for fund raising is permitted, beyond the $10.9-million spending limit per candidate. Thus a candidate theoretically may raise up to half the limit in private funds ($5.5-million), plus $2.2-million for fund-raising purposes, or a total of $7.6-million, and the government matches up to $5.5-million, for a grand total of $13.1-million permitted to be spent by a candidate to achieve nomination. Of course, the government matches only up to $250 per individual contributor, while the law permits contributions of up to $1,000 per individual per candidate. The purpose of matching only up to that level was to encourage candidates to broaden their fund-raising base. But its effect is likely to be that few if any candidates will ever receive as much as $5.5-million in matching funds.

The 1976 Amendments to the FECA, enacted during the prenomination campaigns, changed the law governing termination of a candidacy. In 1976, some of the contenders withdrew from active candidacy but sought to continue to receive matching funds to pay the costs of communicating with delegates or of operating at the convention when the final nomination would be made. Also, some candidates continued to campaign actively despite the fact that they were receiving very small numbers of votes in the primaries. Accordingly, the law was changed to cut off public financing 30 days after two consecutive primaries in which a candidate obtained less than 10 per cent of the votes cast. The revision of the law also denied public funding to a candidate who ceased actively to campaign for the presidential nomination. Such an ex-candidate can continue to receive public funding only for qualified campaign expenses incurred in past primaries.

Upon enactment of the 1976 Amendments in early May, the FEC made a determination that nine candidates were no longer eligible to receive matching funds, except to pay off prior debts. Candidates were given a chance to challenge the FEC's findings and to offer evidence that they were still active candidates. Only one of the nine—Ellen McCormack—became ineligible (some others did so by withdrawing) because she failed to receive 10 per cent or more of the vote in two successive primaries in May.

FEC Certifications

Although the Supreme Court decision approved the law's provisions for government funding, it led to an interruption late in March 1976 in the flow of matching funds to the presidential candidates. As recounted earlier, the candidates were forced to go 61 days, until the FEC was reconstituted, without receiving the funds due them under the law.

The $24.1-million in matching funds that was paid to the 15 qualified candidates by August 26 was triggered by contributions from about 600,000 individuals, indicating that the average matched contribution was about $35.

Another legal way of increasing the amount of matching government funds is for a candidate to ask a person willing to

Table 10-1 FEC Matching Fund Certifications for Presidential Candidates and Parties in 1976*

Candidate	Cumulative Certifications
Birch Bayh	$ 460,973.54
Lloyd Bentsen	511,022.61
Edmund G. Brown Jr.	491,001.89
Jimmy Carter	3,465,584.89
Frank Church	615,126.68
Gerald R. Ford	4,657,007.82
Fred R. Harris	633.099.05
Henry M. Jackson	1,980,554.95
Ellen McCormack	244,125.40
Ronald Reagan	5,088,910.66
Terry Sanford	246,388.32
Milton J. Shapp	299,066.21
Sargent Shriver	285,069.74
Morris K. Udall	1,831,058.55
George C. Wallace	3,291,308.81
Total	$24,100,299.12
Democratic National Committee	$ 1,963,800.00
Republican National Committee	1,963,800.00

*Funds certified through August 26, 1976.

contribute $1,000 to split the gift. For example, such a contributor might ask a spouse and other family members each to contribute $250 of the total. Thus, if four persons contributed the $1,000 total, the government matched the whole $1,000 and not just the first $250 of a single $1,000 gift.

A preliminary compilation of campaign receipts and expenditures for Democratic and Republican candidates for nomination for President indicates that about $64-million was spent in both public and private money since 1973-74 when some of the campaigns started—$38-million by the Democrats and $26-million by the Republican contenders, Ford and Reagan. Consequently, the government-provided matching funds—$24.1-million—accounted for approximately 38 per cent of the total nomination costs of the candidates. About half of the receipts were matching funds; the proportion drops to 33 per cent when related to total receipts from the inception of some 1976 campaigns in 1973, 1974 and 1975.

If the Democratic candidates are considered separately, the $38-million in 1976 compares with $33-million spent by Democratic candidates for the presidential nomination in 1972. However, given the infusion of public money in the matching incentive program ($15-million to Democratic candidates), less private money ($24-million) was raised in 1976 than in 1972. This smaller private dollar total is the result of the $1,000 limit on contributions per candidate per election in effect during 1975 and 1976. But given the inflation factor between 1972 and 1976, the private component bought much less than four years earlier.

Following the primaries but before he was actually nominated, Jimmy Carter asked the FEC to extend beyond the conventions the period for accepting contributions and receiving matching payments to permit him and other candidates to pay off loans and close the books on their prenomination campaigns. He also pointed out that the Republicans would have an extra month to claim matching funds since the Republican convention was in August, a month later than the Democratic one.

Ronald Reagan received the most matching funds ($5.1-million of the potential $5.5-million) of any candidate and about $400,000 more than the Republican nominee, President Ford, who received $4.7-million.

Among the Democrats, Jimmy Carter, the eventual nominee, received the most in matching funds—$3.5-million—while Gov. George C. Wallace received $3.3-million (most of it for contributions made in 1975). Sen. Henry M. Jackson and Rep. Morris K. Udall each received in excess of $1.8-million. Ellen McCormack, the anti-abortion candidate, received the least—$244,125.

TAX CHECKOFF

The money for each of the three phases of federal funding is provided by the so-called tax checkoff. The arrangement provides that every individual whose federal tax liability for any taxable year is $1 or more can designate on his federal income tax form that $1 of his tax money be paid to the Presidential Election Campaign Fund. Those filing joint returns can designate $2 of their tax money. Major party candidates are defined as those nominated by political parties whose presidential candidates received 25 per cent or more of the popular vote in the preceding general election. As mentioned above, a cost-of-living factor is built into the law which will adjust the amount available for future elections.

Minor Party Candidates

A minor party candidate may receive payments before the election if he or another candidate of such a party received between 5 and 25 per cent of the previous presidential vote. If a new party emerges that was not on the ballot four years earlier, or an older minor party is newly successful, the candidate of such a party can qualify retroactively after the November election for a share of the funds if he receives 5 per cent or more of the presidential vote in the current election. The amount of money a minor party candidate may receive in public funds is determined by his share of the popular vote in relation to the average popular vote received by the Democratic and Republican candidates.

Presidential Year Payout

The federal checkoff program operates on a four-year cycle, accumulating money in each tax year with the payout all in the presidential election year. The program has grown in popularity with voters; 1975 income tax returns indicated that about 26 per cent of taxpayers participated, an increase from only 4 per cent in the first year of operation. Percentages and amounts available are shown in Table 10-2. Nonetheless, the program would not provide enough money for government funding of Senate and House campaigns. Congress would be required to make direct appropriations to fully fund a dependable program — or greatly increase the amount that can be checked off.

Some criticism of the checkoff plan has been directed at the matter of allocation—whether the distribution of major vs. minor party funds was constitutional. That concern was put to rest when the Supreme Court sanctioned the methods of public financing the 1974 Amendments provided. Other critics have questioned the drain on the U.S. Treasury in times of economic hardship; the revenue losses which the tax checkoff program entails must be made up in other ways.

Table 10-2   Federal Income Tax Checkoff Response, 1972-1975

Tax Year	Percentage of Taxpayers Using Checkoff	Amount Checked Off (In $ millions)
1972	3.0%	$ 4.0
1972 (retroactive)*	—	8.9
1973	13.6	17.3
1974	24.2	31.9
1975	25.8	33.0
Total Available		$94.1

* In 1974, the checkoff form was inserted on a redesigned front page of the 1040 form. In its first year, as a separate form, the tax checkoff had been overlooked by many taxpayers. The new procedure also allowed taxpayers who had not made a 1972 checkoff to do so retroactively.

A number of persons and groups have worked actively to publicize the tax checkoff program, and their work has had the success indicated in taxpayer response. As Table 10-2 shows, $94.1-million was accumulated over a four-year period, 1972-75, for 1976 payout. The 1976 payout was:

Prenomination matching funds	$24.1-million
National nominating conventions	4.4-million
General election flat grants	43.6-million
Total (approximate)	$72.1-million

The excess of about $20-million is available in case any minor party candidate qualifies. Any surplus may then in part revert to the general treasury, in part be held for the next election. A fund for the 1980 campaigns will then begin to build through checkoffs on 1977 federal income tax returns and continue through the next three years for the 1980 payout.

PRELIMINARY APPRAISAL OF PUBLIC FUNDING

A preliminary appraisal of the nation's first experience with government funding of presidential campaigns in the prenomination or primary stage leads to these comments. Some observers had argued that government funding would produce more candidates than usual. While almost 100 candidates filed with the FEC, only 15 qualified for matching grants. All of the serious candidates organized their fund raising to achieve early eligibility to receive government funds, and once qualified, all accepted them. The President Ford Committee considered not taking the money and going the private route, but it soon decided to go along with the others; the decision paid off as the Ford campaign received the second highest amount of matching funds.

Some observers thought that candidates with only a regional base to start out with, such as Jimmy Carter, would have difficulty qualifying for matching funds; but he, along with other sectional candidates, qualified readily.

Screening Process

Qualifying for the matching grants meant "a kind of license to practice" in the big time, as former North Carolina governor and Democratic hopeful Terry Sanford expressed it.[2] It has become a new threshold, a new screening process, for presidential candidates. It may screen out certain candidates. One theory had it that the difficulty presidential candidates for nomination would have attaining the threshold for public funding would narrow the choices and make for a stronger candidate who could survive the primaries and win nomination on the first ballot. The promise of government funding attracted numerous Democratic candidates who were able to qualify, and it did not lead to factionalization or hopeless division.

The matching funds program was intended to encourage a broadening of the political-financial base and to get and to keep people in the habit of giving. It provides the most insurance for the future because of the link to private giving.

Successfully raising big money in small sums—necessary because of the matching limit of $250—often starts with a network of friends, supporters or business associates willing to help out. Many of those asked to contribute may have given earlier when the candidate ran for another office. The circle widens as friends ask their friends, and the outreach broadens, spreading to other areas and states. A contact in one area holds a fund-raising party. Those who become persuaded not only contribute but also ask others to give. For example, in late 1974, while he was still governor of Georgia, Jimmy Carter's friends raised about $47,000 to start his national campaign. During 1975, Carter was able to raise an additional $700,000, mainly from Georgians. Some direct mail was undertaken, but the most successful events were $100-a-person cocktail parties. Carter was a candidate from the South and not well-known nationally. Nevertheless, he was considered by some to be a means of stopping George Wallace. Accordingly, Carter attracted early support from a nucleus of 1972 McGovern supporters, with ties to people across the country, who were willing to contribute to help him qualify for matching funds. Thus a candidate who was not perceived as a liberal in the McGovern mold was still able to tap into a network of liberals and build a national campaign successfully.

Prolonged Campaigns

Some campaigns that received government funds in 1976 were undoubtedly prolonged as a result of the additional money that was available. One candidate surprised observers by qualifying easily. She was Ellen McCormack, the anti-abortion candidate, who ran essentially a single-issue campaign. McCormack was a political unknown; she was able to qualify because the issue she represented was an emotional one with adherents in a large number of states, and her campaign was well organized to reach them. It was clear, however, that her campaign was designed to attract attention to her cause rather than to nominate her. Other such issue-oriented candidates can be expected in the future.

Despite government funding, seven candidates for the Democratic nomination—Sanford, Bentsen, Bayh, Shapp, Harris, Jackson and Shriver—dropped out by the middle of the primary season when they failed to receive enough votes in several states to be able to continue to contest effectively. However, several of these, although no longer active candidates, remained as favorite sons or in position to keep their options open for a time, drawing additional funding to the extent they were able to raise more money for matching. Then, of course, in May the 1976 Amendments effectively cut off further funding for them. Clearly, however, it is the vote that is overriding: candidates who fail to make good showings in the presidential primaries find it harder to raise money, thus reducing the matching funds, and so the cycle leading to withdrawal from the race begins.

It is clear that the combination of contribution limits and government funding increased the costs of fund raising. The effort to reach out to a wide audience is expensive, especially for matchable sums of $250 or under. Accordingly, fund-raising costs were proportionally higher in 1976 than in previous campaigns where contributions could be solicited in larger amounts. Bookkeeping costs also were high, partly to ensure compliance with the disclosure and limitations sections of the law and partly for preparation of claims submitted for matching funds under procedures required by the FEC.

FEDERAL TAX INCENTIVES

The Revenue Act of 1971 provided tax incentives for political contributions in two ways: (1) political contributors could take a tax credit against their federal income tax for 50 per cent of their contributions, up to a maximum of $12.50 on a single return and $25 on a joint return (the 1974 Amendments to the FECA increased these amounts to $25 and $50, respectively); or alternatively, (2) contributors could claim a tax deduction for the full amount of contributions up to a maximum of $50 on a single return and $100 on a joint return (the 1974 Amendments increased these amounts to $100 and $200, respectively).

Qualifying as contributions are gifts to candidates for election to any federal, state or local elective office in any primary, general or special election and gifts to any committee, association or organization operated exclusively for the purpose of influencing or attempting to influence the election of such candidates.

Contributions do not qualify for the tax incentive program if they are made to "political action committees" engaging in general, political, educational or legislative activities. A campaign committee may be run in conjunction with a political action committee, but contributions must flow from individual taxpayers directly to the campaign committee in order to qualify.

Data from 1972 returns indicate that some $26.5-million was claimed in tax credits (on about 1.8 million returns), nearly $52.3-million in tax deductions (on close to one million returns), while an additional $2.6-million in revenue was earmarked as a result of the tax checkoffs (on 1.5 million returns).[3] It is ironic that the tax incentive program, which cost much more in revenue loss in 1972 should have passed

Congress with little debate, while the checkoff system raised such controversy. The checkoff plan is widely conceded to be the fairer of the two plans since there is equal participation by all who choose to use the checkoff. The checkoff costs less in revenue loss; since it went into effect in 1972, not more than $33-million has ever been checked off in a single tax year.

Tax Deduction. A tax deduction is an allowance granted from gross income before actual computation of tax liability. In effect, it operates on a sliding scale according to the taxpayer's net income bracket. As the income bracket rises, less of the contribution is actually made by the taxpayer, and more of it is borne by the government—in other words, by other taxpayers. Thus, the higher a contributor's income, the more a given deduction will save in taxes. The effects of the provisions which allow deductions for political contributions—both as to cost to the contributor and revenue loss to the government—are determined by the tax brackets of those who take the deduction.

Tax Credit. A tax credit, on the other hand, is an allowance taken from the final tax liability itself. It operates in such a way that every taxpayer, large or small, gets the same benefit for the same size contribution. The revenue loss to the government is a function of the number of contributions made and credits sought on tax returns, not of income level or tax bracket. Thus, when a tax credit is allowed, any contributor can subtract up to the credit limit from his final income tax bill.

The argument in favor of a system of tax deductions often begins that charitable gifts are deducted, not credited, so why should political gifts be treated differently when the purpose is to provide in the political arena the tax incentive that is claimed to be effective in charitable fund raising? A tax deduction for this purpose is simply added to other deductions, or it is, in effect, taken automatically within the standard deduction.[4]

The effect of a tax deduction, however, is a function of the taxpayer's net income bracket. Tax deductions have been criticized for being unfair and discriminatory in application.

For the same amount of contribution, the individual in the higher brackets "saves" a larger proportion of the gift. The increasing cost of the gift dollar, which varies with decreasing amounts of adjusted gross income, acts as a deterrent to giving, the lower one's income. The party or candidate able to attract contributions that qualify at the deductible limit—normally those from higher bracket tax-payers—stands to benefit from the largest subsidy from government; the bias in this mechanism is apparent.[5]

A tax credit, on the other hand, because it is a credit against tax liability, affects the large and the small contributor alike. The advantage is equal because the benefit for the same amount of contribution is the same for each. Similarly, the incentive to contribute—and to take a credit—appears to be about the same for both because of the way the tax credit mechanism operates; in effect, it affords the taxpayer a choice between paying his full tax liability or diverting part of that liability, up to the limited amount of the credit, into political channels.

Government shares half of the cost of a tax credit, up to the limit, and the other half comes out of the pocket of the contributor. Thus contributions totaling $50 would be necessary in order to claim the full $25 credit.

SUMMARY

Three kinds of government funding became available in 1976 for aspects of presidential campaigns: (1) a flat grant for the general election campaign (in 1976 the grant amounted to $21.8-million for each major party candidate); (2) public funding up to $2.2-million for each national convention of a major party; (3) matching funds for candidates for the party nominations for President if they can demonstrate a broad base of support in small contributions.

Major party candidates who accept public support for the general elections cannot raise any other funds privately; although $21.8-million seems a large sum, it is less than McGovern spent in 1972 and only a third of the Nixon campaign total in the same year. The candidate saves on fund-raising costs, however, and his national party can spend up to $3.2-million on his behalf. A Supreme Court ruling in 1976 permitted individuals and groups to spend unlimited amounts for a candidate's cause, so long as their efforts are in no way coordinated with him.

A candidate seeking nomination may receive up to about $5.5-million in matching funds; to qualify he must raise $5,000 in private contributions of $250 or less in each of 20 states. Fifteen candidates qualified in 1976, receiving a total of more than $24.1-million.

The money for federal funding is provided by federal tax checkoff; each taxpayer may designate $1 of his tax money ($2 for joint returns) to be paid to the Presidential Election Campaign Fund. The checkoff plan operates on a four-year cycle, accumulating money for each tax year with the payout all in the presidential election year. For the 1976 election, $94.1-million had built up.

Since 1974, federal law also provides tax incentives for making political contributions: (1) political contributors can take a tax credit against their federal income tax for 50 per cent of their contribution up to $25 ($50 on a joint return); or alternatively, (2) a tax deduction may be claimed for the full amount of contributions up to $100 on a single return ($200 on a joint return). The tax deduction operates to benefit the wealthier contributor (as a taxpayer's income bracket rises, more of the cost of the contribution is borne by the government); the tax credit gives the same benefit to all.

NOTES

1. For extended discussions of public funding, see David W. Adamany and George E. Agree, *Political Money: A Strategy for Campaign Financing in America* (Baltimore: The Johns Hopkins University Press, 1975); George E. Agree, "Public Financing After the Supreme Court Decision," in "Political Finance: Reform and Reality," *The Annals*, vol. 425 (May 1976), pp. 134-142; Thomas J. Schwarz, *Public Financing of Elections: A Constitutional Division of the Wealth*, Special Committee on

Election Reform, American Bar Association (Chicago, Ill., 1975).

2. Christopher Lydon, "Democratic Hopefuls Live Off the Land," *The New York Times,* July 13, 1975.

3. Internal Revenue Service, *Statistics of Income—1972, Individual Income Tax Returns,* doc. no. T22.35/2: In 2/972 (Washington, D.C.: U.S. Government Printing Office, 1974).

4. If taken as a standard deduction, there is no real incentive or saving.

5. For a critical review of tax incentives and a discussion of the categories of taxpayers who benefit, see Adamany and Agree, *op. cit.,* pp. 123-128.

11

The Future of Financing Politics: Reaction and Reality

Well before Watergate unloosed its flood of campaign abuses, the U.S. political system was straining. The dissension, alienation and violence characteristic of America in the 1960s and the early 1970s can be related in part, at least, to a failure to enlist widespread citizen participation in the tasks of reforming and sustaining our democratic processes.

Although the American people are pragmatic, preferring to struggle with realities rather than with theories, until recently they failed to consider seriously better ways to finance and regulate politics. Public financing for presidential elections was provided for the first time in 1976. It came five years after the first major political campaign reforms in almost half a century.

Some of the 50 states have been out in front of the nation as a whole in their efforts to deal with public funding. Eight states currently have checkoff provisions on their income tax forms. In four of the eight, the funds go to political parties for distribution rather than directly to candidates as the federal law provides.

The price of running for public office is rising steadily. An increasingly professional approach to campaigning and a complex and sophisticated political technology have combined to drive up political costs. The campaigner for a major office must find means of financing professional management: consultants, advertising agency assistance, media specialists, accountants, attorneys, surveys and polls. Such a candidate needs expert help to prepare material for the media, negotiate for broadcast time, plan strategy by computer and test public opinion.

The task of raising funds is compounded by the American system of holding federal, state and local elections simultaneously. As this system accentuates competition for money, services and the attention of voters, costs increase enormously. Millionaire candidates willing to spend their own money raise the ante for other candidates. Candidates of the same party compete aggressively for nomination before facing the other party's nominees. In the primary campaigns, candidates and committees of the same party, at different levels, contend against one another for dollars and votes. Moreover, in primary and general elections, politics competes with commercial advertising.

In this competitive market, already exploding with commercial bids for the consumer's notice, the attention of the electorate is constantly and readily distracted. The voter seems to require fresh stimulation almost daily, and the stimulation must build toward a peak just before the election. Because political activity must be intense enough—in a brief political season—to attract the voter and motivate him to go to the polls, costs are high. Those costs are a burden for those who can afford them; they may freeze out those who cannot.

President Kennedy described the dilemma of candidates confronting such costs as "the pressure of opportunity." Politicians who find money knocking at their door may choose not to ask about the source. But if that is their course, they soon find themselves in what President Kennedy called "moral hock"—the condition of one who for need of money tacitly obligates himself to large contributors or special interests.

Traditional methods of financing campaigns had been in themselves obstacles to reform. The system satisfied some interests and many politicians. Big contributors representing commerce, industry, trade associations, labor unions and other groups had relied to a considerable extent for their influence in government on their control of political funds.

When politicians obtain the sums required in other ways, for example from government funding, these groups will seek other ways of influencing legislation. For instance, if their campaign contributions are limited by law, they may turn to more sophisticated lobbying. The quest for scarce political funds still may lead to two unfortunate results: impecunious candidates who may be forced to accept funds from dubious or even illegal sources; and candidates with strong financial resources of their own who may gain such an advantage that their actual qualifications for office become secondary considerations.

Resolving the Special Interest Dilemma

The potential influence of special interest group contributors has raised basic questions about the relationship of the economic substructure to the political superstructure in a pluralistic, democratic society. In developing a model system that is practical and enforceable and will raise levels of public confidence in the electoral system, we need to explore further such questions as: When does a political contribution or gift become a bribe? Is systematic campaign soliciting equivalent to a conspiracy to extort funds? Do incumbents so completely dominate the collections of campaign funds as to prevent truly competitive elections? Do we really spend too much on politics?

By means of improved monitoring and disclosure of relationships between private interests and government, the potential for undue influence by big interests is diminished without restricting their right to participate in the electoral process. Participation by special interest groups provides an important safety valve in the political system. Moreover, a free, flexible and healthy society can stand up against stronger forces within the system than many persons think.

It is well to remember that a single voice may not be heard except through the banding together of like-minded persons or through the use of expensive media. A sense of balance and equilibrium between competing forces in the society, with government playing a moderating but not dominating role, is difficult to achieve.

The ruling of the Supreme Court in *Buckley v. Valeo* equated campaign spending with free speech. The court recognized that to be effectively heard in an environment of mass communication, speech needs to be amplified. The amplification may take the form of purchased air time, space in the print media or other methods. If free speech in politics means the right to speak effectively, the court's decision justifies the use of tax dollars for campaign purposes which enable candidates and parties to reach the electorate. Thus, the ruling would appear to strengthen the argument, advanced by many students of campaign finance: that floors, not ceilings, be established. Floors mean the availability of government funds to ensure a minimum level of access of the candidate to the electorate. Beyond that level, candidates could spend as much private money as they could raise.

Private Financing

Yet even with public financing, a commitment to some forms of private financing seems likely to continue. The need to devise new solicitation and collection systems, and to use the ones in hand more effectively, is also apparent. The improvement of solicitation and collection systems is essential if tax or matching incentives are to work effectively. The political party, of course, is one possible "collection agency." The party can go beyond merely funding party committees to fund its candidates' campaigns as well. Other important collection systems include associational networks existing in membership groups, though some of those groups currently are in disrepute. Labor unions, corporations, dairy cooperatives, trade associations and professional groups can solicit effectively because of two characteristics: (1) they include large groups of like-minded persons, and (2) they have ready-made channels for communicating with their members. Whether at meetings, through field men or even by mail, such groups possess internal and therefore inexpensive means of asking for political money.

Collection systems with bipartisan potential exist at places of employment. With safeguards (perhaps through the use of a neutral trusteeship program), even government employees could be asked on a nonpartisan basis to contribute. While such sources of funds may be controversial, their potential is immense if properly tapped.

No solicitation and collection system—whether door-to-door solicitation, membership organization, payroll withholding or mass mail—will satisfy the financial needs of all parties and candidates. Campaigners will continue to seek funds separately. But labor, trade association and corporate bipartisan fund-raising drives have special advantages: they cost the parties and candidates nothing, and the expense to the sponsoring organizations is minimal.

Carleton Sterling has criticized the political reformer for seeking "...a direct dialogue between candidates and voters both free of outside influences."[1] Politics devoid of the influence of interest groups is not realistic. Politics probably cannot be sterilized and purified to the degree that would satisfy the most zealous reformers. Politics is about people and groups of people, their ideas, interests and aspirations. Since people seek political involvement partly through groups, a politics in which supportive groups are shut out or seriously impaired is difficult to envisage.

Too many ideas of value to society would get lost without the organized participation of groups in electoral politics. Some groups with few members participate mainly through their wealth. As people and groups differ, conflict occurs, but it occurs in a political arena in which government sets the rules and the players are expected to play by them. The government, however, is also a player, and the only fail-safe guarantee against its dominance lies in the ability of groups and interests in society to articulate their demands, to coalesce and to oppose government with the resources, including the money resources, that they command.

In a sense, broadly based political power was conceived to help equalize inequalities in economic resources. That promise is compromised if special interests get undue preferment from candidates and parties are forced to depend on them because alternative sources of adequate funds are not available. But the promise also is compromised if special interests are unduly restricted in presenting their claims; that is why limits and prohibitions, because of their inhibiting effects, require constant evaluation to be certain that significant avenues of expression are not being blocked.

Government subsidies represent one alternative source of funds. But given the struggle to provide public funding at just the presidential level, private solicitation for campaigns at lower levels will be necessary in the indefinite future.

Participation as a Goal

Citizen participation in politics, including pocketbook participation, is one way to thwart concentrated privilege. The citizen who feels that elites make all the decisions in public affairs throws in the towel before the bell rings. The citizen persuaded that only large contributors are influential has been deluded.

Most people agree that money should not determine who holds public office. Thoughtful citizens accept political costs as the price of two-party competition. People can recognize the need for realistic regulation of funds in order to avoid undue political influence by a few persons or groups. They can come to see the wholesome effect of disclosure of sources of political funds, wide publicity for such information and requirements for disclosure of the personal income of candidates and incumbents. Opinion trends augur sympathy for the notion that government should assist candidates and parties to meet legitimate campaign and political expenses. The relative success of federal and state tax checkoffs is testimony to that conclusion.

Money is only one part of a complex political ecology in which voting is the single most important individual act. Persons who would replace private financing with total government funding might succeed unwittingly in changing fundamental balances in the political system. Critics who minimize individual efforts ignore history: a system of free elections cannot survive without voluntarism. In whatever form or quantity elections draw upon government assistance, freely contributed money and services will still be needed.

Success in attracting individuals to charitable giving has not been a matter of accident or a spontaneous result of general good will toward organizations with good causes. Rather, it reflects a serious effort to educate the public in its responsibilities and to organize collection systems. Political responsibilities must be similarly learned.

The value of contributing small sums for political activity is neither taught in schools nor widely understood as an act of good citizenship, although voting is both honored and respected, at least in principle. The challenge is to associate contributing with voting as an act of good citizenship, to upgrade and dignify political giving and to gain for the popular financing of politics the public approval accorded voting.

The major changes in our campaign finance laws in the 1970s have not always resulted in systematic or consistent reform. In part, this is because various aspects of the problem have been dealt with separately and at different times by the major actors in government—Congress, the President, the Federal Election Commission and the Supreme Court.

What the 1971 Federal Election Campaign Act, the 1974 Amendments and many state laws have lacked has been a philosophy about regulation that is both constitutional and pragmatically designed to keep the election process open and flexible rather than rigid, exclusionary and fragmented. It is not yet clear whether the 1976 Amendments or the revisions of state law following *Buckley v. Valeo* will lead to the openness and flexibility a democratic and pluralistic society require.

NOTES

1. Carleton W. Sterling, "Control of Campaign Spending: The Reformer's Paradox," *American Bar Association Journal*, 59 (October 1973), p. 1153.

Appendix

Federal Election Campaign Act of 1971

The Federal Election Campaign Act of 1971 (FECA) was the first comprehensive revision of federal campaign legislation since the Corrupt Practices Act of 1925. The act established detailed spending limits and disclosure procedures. PL 92-225 contained the following major provisions:

General

- Repealed the Federal Corrupt Practices Act of 1925.
- Defined "election" to mean any general, special, primary or runoff election, nominating convention or caucus, delegate selection primary, presidential preference primary or constitutional convention.
- Broadened the definitions of "contribution" and "expenditure" as they pertain to political campaigns, but exempted a loan of money by a national or state bank made in accordance with applicable banking laws.
- Prohibited promises of employment or other political rewards or benefits by any candidate in exchange for political support, and prohibited contracts between candidates and any federal department or agency.
- Provided that the terms "contribution" and "expenditure" did not include communications, non-partisan registration and get-out-the-vote campaigns by a corporation aimed at its stockholders or by a labor organization aimed at its members.
- Provided that the terms "contribution" and "expenditure" did not include the establishment, administration and solicitation of voluntary contributions to a separate segregated fund to be utilized for political purposes by a corporation or labor organization.

269

Contribution Limits

● Placed a ceiling on contributions by any candidate or his immediate family to his own campaign of $50,000 for President or Vice President, $35,000 for senator and $25,000 for representative.

Spending Limits

● Limited the total amount that could be spent by federal candidates for advertising time in communications media to 10 cents per eligible voter, or $50,000, whichever was greater. The limitation would apply to all candidates for President and Vice President, senator and representative, and would be determined annually for the geographical area of each election by the Bureau of the Census.

● Included in the term "communications media" radio and television broadcasting stations, newspapers, magazines, billboards and automatic telephone equipment. Of the total spending limit, up to 60 per cent could be used for broadcast advertising time.

● Specified that candidates for presidential nomination, during the period prior to the nominating convention, could spend no more in primary or non-primary states than the amount allowed under the 10-cent-per-voter communications spending limitation.

● Provided that broadcast and non-broadcast spending limitations be increased in proportion to annual increases in the Consumer Price Index over the base year 1970.

Disclosure and Enforcement

● Required all political committees that anticipated receipts in excess of $1,000 during the calendar year to file a statement of organization with the appropriate federal supervisory officer, and to include such information as the names of all principal officers, the scope of the committee, the names of all candidates the committee supported and other information as required by law.

● Stipulated that the appropriate federal supervisory officer to oversee election campaign practices, reporting and disclosure was the Clerk of the House for House candidates, the Secretary of the Senate for Senate candidates and the Comptroller General for presidential candidates.

● Required each political committee to report any individual expenditure of more than $100 and any expenditures of more than $100 in the aggregate during the calendar year.

● Required disclosure of all contributions to any committee or candidate in excess of $100, including a detailed report with the name and address of the contributor and the date the contribution was made.

● Required the supervisory officers to prepare an annual report for each committee registered with the commission and make such reports available for sale to the public.

● Required candidates and committees to file reports of contributions and expenditures on the 10th day of March, June and September every year, on the 15th and fifth days preceding the date on which an election was held and on the 31st day of January. Any contribution of $5,000 or more was to be reported within 48 hours after its receipt.

● Required reporting of the names, addresses and occupations of any lender and endorser of any loan in excess of $100 as well as the date and amount of such loans.

● Required any person who made any contribution in excess of $100, other than through a political committee or candidate, to report such contribution to the commission.

● Prohibited any contribution to a candidate or committee by one person in the name of another person.

● Authorized the office of the Comptroller General to serve as a national clearinghouse for information on the administration of election practices.

● Required that copies of reports filed by a candidate with the appropriate supervisory officer also be filed with the secretaries of state for the state in which the election was held.

Miscellaneous

● Prohibited radio and television stations from charging political candidates more than the lowest unit cost for the same advertising time available to commercial advertisers. Lowest unit rate charges would apply only during the 45 days preceding a primary election and the 60 days preceding a general election.

● Required non-broadcast media to charge candidates no more than the comparable amounts charged to commercial advertisers for the same class and amount of advertising space. The requirement would apply only during the 45 days preceding the date of a primary election and 60 days before the date of a general election.

● Provided that amounts spent by an agent of a candidate on behalf of his candidacy would be charged against the overall expenditure allocation. Fees paid to the agent for services performed also would be charged against the overall limitation.

● Stipulated that no broadcast station could make any charge for political advertising time on a station unless written consent to contract for such time had been given by the candidate, and unless the candidate certified that such charge would not exceed his spending limit.

Revenue Act of 1971

The Revenue Act of 1971, through tax incentives and a tax checkoff plan, provided the basis for public funding of presidential election campaigns. PL 92-178 contained the following major provisions:

Tax Incentives and Checkoff

- Allowed a tax credit of $12.50 ($25 for a married couple) or a deduction against income of $50 ($100 for a married couple) for political contributions to candidates for local, state or federal office.
- Allowed taxpayers to contribute to a general fund for all eligible presidential and vice presidential candidates by authorizing $1 of their annual income tax payment to be placed in such a fund.

Presidential Election Campaign Fund

- Authorized to be distributed to the candidates of each major party (one which obtained 25 per cent of votes cast in the previous presidential election) an amount equal to 15 cents multiplied by the number of U.S. residents age 18 or over.
- Established a formula for allocating public campaign funds to candidates of minor parties whose candidates received 5 per cent or more but less than 25 per cent of the previous presidential election vote.
- Authorized payments after the election to reimburse the campaign expenses of a new party whose candidate received enough votes to be eligible or to a minor party whose candidate increased its vote to the qualifying level.
- Prohibited major party candidates who chose public financing of their campaign from accepting private campaign contributions unless their shares of funds contributed through the income tax checkoff procedure fell short of the amounts to which they were entitled.
- Prohibited a major party candidate who chose public financing and all campaign committees authorized by the candidate from spending more than the amount to which the candidate was entitled under the contributions formula.
- Provided that if the amounts in the fund were insufficient to make the payments to which each party was entitled, payments would be allocated according to the ratio of contributions in their accounts. No party would receive from the general fund more than the smallest amount needed by a major party to reach the maximum amount of contributions to which it was entitled.
- Provided that surpluses remaining in the fund after a campaign be returned to the Treasury after all parties had been paid the amounts to which they were entitled.

Enforcement

• Provided penalties of $5,000 or one year in prison, or both, for candidates or campaign committees which spent more on a campaign than the amounts they received from the campaign fund or who accepted private contributions when sufficient public funds were available.

• Provided penalties of $10,000 or five years in prison, or both, for candidates or campaign committees who used public campaign funds for unauthorized expenses, gave or accepted kickbacks or illegal payments involving public campaign funds or who knowingly furnished false information to the Comptroller General.

Federal Election Campaign Act
Amendments of 1974

The 1974 Amendments set new contribution and spending limits, made provision for government funding of presidential prenomination campaigns and national nominating conventions, and created the bipartisan Federal Election Commission to administer election laws. PL 93-443 contained the following major provisions:

Federal Election Commission

- Created a six-member, full-time bipartisan Federal Election Commission to be responsible for administering election laws and the public financing program.
- Provided that the President, Speaker of the House and President pro-tem of the Senate would appoint to the commission two members, each of different parties, all subject to confirmation by Congress. Commission members could not be officials or employees of any branch of government.
- Made the Secretary of the Senate and Clerk of the House ex officio, non-voting members of the FEC; provided that their offices would serve as custodian of reports for House and Senate candidates.
- Provided that commissioners would serve six-year, staggered terms and established a rotating one-year chairmanship.

Contribution Limits

- $1,000 per individual for each primary, runoff or general election, and an aggregate contribution of $25,000 to all federal candidates annually.
- $5,000 per organization, political committee and national and state party organizations for each election, but no aggregate limit on the amount organizations could contribute in a campaign nor on the amount organizations could contribute to party organizations supporting federal candidates.
- $50,000 for President or Vice President, $35,000 for Senate, and $25,000 for House races for candidates and their families to their own campaign.
- $1,000 for independent expenditures on behalf of a candidate.
- Barred cash contributions of over $100 and foreign contributions.

Spending Limits

- Presidential primaries—$10-million total per candidate for all primaries. In a state presidential primary, limited a candidate to spending no more than twice what a Senate candidate in that state would be allowed to spend *(see below)*.

● Presidential general election—$20-million per candidate.

● Presidential nominating conventions—$2-million each major political party, lesser amounts for minor parties.

● Senate primaries—$100,000 or eight cents per eligible voter, whichever was greater.

● Senate general elections—$150,000 or 12 cents per eligible voter, whichever was greater.

● House primaries—$70,000.

● House general elections—$70,000.

● National party spending—$10,000 per candidate in House general elections; $20,000 or two cents per eligible voter, whichever was greater, for each candidate in Senate general elections; and two cents per voter (approximately $2.9-million) in presidential general elections. The expenditure would be above the candidate's individual spending limit.

● Applied Senate spending limits to House candidates who represented a whole state.

● Repealed the media spending limitations in the Federal Election Campaign Act of 1971 (PL 92-225).

● Exempted expenditures of up to $500 for food and beverages, invitations, unreimbursed travel expenses by volunteers and spending on "slate cards" and sample ballots.

● Exempted fund-raising costs of up to 20 per cent of the candidate spending limit. Thus the spending limit for House candidates would be effectively raised from $70,000 to $84,000 and for candidates in presidential primaries from $10-million to $12-million.

● Provided that spending limits be increased in proportion to annual increases in the Consumer Price Index.

Public Financing

● Presidential general elections—voluntary public financing. Major party candidates would automatically qualify for full funding before the campaign. Minor party and independent candidates would be eligible to receive a proportion of full funding based on past or current votes received. If a candidate opted for full public funding, no private contributions would be permitted.

● Presidential nominating conventions—optional public funding. Major parties would automatically qualify. Minor parties would be eligible for lesser amounts based on their proportion of votes received in a past election.

● Presidential primaries—matching public funds of up to $5-million per candidate after meeting fund-raising requirement of $100,000 raised in amounts of at least $5,000 in each of 20 states or more. Only the first $250 of individual private contributions would be matched. The matching funds were to be divided among the candidates as quickly as possible. In allocating the money, the order in which the candidates qualified would be taken into account. Only private gifts, raised after Jan. 1, 1975, would qualify for matching for the 1976 election. No federal payments would be made before January 1976.

● Provided that all federal money for public funding of campaigns would come from the Presidential Election Campaign Fund. Money received from the federal income tax dollar checkoff would be automatically appropriated to the fund.

Disclosure and Enforcement

● Required each candidate to establish one central campaign committee through which all contributions and expenditures on behalf of a candidate must be reported. Required designation of specific bank depositories of campaign funds.

● Required full reports of contributions and expenditures to be filed with the Federal Election Commission 10 days before and 30 days after every election, and within 10 days of the close of each quarter unless the committee received or expended less than $1,000 in that quarter. A year-end report was due in nonelection years.

● Required that contributions of $1,000 or more received within the last 15 days before election be reported to the commission within 48 hours.

● Prohibited contributions in the name of another.

● Treated loans as contributions. Required a cosigner or guarantor for each $1,000 of outstanding obligation.

● Required any organization which spent any money or committed any act for the purpose of influencing any election (such as the publication of voting records) to file reports as a political committee.

● Required every person who spent or contributed over $100 other than to or through a candidate or political committee to report.

● Permitted government contractors, unions and corporations to maintain separate, segregated political funds.

● Provided that the commission would: receive campaign reports; make rules and regulations (subject to review by Congress within 30 days); maintain a cumulative index of reports filed and not filed; make special and regular reports to Congress and the President; and serve as an election information clearinghouse.

● Gave the commission power to render advisory opinions; conduct audits and investigations; subpoena witnesses and information; and go to court to seek civil injunctions.

● Provided that criminal cases would be referred by the commission to the Justice Department for prosecution.

● Increased existing fines to a maximum of $50,000.

● Provided that a candidate for federal office who failed to file reports could be prohibited from running again for the term of that office plus one year.

Miscellaneous

- Set Jan. 1, 1975, as the effective date of the act (except for immediate pre-emption of state laws).
- Removed Hatch Act restrictions on voluntary activities by state and local employees in federal campaigns, if not otherwise prohibited by state law.
- Prohibited solicitation of funds by franked mail.
- Pre-empted state election laws for federal candidates.
- Permitted use of excess campaign funds to defray expenses of holding federal office or for other lawful purposes.

Federal Election Campaign Act Amendments of 1976

The 1976 Amendments revised election laws following the Supreme Court decision in *Buckley v. Valeo*. The Amendments reopened the door to large contributions through "independent expenditures" and through corporate and union political action committees. PL 94-283 contained the following major provisions:

Federal Election Commission

● Reconstituted the Federal Election Commission as a six-member panel appointed by the President and confirmed by the Senate.

● Prohibited commission members from engaging in outside business activities; gave commissioners one year after joining the body to terminate outside business interests.

● Gave Congress the power to disapprove individual sections of any regulation proposed by the commission.

Contribution Limits

● Limited an individual to giving no more than $5,000 a year to a political action committee and $20,000 to the national committee of a political party (the 1974 law set a $1,000 per election limit on individual contributions to a candidate and an aggregate contribution limit for individuals of $25,000 a year.)

● Limited a multi-candidate committee to giving no more than $15,000 a year to the national committee of a political party (the 1974 law set only a limit of $5,000 per election per candidate).

● Limited the Democratic and Republican senatorial campaign committees to giving up to $17,500 a year to a candidate (the 1974 law had set a $5,000 per election limit).

● Allowed campaign committees set up to back a single candidate to provide "occasional, isolated and incidental support" to another candidate. (The 1974 law required a campaign committee to spend money only on behalf of the single candidate for which it was formed.)

● Restricted the proliferation of membership organization, corporate and union political action committees. All political action committees established by a company or an international union would be treated as a single committee for contribution purposes. The contributions of political action committees of a company or union would be limited to no more than $5,000 overall to the same candidate in any election.

Spending Limits

● Limited spending by presidential and vice presidential candidates to no more than $50,000 of their own, or their family's money, on their campaigns, if they accepted public financing.

● Exempted from the law's spending limits payments by candidates or the national committees of political parties for legal and accounting services required to comply with the campaign law, but required that such payments be reported.

Public Financing

● Required presidential candidates who received federal matching subsidies and who withdrew from the prenomination election campaign to give back leftover federal matching funds.

● Cut off federal campaign subsidies to a presidential candidate who won less than 10 per cent of the vote in two consecutive presidential primaries in which he ran.

● Established a procedure under which an individual who became ineligible for matching payments could have eligibility restored by a finding of the commission.

Disclosure and Enforcement

● Gave the commission exclusive authority to prosecute civil violations of the campaign finance law and shifted to the commission jurisdiction over violations formerly covered only in the criminal code, thus strengthening its power to enforce the law.

● Required an affirmative vote of four members for the commission to issue regulations and advisory opinions and initiate civil actions and investigations.

● Required labor unions, corporations and membership organizations to report expenditures of over $2,000 per election for communications to their stockholders or members advocating the election or defeat of a clearly identified candidate. The costs of communications to members or stockholders on issues would not have to be reported.

● Required that candidates and political committees keep records of contributions of $50 or more. (The 1974 law required records of contributions of $10 or more.)

● Permitted candidates and political committees to waive the requirement for filing quarterly campaign finance reports in a nonelection year if less than a total of $5,000 was raised or spent in that quarter. Annual reports would still have to be filed. (The exemption limit was $1,000 under the 1974 law.)

● Required that political committees and individuals making an independent political expenditure of more than $100 that advocated the defeat or election of a candidate file a report with the election commission. Required the committee and individual to state, under penalty of perjury, that the expenditure was not made in collusion with a candidate.

● Required that independent expenditures of $1,000 or more made within 15 days of an election be reported within 24 hours.

● Limited the commission to issuing advisory opinions only for specific fact situations. Advisory opinions could not be used to spell out commission policy. Advisory opinions were not to be considered as precedents unless an activity was "indistinguishable in all its material aspects" from an activity already covered by an advisory opinion.

● Permitted the commission to initiate investigations only after it received a properly verified complaint or had reason to believe, based on information it obtained in the normal course of its duties, that a violation had occurred or was about to occur. The commission was barred from relying on anonymous complaints to institute investigations.

● Required the commission to rely initially on conciliation to deal with alleged campaign law violations before going to court. The commission was allowed to refer alleged criminal violations to the Department of Justice for action. The Attorney General was required to report back to the commission within 60 days on action taken on the apparent violation and subsequently every 30 days until the matter was disposed of.

● Provided for a one-year jail sentence and a fine of up to $25,000 or three times the amount of the contribution or expenditure involved in the violation, whichever was greater, if an individual was convicted of knowingly committing a campaign law violation that involved more than $1,000.

● Provided for civil penalties of fines of $5,000 or an amount equal to the contribution or expenditure involved in the violation, whichever was greater. For violations knowingly committed, the fine would be $10,000 or an amount equal to twice the amount involved in the violation, whichever was greater. The fines could be imposed by the courts or by the commission in conciliation agreements. (The 1974 law included penalties for civil violations of a $1,000 fine and/or a one-year prison sentence.)

Miscellaneous

● Restricted the fund-raising ability of corporate political action committees. Company committees could seek contributions only from stockholders and executive and administrative personnel and their families. Restricted union political action committees to soliciting contributions only from union members and their families. However, twice a year permitted union and corporate political action committees to seek campaign contributions only by mail from all employees they are not initially restricted to. Contributions would have to remain anonymous and would be received by an independent third party that would keep records but pass the money to the committees.

● Permitted trade association political action committees to solicit contributions from the stockholders and executive and administrative personnel and their families of member companies.

● Permitted union political action committees to use the same method to solicit campaign contributions that the political action committee of the company uses. The union committee would have to reimburse the company at cost for the expenses the company incurred for the political fundraising.

Selected Bibliography

Books

Adamany, David. *Campaign Finance in America*. North Scituate, Mass. Duxbury Press, 1972.

———, and Agree, George E. *Political Money: A Strategy For Campaign Financing In America*. Baltimore: The Johns Hopkins University Press, 1975.

Agranoff, Robert. *The Management of Election Campaigns*. Boston: Holbrook Press, Inc., 1976.

———. *The New Style in Election Campaigns*. Boston: Holbrook Press, Inc., 1976.

Alexander, Herbert E. *Financing the 1960 Election*. Princeton, N.J.: Citizens' Research Foundation, 1970.

———. *Financing the 1964 Election*. Princeton, N.J.: Citizens' Research Foundation, 1968.

———. *Financing the 1968 Election*. Lexington, Mass.: Lexington Books, D.C. Heath and Company, 1971.

———. *Financing the 1972 Election*. Lexington, Mass.: Lexington Books, D.C. Heath and Company, 1976.

———. *Money in Politics*. Washington, D.C.: Public Affairs Press, 1972.

———, ed. *Campaign Money: Reform and Reality in the States*. New York: The Free Press, 1976.

Amick, George. *The American Way of Graft*. Princeton, N.J.: The Center for Analysis of Public Issues, 1976.

Barber, James David, ed. *Choosing the President*. Englewood Cliffs, N.J.: Prentice-Hall, Inc., 1974.

Beard, Edmund, and Horn, Stephen. *Congressional Ethics: A View From the House.* Washington, D.C.: The Brookings Institution, 1975.

Bernstein, Carl and Woodward, Bob. *All the President's Men.* New York: Simon and Schuster, 1974.

Bickel, Alexander M. *Reform and Continuity: The Electoral College, the Convention, and the Party System.* New York: Harper & Row, Publishers, 1971.

Broder, David S. *The Party's Over: The Failure of Politics in America.* New York: Harper & Row, Publishers, 1972.

Caddy, Douglas. *The Hundred Million Dollar Payoff.* New Rochelle, N.Y.: Arlington House, Publishers, 1974.

Chester, Edward W. *Radio, Television and American Politics.* New York: Sheed and Ward, 1969.

Claude, Richard. *The Supreme Court and the Electoral Process.* Baltimore: The Johns Hopkins Press, 1970.

Clem, Alan L. *The Making of Congressmen: Seven Campaigns of 1974.* North Scituate, Mass.: Duxbury Press, 1976.

Cressey, Donald R. *Theft of the Nation: The Structure and Operations of Organized Crime in America.* New York: Harper & Row, Publishers, 1969.

Demaris, Ovid. *Dirty Business: The Corporate-Political Money-Power Game.* New York: Harper's Magazine Press, 1974.

DeVries, Walter and Tarrance, Lance, Jr. *The Ticket-Splitter: A New Force in American Politics.* Grand Rapids, Mich.: William B. Eerdmans Publishing Company, 1972.

Domhoff, G. William. *Fat Cats and Democrats: The Role of the Big Rich in the Party of the Common Man.* Englewood Cliffs, N.J.: Prentice-Hall, 1972.

Dorman, Michael. *Payoff: The Role of Organized Crime in American Politics.* New York: David McKay Company, Inc., 1972.

Dunn, Delmer. *Financing Presidential Campaigns.* Washington, D.C.: The Brookings Institution, 1972.

Epstein, Edwin M. *The Corporation in American Politics.* Englewood Cliffs, N.J.: Prentice-Hall, Inc., 1969.

Gilson, Lawrence. *Money and Secrecy: A Citizen's Guide to Reforming State and Federal Practices.* New York: Praeger Publishers, 1972.

Heard, Alexander. *The Costs of Democracy.* Chapel Hill, N.C.: University of North Carolina Press, 1960.

Heidenheimer, Arnold J., ed. *Comparative Political Finance: The Financing of Party Organizations and Election Campaigns.*

Lexington, Mass.: Lexington Books, D.C. Heath and Company, 1970.

Hershey, Marjorie Random. *The Making of Campaign Strategy.* New York: D.C. Heath, 1974.

Hess, Stephen. *The Presidential Campaign: The Leadership Selection Process After Watergate.* Washington, D.C.: The Brookings Institution, 1974.

Hiebert, Ray, Jones, Robert, Lotito, Ernest and Lorenz, John, eds. *The Political Image Merchants: Strategies in the New Politics.* Washington, D.C.: Acropolis Books Ltd., 1971.

Kelley, Stanley, Jr. *Political Campaigning: Problems in Creating an Informed Electorate.* Washington, D.C.: The Brookings Institution, 1960.

———. *Professional Public Relations and Political Power.* Baltimore: The Johns Hopkins Press, 1956.

Kraus, Sidney. *The Great Debates: Background—Perspective—Effects.* Bloomington, Ind.: Indiana University Press, 1962.

Lang, Kurt and Lang, Gladys Engel. *Politics and Television.* Chicago: Quadrangle Books, 1968.

Leonard, Dick. *Paying for Party Politics: The Case For Public Subsidies.* London: PEP, 1975.

Leuthold, David A. *Electioneering in a Democracy: Campaigns for Congress.* New York: John Wiley and Sons, 1968.

McCarthy, Max. *Elections for Sale.* Boston: Houghton-Mifflin Company, 1972.

McGinniss, Joe. *The Selling of the President, 1968.* New York: Trident Press, 1969.

MacNeil, Robert. *The People Machine: The Influence of Television on American Politics.* New York: Harper & Row, Publishers, 1968.

May, Ernest R. and Fraser, Janet, eds. *Campaign '72: The Managers Speak.* Cambridge: Harvard University Press, 1973.

Mazmanian, Daniel A. *Third Parties in Presidential Elections.* (Studies in Presidential Selection.) Washington, D.C.: The Brookings Institution, 1974.

Mickelson, Sig. *The Electric Mirror: Politics in an Age of Television.* New York: Dodd, Mead & Company, 1972.

Milbrath, Lester W. *Political Participation: How and Why Do People Get Involved in Politics?* Chicago: Rand McNally & Company, 1965.

Minow, Newton N., Martin, John Bartlow and Mitchell, Lee M. *Presidential Television.* New York: Basic Books, 1973.

Napolitan, Joseph. *The Election Game and How to Win It.* Garden City, New York: Doubleday & Company, Inc., 1972.

Nichols, David. *Financing Elections: The Politics of an American Ruling Class.* New York: New Viewpoints, A Division of Franklin Watts, Inc., 1974.

Nie, Norman H., Verba, Sidney and Petrocik, John R. *The Changing American Voter.* Cambridge: Harvard University Press, 1976.

Nimmo, Dan. *The Political Persuaders.* Englewood Cliffs, N.J.: Prentice Hall, 1970.

Overacker, Louise. *Money in Elections.* New York: The Macmillan Company, 1932.

Patterson, Thomas E. and McClure, Robert D. *The Unseeing Eye: The Myth of Television Power in National Politics.* New York: G.P. Putnam's Sons, 1976.

Peabody, Robert L., Berry, Jeffrey M., Frasure, William G. and Goldman, Jerry. *To Enact A Law: Congress and Campaign Financing.* New York: Praeger Publishers, 1972.

Pollock, James K., Jr. *Party Campaign Funds.* New York: Alfred A. Knopf, 1926.

————. *Money and Politics Abroad.* New York: Alfred A. Knopf, 1932.

Rae, Douglas W. *The Political Consequences of Electoral Laws.* New Haven: Yale University Press, 1967.

Ranney, Austin. *Curing the Mischiefs of Faction: Party Reform in America.* Berkeley: University of California Press, 1975.

Ripon Society and Brown, Clifford W., Jr. *Jaws of Victory: The Game-Plan Politics of 1972, The Crisis of the Republican Party, and The Future of the Constitution.* Boston: Little, Brown and Company, 1974.

Rosenbloom, David Lee. *The Election Men: Professional Campaign Managers and American Democracy.* New York: Quadrangle Books, 1973.

Saloma, John S., III and Sontag, Frederick H. *Parties: The Real Opportunity for Effective Citizen Politics.* New York: Alfred A. Knopf, 1972.

Shannon, Jasper B. *Money and Politics.* New York: Random House, 1959.

Steinberg, Arnold. *Political Campaign Management: A Systems Approach.* Lexington, Mass.: Lexington Books, D.C. Heath and Company, 1976.

————. *The Political Campaign Handbook: Media, Scheduling, and*

Advance. Lexington, Mass.: Lexington Books, D.C. Heath and Company, 1976.

Stewart, John G. *One Last Chance: The Democratic Party, 1974-76.* New York: Praeger Publishers, 1974.

Sundquist, James L. *Dynamics of the Party System: Alignment and Realignment of Political Parties in the United States.* Washington, D.C.: The Brookings Institution, 1973.

Thayer, George. *Who Shakes the Money Tree?: American Campaign Financing Practices from 1789 to the Present.* New York: Simon and Schuster, 1973.

Van Doren, John. *Big Money in Little Sums.* Chapel Hill: Institute for Research in Social Science, University of North Carolina, 1956.

White, Theodore H. *The Making of the President, 1960.* New York: Atheneum Publishers, 1961.

_____. *The Making of the President, 1964.* New York: Atheneum Publishers, 1965.

_____. *The Making of the President, 1968.* New York: Atheneum Publishers, 1969.

_____. *The Making of the President, 1972.* New York: Atheneum Publishers, 1973.

Woodward, Bob and Bernstein, Carl. *The Final Days.* New York: Simon and Schuster, 1976.

Reports and Articles

AEI Round Table, Alexander M. Bickel, Chairman. *Watergate, Politics, and the Legal Process.* Washington, D.C.: American Enterprise Institute for Public Policy Research, March 13 and 14, 1974.

Alexander, Herbert E., ed. "Political Finance: Reform and Reality," *The Annals,* vol. 425, Philadelphia: The American Academy of Political and Social Science, May 1976.

Alexander, Herbert E. and Molloy, J. Paul. *Model State Statute: Politics, Elections and Public Office.* Princeton, N.J.: Citizens' Research Foundation, August 1974.

The American Bar Association, Special Committee on Election Reform. *Symposium on Campaign Financing Regulation.* Tiburon, Calif., April 25-27, 1975.

Analysis of Federal and State Campaign Finance Law: Summaries. Prepared for the Federal Election Commission by American Law Division of the Congressional Research Service, Library of Congress. June 1975.

"Developments in the Law—Elections," *Harvard Law Review.* vol. 88, no. 6, Cambridge, Mass.: Gannett House, April 1975.

Electing Congress: The Financial Dilemma. Report of the Twentieth Century Fund Task Force on Financing Congressional Campaigns. (Background Paper by David L. Rosenbloom) New York, 1970.

Financing a Better Election System. A Statement on National Policy by the Research and Policy Committee of the Committee for Economic Development. New York: Committee for Economic Development, December 1968.

Financing Presidential Campaigns. Report of the President's Commission on Campaign Costs. Washington, D.C., April 1962.

Kirby, James C., Jr. *Congress and the Public Trust.* Report of the Association of the Bar of the City of New York Special Committee on Congressional Ethics. New York: Atheneum, 1970.

Moore, Jonathan and Albert C. Pierce, eds. *Voters, Primaries and Parties.* Selections from a Conference on American Politics. Institute of Politics, John Fitzgerald Kennedy School of Government, Harvard University, 1976.

1972 Congressional Campaign Finances. Prepared by The Campaign Finance Monitoring Project, 3 vols., Washington, D.C.: Common Cause, 1974.

1972 Federal Campaign Finances: Interest Groups and Political Parties. Prepared by The Campaign Finance Monitoring Project, 10 vols., Washington, D.C.: Common Cause, 1974.

1974 Congressional Campaign Finances. Prepared by the Campaign Finance Monitoring Project, 5 vols., Washington, D.C.: Common Cause, 1976.

Nomination and Election of the President and Vice President of the United States. Compiled by Thomas M. Durbin, Rita Ann Reimer and Thomas B. Riby, Congressional Research Service, Library of Congress for the United States Senate Library, under the direction of Francis R. Valeo, Secretary of the Senate. Washington, D.C.: U.S. Government Printing Office, 1976.

Penniman, Howard R. and Winter, Ralph K., Jr. *Campaign Finances: Two Views of the Political and Constitutional Implications.* Washington, D.C.: American Enterprise Institute for Public Policy Research, 1971.

"The Political Money Tree," *In Common.* vol. 7, no. 2, Washington, D.C.: Common Cause, Spring 1976.

Rose, Richard and Heidenheimer, Arnold J., eds. "Comparative Political Finance: A Symposium," *Journal of Politics,* vol. 25, no. 3, August 1963.

Rosenthal, Albert J. *Federal Regulation of Campaign Finance: Some Constitutional Questions.* Milton Katz, ed. Princeton, N.J.: Citizens' Research Foundation, 1972.

Schwarz, Thomas J. *Public Financing of Elections: A Constitutional Division of the Wealth.* Chicago: American Bar Association, Special Committee on Election Reform, 1975.

Tufte, Edward R., ed. "Symposium on Electoral Reform," *Policy Studies Journal,* vol. 2, no. 4, Urbana, Ill.: Political Science Department and the Institute of Government and Public Affairs at the University of Illinois, Summer 1974.

U.S. Congress. *Special Report* of the Joint Committee on Congressional Operations. Pursuant to Section 402(a)(2) of the Legislative Reorganization Act of 1970. Identifying Court Proceedings and Actions of Vital Interest to the Congress. Decision of the United States Supreme Court, *Buckley v. Valeo, January 30, 1976.* Committee Print. 94th Cong., 2d sess. Washington, D.C.: U.S. Government Printing Office, 1976.

U.S. Congress, Senate. Select Committee on Presidential Campaign Activities. *Final Report.* Pursuant to S. Res. 60, February 7, 1973. Senate Report No. 93-981. 93rd Cong., 2d sess. Washington, D.C.: U.S. Government Printing Office, 1974.

U.S. Congress, Senate. Select Committee on Presidential Campaign Activities. *Election Reform: Basic References.* Pursuant to S. Res. 60. Committee Print, 93rd Cong., 1st sess. Washington, D.C.: U.S. Government Printing Office, 1973.

Voters' Time. Report of the Twentieth Century Fund Commission on Campaign Costs in the Electronic Era. New York, 1969.

Winter, Ralph K., Jr. *Watergate and the Law: Political Campaigns and Presidential Power.* (Domestic Affairs Study No. 22.) Washington, D.C.: American Enterprise Institute for Public Policy Research, 1974.

_____, in association with John R. Bolton. *Campaign Financing and Political Freedom.* (Domestic Affairs Study No. 19.) Washington, D.C.: American Enterprise Institute for Public Policy Research, 1973.

Index

A

B

N, O

P, Q